Analysis

With the volatile nature of today's workplaces, analysis tools are more valuable than ever: this book provides those tools to capture human expertise before it leaves the organization.

The concepts of analysis may be timeless, but recent years have seen massive changes in terms of organizational structures, work systems, and worker requirements, such as remote working and increased employee turnover. This book covers the theory and concepts behind performance improvement, and then turns to the real-world work of performance diagnosis, process improvement, and task documentation, introducing cross-functional task analysis, which recognizes the changing nature of work as more of today's tasks are extensive and require collaboration across jobs. Each chapter can stand alone if organizations need to focus on a particular area, and includes examples that reflect contemporary work, from job descriptions to task inventories and specific task analyses.

One of the only texts providing the tools and processes necessary to analyze workplace performance, document human expertise, and develop training materials, this book is intended for managers, executives, students, and any workplace or organization development professional interested in human expertise and how to manage it.

Dr. Richard A. Swanson is Professor Emeritus of Human Resource Development at the University of Minnesota. Following that tenure, he served as Distinguished Research Chair in the College of Business and Technology, University of Texas at Tyler. Swanson has published extensively and has consulted with organizations in the Americas, Europe, Asia, and Africa.

Dr. Thomas J. Chermack is Professor of Organizational Learning, Performance and Change at Colorado State University. His research focuses on the outcomes of scenario planning and he has published extensively on the topic. He has consulted with organizations worldwide and directs the Ph.D. program at Colorado State University.

Analysis

The Key to Improving Organizational and Individual Performance

Richard A. Swanson and
Thomas J. Chermack

Routledge
Taylor & Francis Group

NEW YORK AND LONDON

Designed cover image: Getty

First published 2025
by Routledge
605 Third Avenue, New York, NY 10158

and by Routledge
4 Park Square, Milton Park, Abingdon, Oxon, OX14 4RN

Routledge is an imprint of the Taylor & Francis Group, an informa business

ISBN: 978-1-032-85522-6 (hbk)
ISBN: 978-1-032-85262-1 (pbk)
ISBN: 978-1-003-51853-2 (ebk)

DOI: 10.4324/9781003518532

Typeset in Galliard
by KnowledgeWorks Global Ltd.

Dedicated to young problem-solvers focused on making the world a better place.

Contents

List of Figures

About the Authors

Dr. Richard A. Swanson is Professor Emeritus of Human Resource Development and Adult Education at the University of Minnesota, where he served on the faculty for 25 years. Following that tenure, he served as Distinguished Research Professor of Human Resource Development and the Sam Lindsey Chair in the College of Business and Technology, University of Texas at Tyler. Swanson received his bachelor's and master's degrees from the College of New Jersey and his doctorate from the University of Illinois. Swanson has published extensively and has consulted with organizations in the Americas, Europe, Asia, and Africa. He is the founding editor of both the *Human Resource Development Quarterly* and *Advances in Developing Human Resources.* Swanson is one of the Academy of Human Resource Development founders and served as an early president. In 1995, the academy established the Richard A. Swanson Award for Excellence in Research and inducted him into the HRD Scholar Hall of Fame in 2004. He was also inducted into the International Adult and Continuing Education Hall of Fame in 2001 and received a University of Illinois Education Alumni Association Distinguished Alumni Award in 2003. Swanson lives in St. Paul, Minnesota.

Dr. Thomas J. Chermack is Professor of Organizational Learning, Performance, and Change at Colorado State University. He has studied and practiced scenario planning for over 20 years. Tom has consulted on scenario projects through his company Chermack Scenarios with organizations worldwide, including many Fortune 50 companies in the United States, among others. These projects have yielded significant insights for organization leaders resulting in new perceptions of their organizations, environments, and capabilities. He has published over 100 refereed articles and is the author of three books (*Scenario Planning in Organizations, Foundations of Scenario Planning: The Story of Pierre Wack and Using Scenarios*). He is also the co-author of *Theory Building in Applied Disciplines* with Richard A. Swanson. Tom's research focuses on the theoretical foundations and outcomes of scenario planning. He has published widely on the theory and practice of scenario planning, including numerous studies that demonstrate its benefits. Tom's research has appeared in numerous scholarly journals as well as books and magazines. He teaches courses on scenario planning as well as human expertise, evaluation and assessment, analysis in organizations, change management, and organization development.

Preface

The fundamental premise of *Analysis* is that systematic and thorough organization performance diagnosis and documentation of workplace expertise provides the true basis for improving performance at the organization, process, team, and worker levels. This is a book about mastering performance improvement using proven analysis tools. and the work, not mastering the worker.

The tools presented in this book have never been more important. The after-effects of the "Pandemic," the "Great Resignation," the "Silver Wave" of retiring baby boomers, and the incredible shift in technology with the invasion of artificial intelligence are all signs that analysis is a priority. Analysis focused on performance improvement is critical to ensure the survival of organizations amidst unprecedented market volatility and talent shortages. As workplace demands shift from more traditional well-established roles to more fluid and flexible positions, the analysis tools in this book are the key to improving performance in today's modern organization. Arguably, there has been no other time during which people have left their roles or transitioned to other jobs at the present rate. The results are more frequent disruptions due to unanticipated staff departures, increased loss of organization knowledge and expertise, and higher cost risks associated with a lack of clarity around the tasks that drive performance improvement.

Therefore, an additional premise of this book is very simple: Capturing the knowledge of experts before they leave the organization creates an important competitive advantage. This book provides the tools you need to do exactly that.

Organization efforts at improving performance—such as organization development, training, quality improvement, reengineering, human resource development, and performance technology—are exhibited in various ways. One way clearly recognizes the organization's core processes and their connectedness to basic inputs and outputs for adding value. The other important approach to improving performance is uncovering patterns of independent activities taking place apart from the core organizational inputs and outputs that have connections to organization performance measures.

Regardless of the specific approach used, standard performance improvement models include four to six phases, from analysis to evaluation. One standard version is analysis, design, development, implementation, and evaluation. However, it is how the analysis phase is carried out that determines whether performance improvement efforts support core organization and work processes. Years ago, core organization processes were relatively simple, as they reflected the complexity of technology at the time. Technological advancements in automation, programming, and artificial intelligence demand an increase in tasks requiring interaction with systems and knowledge. Despite these dramatic changes in technology, analyzing tasks to clarify their alignment with an organization's performance goals, remains steadfast and unchanged. These analysis tools are technology timeless. Even though analysis practices are diverse, a universal analysis vocabulary has developed. Almost everyone claims that the up-front analysis phase is important, even though professional practices leave much to be desired. Thus, the easy talk about analysis—at both the diagnosis of performance and documentation of expertise levels—can mean intense investigation from one perspective or a fairly simple "armchair" activity from another.

Our position, backed by research and experience, is that the analysis phase, and its requirements of organization diagnosis and expertise documentation, is the most critical phase of the performance improvement process. It is also the phase that is most poorly executed. The results of poorly executed up-front analysis have significant implications for performance outcomes, much of which can be fixed by applying the tools described in this book.

Most performance improvement interventions are driven by employee perceptions of organizational health that get connected to "feel-good" outcomes or "compliance" concerns versus mission/goal-related outcomes. While there is a growing body of research that acknowledges the positive impact organizational health can have on performance, it is peripheral at best. Those efforts, despite their role in employee well-being, do not result in significant or easily measurable performance improvements. The interventions presented in this book do. The activity-oriented view, with its emphasis on perception and program delivery, does not focus on the analysis phase, it is more concerned with implementation and evaluation phases. It relegates analysis to opinion surveys, resulting in choosing interventions based on popularity ratings that may improve culture, but offer no assurance of improving performance. All organizations struggle with competing priorities for investment. When resources are scarce and unstable, as they often are, the future of an organization depends on the impact of its business interventions. The interventions that reliably deliver measurable performance improvements and focus on expertise are the ones that ensure survival.

Overview of the Contents

Analysis: The Key for Improving Organization and Individual Performance works on the assumption that performance improvement efforts if they are going to add value to the organization, require an emphasis on the analysis phase. The analysis phase is the content of this book. To meet these ends, we present practical tools in two major arenas: (1) diagnosis of performance and (2) documentation of expertise.

Diagnosis of performance analyzes the performance variables (mission/ goals, processes, motivation, capacity, and expertise) at the organization, process, team, and individual performance levels. Documentation of expertise requires analysis of the work expertise needed to achieve optimal work performance. This analysis involves the components of job description, task inventories, and the detailed analysis of varying tasks (procedure, systems, and knowledge work tasks). In this book, an effort has been made to provide examples that will resonate with a new generation of performance improvement professionals and executive leaders. Again, the fundamental premise of this book is that rigorous workplace diagnosis and documentation provide the true basis for improving performance. This is not a book about organization strategy focusing on alternative future states of the organization. Yet, we know of several instances where organizations using the analysis tools in this book came to understand that their performance improvement issues demanded that they stop and reconsider their futures, from going out of business to modifying the fundamental purpose of the businesses (Chermack, 2011).

At first glance, these tools may appear to be complex. They are easily learned and highly effective. In most instances, we provide both process and thinking models to explain each tool. The process models describe the steps and flow of the processes and the thinking models present the dimensions that need to be considered. They are tools that can be learned to some degree by anybody committed to the goal of performance improvement. The opportunity to engage analysis work teams of stakeholders can pay off in gaining time and commitment. The output of careful analysis is the critical information that accurately defines, frames, and guides effective performance improvement interventions.

The Sextant as the Icon

Navigating boats in open seas overwhelms and distorts the senses, much like the analysis challenge facing professionals wanting to improve performance in organizations.

Without accurate reference points, ships and sailors are easily lost. The sextant was a navigation instrument invented in the nineteenth century.

It measured the altitudes of celestial bodies to determine precise latitude and longitude positioning—triangulation of data. The sextant provided position and direction, like the tools in this book. A vintage sextant still works with exactly the same accuracy and reliability as it did centuries ago while today, we rely on global positioning system (GPS) technology for navigation purposes.

The analysis for performance tools provides position and direction that allows the performance improvement professional to analyze, navigate, and improve complex organizations. The sextant was selected as an icon for the critical up-front analysis theory, methods, and tools presented in this book.

The cover image depicts an 18th-century brass sextant by the English School (©Private collection/The Bridgeman Art Library).

Acknowledgments

A number of people and organizations have provided support for the ideas, research, development, and writing that led to this book. Most recently, Laura M. Coons and Jessica M. Serkey Bishop have made important contributions.

Important research funds were made available by Manville Corporation, with the full support of Gary R. Sisson and Gil Cullen, former executives of that firm. Additional organizations provided support over the years, including 3M, CIGNA, Citicorp, Kellogg Company, Onan Corporation, Scoville Press, Xcel Energy, University of Minnesota, University of Texas at Tyler, and Colorado State University.

Contributions to the ideas presented in the book have come from Deane B. Gradous, Timothy McClernon, Gary R. Sisson, Barbara L. Swanson, and Richard J. Torraco, The results of intellectual exchanges with David C. Bjorkquist, Gary M. Geroy, Richard Herling, Ronald L. Jacobs, Russell Korte, Susan A. Lynham, Joseph T. Martelli, Laird McLean, Rochell McWhorter, Brian P. Murphy, Willis P. Norton, David L. Passmore, Steve Piersanti, Gene W. Poor, Wendy E. A. Ruona, and Catherine M. Sleezer have also made their way into the pages of this book. We sincerely thank them all, because each has had a positive impact on our lives and on this book.

Richard A. Swanson
St. Paul, Minnesota
Thomas J. Chermack
Fort Collins, Colorado

Part I

Analysis Basics

Chapter 1

Linking Improvement Programs to Important Organization Goals

Chapter Sections

- **When Leaders Decide to Follow-Up**
- **Four Performance Questions about Outputs**
- **Analysis Work Is Important**
- **Long-Term Success**
- **Conclusion**

The role of performance improvement in organizations is one of the most critical strategic considerations in human resource development, quality improvement, process improvement, reengineering, knowledge management, technology, and take-charge management. Organizational leaders should focus considerable energy in this area. Their organizations spend millions of dollars each year on development efforts aimed at their systems, employees, and customers. While much is to be gained in terms of increased performance, money spent hastily on programs based on erroneous assumptions yields very little for the organizations and individuals participating in them.

Global events continue to dramatically reshape the nature of the workforce. Leaders must contend with transformation on an ever-more rapid pace and ever-more revolutionary scale. While the lasting changes stemming from the *Great Resignation*, *Great Reshuffle*, *Great Reset*, or *Artificial Intelligence* won't be known for many years, these phenomena seem not to be the *beginning* of massive change, but the culmination of decades of long-simmering challenges.

Many studies on employee engagement suggest that even before the pandemic, at best, roughly 20% of people felt fully engaged at work (Buckingham, 2022). Trends over the last few years suggest employees do not trust their leaders, do not feel resilient about overcoming work challenges, and generally do not believe their organizations truly care about their personal growth and development (Buckingham, 2022). Not surprisingly, the rate at which workers

DOI: 10.4324/9781003518532-2

leave organizations is increasing. In 2016, about 34% of employees changed companies every five years. In 2020, 42% did so (McLean & Company, 2022). The Bureau of Labor Statistics reports similar increases in voluntary turnover—from 20% per year in 2013 to 25% per year in 2020 (BLS, 2022). Historically, low unemployment compels leaders to devise ever more inventive incentives to attract talent—but retaining those individuals is not currently positively impacted by those benefits (Miller, 2021). The general chaos created by current uncertainty around remote, hybrid, and in-person work experiences is further exacerbating these challenges, and no one has a clear answer on steps that might meaningfully make a difference (Goldberg, 2022).

Why do employee engagement, trust, resilience, and office experiences have a bearing on a discussion about performance improvement? The Work Institute (2022) estimates voluntary turnover costs companies in the US $630 billion annually. Consistently, when they share what would make a difference in their experience at work, employees share clear expectations, connected to clear performance outcomes, linked to meaningful development are top of mind (Gallup, 2022). Further, if the highly mobile nature of the workforce does not change no matter what companies do, performance improvement documentation is even more important. Capturing the expertise of skilled workers and creating accurate job/task details to help demystify what is expected in roles are vital steps.

Performance improvement professionals often find themselves in awkward positions. They face many conflicting demands on their services. When executives attend seminars, they sometimes hear motivational speakers, which can be a useful event though usually it is not. Hooked by the fiery delivery and the bold promises of the management evangelists, many executives become enthusiastic about bringing new messages home to their organizations and demand, "Hire the consultant and see that everyone in headquarters goes through the program." Or even worse "We should order 2,000 copies of that book and demand that all of our managers read it." Then, after a large investment in time and money, everyone in the organization has the language of the consultant, but nothing else in the organization has substantially changed. Under highly dynamic workforce conditions, the leaders who sought such programming may be gone from the organization before the full deployment is achieved. The original vision typically departs with them. Who, then, holds the organization accountable to the new processes and practices? Nutt (2003) described the failure to reconcile claims and reality as a common trap that decision-makers fall into. They contract for performance gains and are provided intensive development activities but fail to acquire evidence of results.

The performance improvement manager who dutifully responds to line manager requests by charging out to hire an external expert is simply fulfilling the whims of his or her boss. Instead, the performance improvement leader should be investigating business performance issues and offering sound proposals for development efforts that directly address important organizational goals. For example:

- What is creating the quality problem at the Boise facility?
- Why are our engineers unable to integrate their CAD/CAM files with those of the customers' engineers?
- How can we reduce cycle time for our highest-demand product?
- Why can only two of our twelve financial investors regularly put together sound financial deals?

Each organization is unique. Each has its own mission, strategies, performance goals, and challenges. Often these are not well-articulated or described. Seldom is a scope, schedule, or budget aligned to the various missions or strategies. Faddish, one-size-fits-all performance improvement efforts are not likely to fit a specific organizational physique. With considerable confidence, we can say that in the short or long run, performance improvement efforts not accurately connected to an important organizational goal will be seen as the ill-fitting garments they are and will be tossed out of the organization. Nohria and Berkley (1998) sum up the situation by stating, "The manager's job is not to seek out novelty but to make sure the company gets results" (p. 203).

When Managers Decide to Follow-Up

It is discouraging to discover how rarely leaders provide support for participants following expensive employee development programs (Holton & Baldwin, 2003; McLagan, 2003). Leaders have historically done little to ensure that the on-the-job performance of employees reflects what they have learned in organization-sponsored development programs (Parker, 1986). This may be because they themselves did not participate fully in the program and cannot model the behavior, or because they are pulled in so many directions, they are unable to create the norms that would drive consistent application of the learning. Further, expensive training programs without a full organization-wide deployment strategy are doomed. When only some associates know the new approach, successfully implementing that approach is practically impossible. Meanwhile, the same leaders often say they want hard numbers about the contributions that development programs have made to organizational success. Leaders also say they would provide more support for development efforts if such evidence were made available (Kusy, 1986). When upper management does decide to follow performance improvement programs with evaluation, they often do not like what they find:

- The effort did not fill a current or future business need.
- The program did not fit the culture of the organization.

- The principles and systems covered in the program did not reflect the expected work performance.
- Participants did not develop their expertise to the level of mastery required to perform on the job.
- Participants were punished by leaders or peer groups for implementing new ideas and expertise back on the job.

Four Performance Questions about Outputs

Four simple performance questions, if they were asked at the outset of planning for improvement efforts, could radically change the role and contributions of the development functions in most organizations.

1 Will the individual perform better after the intervention?
2 Will the process perform better after the intervention?
3 Will the work team perform better after the intervention?
4 Will the organization perform better after the intervention?

All four questions focus on outputs. All four link development to the primary mission of the organization.

Top decision-makers work hard at setting mission, strategy, and goals for the organization. Increasingly, performance improvement professionals are becoming members of this team. The aim, of course, is to maximize productivity and economic return by producing and delivering quality goods and services required by the customer. Managing the core enterprise of most organizations is subject to many uncertainties. The internal environment of the organization reflects the complexity and fluidity of its external environment. Within a context of changing culture, politics, and technologies (Brache, 2002; Drazin, Glynn, & Kazanjian, 2004; Swanson, 1999), management's decisions to invest in development efforts are too often made apart from the four questions about performance improvement.

Performance improvement leaders, too, are often distracted from focusing on the organization, process, work team, and job performance questions. Two factors seem to be the source of the distractions that pull professionals away from their focus on performance. The first factor arises from management itself. Many general leaders know little or nothing about sound performance improvement practices, yet they strongly attempt to control new efforts and processes. In the absence of a true understanding of the proper role of development, such leaders let their personal agendas take over. The second factor arises from developers themselves. Many are ill-equipped to advocate for or implement a sound development process for responsibly connecting their contributions to the mission, strategies, and performance goals of their organizations. As a result, many development decisions are based, by default, on a consultant's promises or management's wants and preferences, rather than on careful analyses of organization, process, work team, and individual performance issues and the variables that impinge on them.

Competent, responsible leaders ought to be asking the organizational, process, work team, and individual performance questions. Performance improvement managers should be skillful in accessing the information required to answer these questions. Performance improvement efforts that are based on sound analyses will almost always stand up to inquiry by decision-makers when they ask any of the four performance questions—relating to organization, process, work team, or individual performance—or all four together. Development leaders ought to be able to show that their programs make a positive difference in their organizations in the form of improved performance.

Responsible performance improvement efforts are realized through an orderly process that *starts* with:

- specifying an important performance goal,
- determining the underlying performance variables,
- documenting work processes, and
- documenting the workplace expertise required of the performance goal.

These four components comprise the analysis phase of the systematic performance improvement process and the scope of this book. Beyond the analysis phase, the other phases address the design, development, implementation, and evaluation of the performance improvement effort. Because the analysis phase defines, frames, and directs the remaining steps, it is considered the most critical. Thus, learning how to diagnose organizational performance and document workplace expertise pays off for analysts, their organizations, and the integrity of the improvement effort.

Analysis Work Is Important

Most development and performance improvement programs based on the whims of organization decision-makers die out within a year or two. Performance improvement professionals must be able to carry out analysis work. They must be able to analyze performance at the organization, process, work team, and job levels and they must know how to interpret the resulting requirements for workplace improvement before implementing development solutions. Their expertise and comfort levels increase by using proven diagnostic and documentation tools, thereby providing a solid foundation on which to build responsible performance improvement solutions. The goal is to develop interventions that have an impact on individual, process, work team, and/or organization performance. The future of most

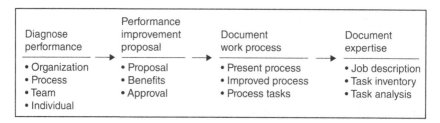

Diagnose performance	Performance improvement proposal	Document work process	Document expertise
• Organization	• Proposal	• Present process	• Job description
• Process	• Benefits	• Improved process	• Task inventory
• Team	• Approval	• Process tasks	• Task analysis
• Individual			

Figure 1.1   Overview of Analysis for Improving Performance Process

performance improvement functions depends, at least in part, on managers and development professionals learning to work in partnership to achieve greater positive returns from performance improvement activities (McLean, 2005; Swanson, 1999). Careful analysis and follow-through are the means for accomplishing high-performance returns.

Long-Term Success

The work of performance improvement professionals should be no different than that of other competent business leaders. The careful analytical processes that are expected and regularly performed in areas of strategic and tactical planning, product development, marketing, and systems engineering can also be applied to performance improvements. Yet, they are rarely taken with the same level of seriousness. The content boundary for this book is devoted to sound and systematic tools for diagnosing and documenting workplace performance and expertise. The book's core content focal points are displayed in Figure 1.1. Analyzing organization performance for goal attainment at one or more of the four levels culminates in a performance improvement proposal. That proposal leads to work process analysis and documentation of the expertise required for performance improvement.

Conclusion

The case for engaging in front-end analysis is a practical and compelling one. As a reminder, there has never been a more important and relevant time for the kind of work described in the following chapters. It results in an accurate connection to important and attainable performance gains. It is not an empty promise of performance. Analysis reduces the amount of perceived chaos in the organization through professional expertise and purposeful inquiry. Analysis takes time and money but ends up saving much more time and money than it consumes.

This is not a book about one perspective or technique promising to improve performance (e.g., total quality management, reengineering, and knowledge management). This is a book focused on outcomes and performance. This is a book that presents a variety of tools for directing performance improvement efforts. This is a book for take-charge leaders, performance improvement specialists, and workers wanting to improve their organizations. This is a book that facilitates team effort and commitment to organization-specific performance improvement efforts. And, it will provide the ability to capture expertise before it exits with key workers.

The next chapter steps back to provide the deeper theoretical basis that underlies performance improvement in complex organizations. The remaining chapters provide the "real-world" knowledge, tools, examples, and exercises aimed at developing your expertise in diagnosing organizational performance and documenting workplace expertise—the keys to long-term organization success.

Chapter 2

Foundations of Performance Improvement

Chapter Sections

- Purpose of This Chapter
- The Performance Improvement Theory Stool
- Functional Models of Performance
- Conclusion

Make no doubt about it—there is a great deal to learn about change, management, and performance improvement. Theories in all these realms are works in progress. While this research is going on, thousands of charlatans and well-intentioned practitioners are trying to fill the void. Fortunately, we know enough about the theoretical aspects of performance improvement in organizations to be doing much better than most present-day practices (Swanson & Chermack, 2013). Armed with a theoretical understanding of performance improvement, practitioners are better able to resist the charlatans and create truly successful interventions.

This observation is not intended to disregard experience. Experience is an important part of sound theory, but is inadequate by itself (Swanson, 1990a). Gagne's (1962) classic research on training reported that people do not improve, let alone get to excellence, through experience alone. He goes on to say that without serious study, reflections, and the creation of foundational concept/theories, we will continue to repeat our failed experiences without learning from them.

As a result, critics of management scholarship and practice have harsh things to say. They reach back for classic examples such as the book *In Search of Excellence* (Peters & Waterman, 1982), which identified forty-three excellent companies and tried to distill their secret to organizational success. But less than five years after the book's publication, two-thirds of the companies have ceased to be excellent (Micklethwait & Wooldridge, 1996). Apparently, the excellent companies did not have a key to excellence, and those that tried to replicate the excellent practices identified through superficial investigation were most likely even worse off.

DOI: 10.4324/9781003518532-3

Single-dimension views of organizations often become a roadblock to the theoretical foundation of performance. Such views, while obviously easier to understand, are overgeneralizations in terms of their utility for understanding the true complexity of organizations, work processes, work teams, and individuals. Descriptions of four common single-dimension views follow.

- **Power-Oriented View:** Some analysts consider powerful leaders in the organization to be the instruments for change—the power-oriented view. In power-driven organizations, managers assume that their job is to plan, organize, and control organizational processes. The performance improvement professional's role is to respond to line manager requests for activities and programs. Satisfying line managers is the major goal. Given this power view, developers primarily serve at the beck and call of powerful organizational leaders and decision-makers.
- **Economic View:** Some analysts view organizations as instruments for increasing the wealth of shareholders—the economic view. In economically driven organizations, managers assume that their job is to ensure high returns on all investments. Here the developer's role is to apply solutions that will yield high returns on investments. Increasing the quality or quantity of individual worker outputs is a major development goal. Given this economic view, performance improvement professionals adjust themselves to adhere to and assist in implementing the economic agenda of the organizations.
- **Mechanistic View:** Some analysts regard organizations as machines in which the goal is obtaining the maximum quantity and quality of outputs through smoothly running maximally efficient organization processes— the mechanistic view. In mechanistic organizations, managers assume that their job is to ensure that organization processes are highly efficient. The role for developers in this context is to respond to calls for improved work methods and for workers' adherence to ever-higher performance standards and goals. Given this mechanistic view, development is primarily a tool for improving the effectiveness and efficiency of established work processes.
- **Humanistic View:** Some analysts view organization as social entities in which a high quality of work life is a major goal—the humanistic view. In humanistic organizations, managers assume that their job is to guarantee the high morale of workers, which will then logically lead to increased outputs of goods and services on the part of satisfied workers. Here the developers' role is to assist managers and workers in building their interpersonal skills. Given this humanistic view, development is primarily a tool for improving the relationships between people up, down, and across the organization hierarchy.

These organizational views, whether applied singly or in partial combinations, provide inadequate foundations for organization problem-solving. Holders of these single-dimension views will tend to restrict themselves to a narrow set of problem situations and their solutions. They limit what they will see or do as they work with managers and others on organizational change.

- The power-oriented analyst will tend to focus on political strategies—on pleasing top managers.
- The economically oriented analyst will tend to focus on strategies to optimize financial return on organizational investments.
- The mechanistically oriented analyst will tend to focus on strategies for getting more and more output per worker or process.
- The humanistically oriented analyst will tend to focus on creating harmony in the workplace and on making work life more pleasant.

Purpose of This Chapter

The purpose of this chapter is to provide a theoretical foundation for improving performance within an organization context. Such a foundation is important for performance improvement practitioners because it grounds actions in a unifying model of reality. Two major sections follow.

First, a theoretical foundation for those wishing to understand and analyze organizations is presented. A thinking model in the form of a three-legged stool is used as a visual metaphor with a leg each for economic, psychological, and systems theories' contribution to a theory of organization performance. The stool sits on an ethical rug.

Second, a taxonomy for performance and a system/process model are presented in graphic form to illustrate the taxonomic levels of performance and a systems view of the organization that includes the processes within it and the external forces. These models, anchored in sound theory and practice, provide a vehicle for conceptually moving around during the process of improving performance. They help in mentally drilling down, pulling back, or moving back and forth over time in the performance improvement process.

The Performance Improvement Theory Stool

Many disciplines and fields of practice have biases about organization performance. The four single-dimension views of organizations presented earlier illustrate this point. The pool of potential theories claiming to inform organization understanding is huge. Through our research and years of consulting work we determined that:

- foundational theory is important to the practical work of analysis for improving performance;
- organizations are human-made entities having unique goals of producing goods or services; and

- a limited number of highly relevant core theories and their integration should serve as the theoretical foundation of performance improvement.

Performance from an organization, process, team, and individual contributor perspective is broader than any single disciplinary theory. Reflecting the reality that most successful strategies for system and subsystem improvement require multifaceted interventions, the theory of performance improvement is best derived from multiple core disciplines.

"A theory simply explains what a phenomenon is and how it works" (Torraco, 1997, p. 115). The beliefs about performance tend to range from single-dimension to an "anything goes" mentality.

Theory versus Model

Models to improve performance have been developed and disseminated through books, seminars, and consulting projects. Several of these models are based on extensive practical experience with improving performance (Nadler et al., 1992; Rummler & Brache, 2012). Other models for improving performance have been embraced as ways to solve performance problems by addressing them as multidimensional problems that demand multidimensional solutions. Some models for performance improvement are little more than diagrams based on the author's most recent consulting experience.

Armed with a flowchart and a description of its components, performance improvement professionals march into the workplace to effect change. While these models may be powerful enough to effect some change, they are most likely too superficial to explain the complex dynamics of organization performance. A model derived from logic is no substitute for sound theory. Such models can guide improvement efforts through hypothesized relationships without having those relationships ever tested. You can have a model and no theory, you can have a theory with no model, and you can have a theory accompanied by a supporting model. A model by itself is not theory (Swanson & Chermack, 2013).

Disciplinary Theory for Performance Improvement

Presently there is no universal view or agreement on the theory or multiple theories that support performance improvement. In the past, some have called for systems theory to serve as a unifying theory to access all useful theories when required (Gradous, 1989; Jacobs, 1989; McLagan, 1989). Alternatively, many have proposed sets of principles in the forms of comparative lists of added value, products, processes, and expertise (Gilley, Dean, & Bierma, 2000).

The option to having a sound theoretical and disciplinary base for the performance improvement profession is a rudderless state of random activity that is aggressively sponsored by atheoretical professional associations and greedy consultants (Micklethwait & Wooldridge, 1996; Swanson, 1997a). This approach celebrates short-term reactions and proxy results without having a deep understanding or the ability to replicate results.

For this reason, a discrete and logical set of theories as the foundation of performance improvement is proposed. It is comprised of (1) psychological theory, (2) economic theory, and (3) systems theory (Passmore, 1997; Swanson, 1995). Economic theory is recognized as a primary driver and survival metric of organizations; systems theory recognizes purpose, pieces, and relationships that can maximize or strangle systems and subsystems; and psychological theory acknowledges human beings as brokers of productivity along with their cultural and behavioral nuances. Each of these three theories is unique, complementary, and robust. Together and integrated, they form the theoretical basis of performance improvement capable of responding to the realities of practice.

The theories have been visually presented as comprising a three-legged stool, with the three legs providing great stability as a discipline and field of practice functioning in the midst of uneven and changing conditions (see Figure 2.1). In recent years, particularly with the advance of the global economy and an unbridled free market condition, the stool has been positioned on an ethical rug—a filter, if you will— between its three theories and the context in which performance improvement functions. Thus, the

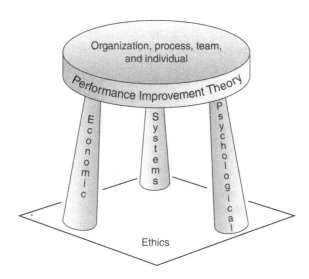

Figure 2.1 Theoretical Foundations of Performance Improvement

three theories are at the core of the profession, and ethics plays an important moderating role.

Economic Theory Foundation

Minimizing economic theory in performance improvement is untenable. While the field of management would position the economic leg as the dominant leg, the widely used book on organization development, *Organization Development and Change* (Cummings & Worley, 2016), does not even have the words economic, financial, or cost–benefit analysis in its index. Amazingly, much of the change, organization development, and improvement literature ignores the economic leg. In a similar vein, almost all business strategy literature ignores the human resource and psychological leg. Economists Bassi and McMurrer (2006) note that the companies investing in the development of their workforce consistently outperform their sector competition, yet business and stock market accounting ignores this fact.

Although there is still much to be learned, a substantial amount of information about the economics of short-term interventions (Swanson, 2001) and broader-based investments is available (Bassi & McMurrer, 2006; Lyau & Pucel, 1995).

How could responsible performance improvement not include direct analysis, action, and measurement of economic outcomes? Over time, organizations must generate more income than they spend in order to exist. Unless performance improvement expenditures contribute to the viability and profitability of an organization, those expenditures will almost certainly be cut back or eliminated. Three specific economic theory perspectives are believed to be most appropriate to performance improvement: (1) scarce resource theory, (2) sustainable resource theory, and (3) human capital theory.

Scarce Resource Theory. Scarce resource theory informs us that there are limitations to everything. The limitations in money, raw materials, time, and so on, require us to make choices as to how capital will be utilized in order to gain the greatest return. Decision-makers choose among options based on their forecasted return on investment. This is a simple and powerful notion that forces decision-makers to separate the most valuable and worthy initiatives from the many things that they could do if there were no resource limitations (Swanson, 2001; Swanson & Gradous, 1986).

Sustainable Resource Theory. Sustainable resource theory is much like scarce resource theory except for one major point: the concern for the long-term versus short-term agenda. Years ago Thurow (1993) informed us that "in the future, sustainable advantage will depend on new process technologies and less on new product technology. New industries of the future depend ... on brain power. Man-made competitive advantages replace the comparative advantage of Mother Nature (natural-resources endowment) or history (capital endowments)" (p. 16).

Human Capital Theory. Becker's (1993) classic book, *Human Capital: A Theoretical and Empirical Analysis with Special Reference to Education,* illustrates this domain. Becker implores the reader:

> I am going to talk about a different kind of capital. Schooling,
>
> a computer training course, expenditures on medical care, and
>
> lectures on the virtues of punctuality and honesty are capital too,
>
> in the true sense that they improve health, raise earnings, or add to
>
> a person's appreciation of literature over a lifetime. Consequently,
>
> it is fully in keeping with the capital concept as traditionally
>
> defined to say that expenditures on education, training, and
>
> medical care, etc., are investments in capital.
>
> (pp. 15–16)

These are not simply costs but investments with valuable returns that can be calculated.

Summary. Economist Alfred Marshall (1949) argues that "the most valuable of all capital is that invested in human beings." Since the performance improvement considered here takes place in organizations that are economic entities, economic theory is essential to understanding performance improvement. In addition, management theories and methods should be properly viewed as useful derivatives of economic theory (see Drucker, 1964).

Psychological Theory Foundation

The psychological theory from which performance theory can draw is immense. It includes theories of learning, human motivation, information processing, and group dynamics along with psychology-based theories of how we make decisions and behave in organizations. Yet, it has been poorly interpreted by the profession. Most practitioners grab onto a small and relatively irrelevant slice of psychological theory and act on it in exaggerated ways. Examples include fascination with reward theory and personality types. Passmore (1997) informs us that "psychology is the science of behavior and mental processes of humans and other animals. Beyond that, we have something that resembles a teenager's closet" (p. 210).

While psychological theory may have something for everybody, the performance improvement profession has yet to fully capitalize on its psychology leverage to improve performance. Unfortunately, the profession relies almost exclusively focused on the behaviorist school of psychology and does not deal in any meaningful way with Gestalt psychology or cognitive psychology (purposive behaviorism). At best, the professional literature addresses the psychological theory leg of the theory stool in an unpredictable manner. Add to this the fact that performance improvement interventions are not regularly and systematically connected to the economic agenda via an analysis of the organization and its goals (Swanson, 2001). It is no wonder, then, that interventions based only on psychological theory are often dismissed as irrelevant by organization leaders unless they mirror the psyche of the top leader.

Fascination appears be the watchword of the psychological leg as questions from psychology are typically narrow and/or disconnected from the core purpose of the organization, the work process, and often even the individual. For example, the continued intrigue of such topics as transfer of training from the psychology perspective primarily focuses on the individual and individual perceptions. The response to this limited perspective is mainly focused on follow-up activity for situations that might be better understood through systems and economic theory—not by psychological theory alone (Holton, 1996).

How could responsible performance improvement professionals not integrate and use the vast body of knowledge from psychological theory? With such vast and divergent psychological theory available, it is more appropriate to focus on core understandings related to behavior and learning rather than fringe psychology theories and techniques. Three specific psychological theory perspectives are proposed here to be most appropriate to the discipline: (1) Gestalt psychology, (2) behavioral psychology, and (3) cognitive psychology (purposive behaviorism).

Gestalt Psychology. Gestalt is the German term for "configuration" or "organization." Gestalt psychologists inform us that we do not see isolated stimuli but stimuli gathered together in meaningful configurations. We see people, chairs, cars, trees, and flowers—not lines and patches of color. Gestaltists believe that people add something to experience that is not contained in the sensory data and that we experience the world in meaningful wholes (Hergenhahn & Olson, 1993). Thus, learning involves moving from one whole to another. Words associated with Gestalt psychology include introspection, meaning, closure, insight, life space, field theory, humanism, phenomenology, and relational theory. The holistic view of individuals and their own need for holistic understanding is in sharp contrast to a mechanistic and elemental view of human beings.

Behavioral Psychology. Behavioral psychology is concerned with what can be seen, and therefore behavior is what is studied. Behavioral psychologists tell us that individuals respond the only way they can, given their capacity, experience, and present forces working on them. No more introspection, no more talk of instinctive behavior, and no more attempts to study the vague notions of human conscious or unconscious mind. Words associated with behaviorism include readiness, law effect, exercise, recency, frequency, stimulus, response, reinforcement, punishment, programmed learning, and drives.

Cognitive Psychology. Tolman's (1932) term purposive behaviorism has been selected as the exemplar of this third important perspective from psychology. Purposive behaviorism attempts to explain goal-directed behavior and the idea that human beings organize their lives around purposes. Purposive behaviorism (and other cognitive psychologies) attempts to integrate theory from Gestalt and behavioral psychology.

"For purposive behaviorism, behavior, as we have seen, is purposeful, cognitive, and molar, i.e., 'Gestalted.' Purposive behaviorism is molar, not a molecular" (Tolman, 1932, p. 419). Words associated with cognitive psychology, including purposive behaviorism, include drive discriminations, field-cognition modes, cognitive map, learning by analogy, learned helplessness, structuring, information processing, short-and long-term memory, and artificial intelligence.

Summary. Since performance improvement takes place in organizations that are psychologically framed by those who invented them, operate in them, and renew them, practitioners must call on psychology as also being essential to its theory (see Argyris, 1993; Bereiter & Scardamalia, 1993; Pfeffer & Sutton, 2000). In addition, learning theories such as constructivism and situated cognition should be properly viewed as useful derivatives of psychological theory. Performance cannot be improved if people choose not to perform, put forth little effort, or do not persist in their efforts (Bereiter & Scardamalia, 1993). Moreover, systematically designed development experiences and workplace systems provide a durable foundation for performance improvement. Thus, theories of learning, human motivation, information processing, and other psychologically based theories provide a core theoretical foundation for performance improvement.

Systems Theory Foundation

Systems theory, a relatively small body of knowledge compared with economics and psychology, contains a harvest of low-hanging performance improvement fruit. From a systems theory perspective, a wide range of systemic disconnects adversely affects performance. Two examples are (1) not being able to clearly specify the required outcomes of the host organization and (2) not having a systematically defined performance improvement process (see Rummler & Brache, 2012).

Systems theory is a relatively young discipline made up of "a collection of general concepts, principles, tools, problems and methods associated with systems of any kind" (Passmore, 1997, pp. 206–207). Gradous's (1989) classic monograph sets the stage for serious consideration of systems theory by the human resource development profession. The quality improvement profession recognizes the classic works of Deming (1986) and Juran (1992) when it comes to systems theory applications to processes and the organizations in which they reside.

Three specific systems theory perspectives are proposed here as appropriate to performance improvement: (1) general systems theory, (2) chaos theory, and (3) futures theory.

General Systems Theory. At its core, general systems theory forces us to talk intelligently about inputs, processes, outputs, and feedback. Furthermore, general systems theory informs us of the reality of open systems (vs. closed systems) in comparison to system engineering that focuses on the less dynamic aspects of the organization and the limitations of a single theory in predicting outcomes (Bertalanffy, 1962).

Boulding's (1956) classic article on general systems theory describes the paradox of a theory so general as to mean nothing and the seeming inability of a single theory from a single field of study to ever reach a satisfactory level of theory generality. He goes on to talk about the power of a "spectrum of theories," a "system of systems" that would perform the function of a "Gestalt" in theory building (Boulding, 1956). "General Systems Theory may at times be an embarrassment in pointing out how far we still have to go" (p. 10)—thus the need to go beyond general systems theory.

Chaos Theory. "Where chaos begins, classical science stops.... Chaos is a science of process rather than a state, of becoming rather than of being" (Gleick, 1987, pp. 3, 5). Chaos theory confronts Newtonian logic head-on by offering a revised motto away from determinism to something much softer: "Given an approximate knowledge of a system's initial conditions and an understanding of natural law, one can calculate the approximate behavior of the system" (Gleick, 1987, p. 15). Chaos theory purposefully acknowledges and studies phenomena that are unsystematic—that do not appear to follow the rules.

Futures Theory. Futures theory is "not necessarily interested in predicting the future, it is about the liberation of people's insights" (Schwartz, 1991, p. 9). Thus, futures theory, in the context of planning for the future in uncertain conditions, in no way resembles the reductionist view of most strategic planning efforts that end up with a single strategy. The language and tools of alternative futures and scenario building are intended to create a true picture of the facts, the potential flux in those facts, and the decision-making agility required of the future. Futures theory is critical for sustainable performance in that it prepares one to recognize and cope with an evolving future state (Chermack, 2003).

Summary. Since systematic performance improvement takes place in organizations that are themselves systems and subsystems functioning within an environmental system that is ever-changing, systems theory is logically at its core (see Buckley, 1968; Gradous, 1989). In addition, engineering technology theories and methods should be properly viewed as useful derivatives of systems theory (see Davenport, 1993; FitzGerald & FitzGerald, 1973).

Ethics

As noted earlier, ethics is viewed as the critical supporting theory for performance improvement. It serves as the filter between the three core theories of economics, psychology, and systems and the context within which performance improvement efforts take place.

Julliard (2004) notes that the social dimension of organizations elevates the role of ethics in quality management. Additionally, the Academy of Human Resource Development established Academy of Human Resource Development Standards on Ethics and Integrity in 1999, and the Academy of Management composed The Academy of Management Code of Ethical Conduct in 2004.

From the ethical beliefs perspective, some argue about the exploitive nature of organizations and would criticize performance improvement professionals as unthinking arms of management (Korten, 1995), challenging them to act as the agent of democracy and equity (Dirkx, 1996). Others argue that exploitation is a much more expansive concept (e.g., employees can exploit their employers) and that it must be dealt with as such (Swanson, Horton, & Kelly, 1986). The bogeyman in the performance picture is not the pursuit of improved performance; rather, it is the possibility of inequitable distribution of the spoils of any gains in performance that have occurred.

Functional Models of Performance

The levels of performance and a systems view of the organization, the processes within, and the external forces from outside are presented in this section. These relatively simple and functional models, anchored in sound theory, provide a vehicle for conceptually shifting around during the process of improving performance. These models help while you are engaged in the performance improvement process to mentally drill down, pull back, or move your thinking around without getting lost.

Taxonomy of Performance

The Taxonomy of Performance provides a lens that helps operationalize performance improvement theory for those who work in complex organizations. It lays out five tiers of performance: understand, operate, troubleshoot, improve, and invent (Figure 2.2). This taxonomy is more generally divided into two categories of effort: maintaining the system and changing the system.

While systems theorists assure us that business and industry conceptually operate as an open system—one that interfaces with other systems and is continually influenced by those systems (Senge, 1990, 1993)—the practical organizational goal is the attempt to establish closed systems, as short-lived as they might be, for producing and delivering goods and services. These temporary, closed systems are mastered and maintained at the understanding, operational, and troubleshooting levels. The closed system is imperfect, and thus the change tiers of the taxonomy of performance (improve and invent) provide the added dimensions to sort out the full range of possible performance issues facing the diagnostician.

However, since almost all organizations are regularly struggling with the two categories, they often get them mixed up. The result of undisciplined jumping from one tier in the taxonomy of performance to another can result in performance improvement in schizophrenia. We consistently observe

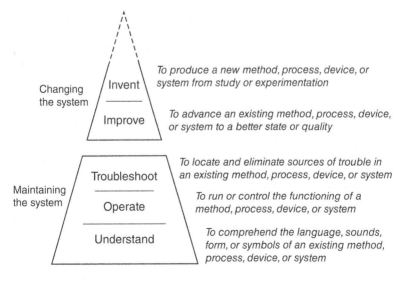

Figure 2.2 Taxonomy of Performance

organizations delivering support and resources at one level and expecting performance at another level. This is done without realizing the built-in discrepancy between their performance expectations and their interventions.

For example, a quality improvement effort to "change the system" could hit a brick wall because there is no documentation of the expertise required to "maintain the existing system." Thus, moving from the performance concern of change to the issue of how to maintain the system may be the critical first improvement step.

At the simplest level, it is no surprise to the experienced diagnostician that organizations that value, establish, and reward people for following rules have a hard time involving them in changing the system. Also, individuals who are trained to simply follow operational steps end up not understanding the system in which they operate and are not able to troubleshoot those systems, let alone improve them or invent new systems.

Thus, an important step in understanding a performance issue is to classify the problem or opportunity in terms of the taxonomy of performance. For example, shortcomings within an existing system level (e.g., maintaining) will require a much different response than moving the present performance from one level to another (e.g., maintaining to improving). Asking the general question as to what is going on here with the taxonomy in mind (understand, operate, troubleshoot, improve, and invent) can lead to an initial judgment that will save a great deal of analysis time.

Systems Model of Performance Improvement

This section presents a system/process model in graphic form that illustrates the organization, the processes within it, and the external forces from outside. This relatively simple but holistic model provides a vehicle for conceptually moving around during the process of improving performance. It helps in mentally visualizing the overall system, process, and context of performance improvement (see Figure 2.3).

Perceptions of Performance

Organizational performance is mediated through human expertise and effort. In contrast to this belief, the performance scorecards available to organizational decision-makers generally ignore these elements. The most evident example is the short-term financial view of company performance as judged by daily stock market data.

The journey of understanding performance for those who share the "human lens" has not been easy. The range of performance perspectives forces the profession to face the realities of how others strategically view us and how we view ourselves (Swanson, 1995; Torraco & Swanson, 1995). It

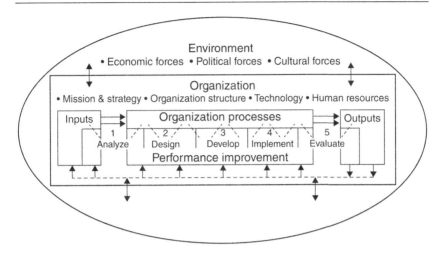

Figure 2.3   Systems Model of Performance Improvement

appears as though there has been a detour during the past seventy years. The massive "Training within Industry" (TWI) project that culminated with the ending of World War II is seen as the origin of contemporary performance improvement (Dooley, 1945; Ruona & Swanson, 1998; Swanson & Torraco, 1994). The performance language was simpler then—"Is it a production problem?" they would ask. If yes, they would use performance improvement tools that were masquerading under the name of "training." Besides operating under a training title that they quickly outgrew, the TWI project delivered organization, process, and individual performance outputs using simple and powerful tools called job instruction, job relations, and job methods. Paralleling this history, the quality improvement history reports a quality erosion after World War II, the adoption of improvement practices in Japan under the leadership of Joseph Juran and Edward Deming, and the return of their methods to US companies in the 1980s.

The reality is that most leaders in organizations pursue performance improvement without special professional interventions. The simple decision to start with the host organizational system as the primary avenue to performance alters the models, thinking, and tools of a performance improvement effort. Without this broad orientation beyond isolated individual, team, and process interventions, the performance lens will likely remain myopic.

Real Performance Is Output

To perform is "to fulfill an obligation or requirement; accomplish something as promised or expected" (Merriam-Webster's Collegiate Dictionary,

2003, p. 1015). Performance is not system design, capability, motivation, competence, or expertise. These, or other similar performance taxonomies, can best be thought of as performance variables, but not performance. Performance may be identified within missions, goals, and strategies—but not always. Performance is the valued productive output of a system in the form of goods or services. The actual fulfillment of the goods and/or services requirement is thought of in terms of units of performance. These goods and/or services units of performance are typically measured in terms of features of production quantity, time, and quality.

Chasing after individual or organization change without first specifying a valid unit of performance is foolhardy and a waste of time. This is because change can take place while "real" performance decreases! One example is to pursue employee satisfaction with the assumption that production will increase. Numerous studies have demonstrated that employee satisfaction can increase while actual production decreases or remains the same. The reengineering fad is another example of the pursuit of change with the majority of instances ending up in performance losses instead of gains (Micklethwait & Wooldridge, 1996). There are those in the profession speaking directly to the topic of performance in an attempt to clarify the relationships among performance drivers (Holton, 1998, 2001) and/or performance variables (Swanson, 1997b).

Systems theory informs us that (1) there are systems and subsystems and (2) all systems are open systems. The realization that there are tiers of subsystems and larger host systems and that systems are open entities constantly changing is humbling. These realizations help prevent professionals from thinking and acting simply and mechanically. Performance improvement practitioners and scholars should not lose sight of the constantly evolving state of overall systems.

The larger frame in which performance improvement functions includes organizations and the milieu in which they function. Organizations are the host systems for the activity. Some of these systems are profit-making organizations that produce goods and/or services for consumers. Some are nonprofit organizations that produce goods and/or services for consumers. Some are publicly owned, some are shareholder-owned and publicly traded, and some are owned by individuals or a group of individuals. All these organizations function in an ever-present political, cultural, and economic milieu. Each has its own mission/strategy, structure, technology, and human resource mix. And, each has core processes related to producing goods and services.

The expectation is that performance improvement efforts will logically culminate with important positive gains in performance for its host organization. Additionally, performance improvement can be viewed as a process functioning within the host organization. All of this is graphically portrayed in Figure 2.3 as a systems model of performance improvement, a process working with other core processes within the organization, all functioning in the larger organizational context. The final phase is focused on the assessment of performance results to heighten the intent of the performance improvement process.

Performance issues will demand concrete actions. Performance improvement is not simply abstract notions about desirable ways to reach a better state. In every workplace, the concrete determinants of performance are reflected in people, their ideas, and the material resources through which their ideas reach the marketplace. Performance cannot be described or improved without specifying its determinants, accounting for the sophisticated processes through which performance is expressed (e.g., human behavior, work process innovation, stock market performance), and making some judgment about whether performance has, in fact, improved. Performance improvement can only be manifested through outputs and change in outputs can only be assessed through some form of measurement. Thus, performance can be systematically operationalized in any organization when we set out to demonstrate whether or not it has improved.

The Systems View ... Again

Most performance improvement professionals have accepted the view of organizations as complex, open systems. Assuming that the challenge is to design and create high-performing organizations, all the parts and subsystems need to work together to achieve the purpose of the whole organization. Developers work with managers in applying sociotechnical principles to organizational problems and opportunities. Given this holistic view, many tools for intervening wisely exist at the organization, process, team, and job performer levels (Brache, 2002). The analyst who takes a systems view will likely see the limitations of other views of the organization. The systems thinker achieves strategic benefits by applying systems solutions to systems problems and opportunities. The systems-oriented developer will tend to focus on (1) defining the organization or system broadly enough to include the root cause of the performance issue and (2) identifying the primary source of the power to take advantage of a performance opportunity. At the same time, the analyst taking this approach will acknowledge the power, economic, mechanistic, and humanistic contributions to the performance problems, opportunities, and solutions.

Basic Systems Thinking

Systems theory was first applied by Ludwig von Bertalanffy (1968) to the field of biology and has since spread to influence a multitude of fields. Systems theorists believe that all configurations of things in the world should be viewed as wholes, rather than being taken apart and examined piece by piece. In systems such as the human mind, the human body, or the human organization, all the parts, or elements, affect each other in complicated and nonobvious ways. Studying the parts individually can disrupt their usual interaction so much that the isolated part will look and act very different from its normal pattern in its normal context. For this reason, it is extremely important to study the whole system at the same time one studies an element, or elements, of that system. Analysis work can be either the decomposition of a whole into its component parts or the piece-by-piece synthesis of component parts into a whole system. Both types of analysis work are important to performance improvement professionals.

All complex systems have certain properties in common, which make them appropriate for study (Clarke & Crossland, 1985). First, systems are assemblies of parts or elements that are connected in an organized way. That is, to focus on a single element and blame it for systems failure is counterproductive. All the elements in a system interact. Second, systems can be identified by their purpose. That is, a good way to identify the elements and interactions of a system of interest is to begin by identifying their collective output. Third, they stop doing whatever they were doing in the system whenever you remove them from the system. Fourth, systems do work. That is, complex systems exist to carry out a process of transforming inputs into outputs. Fifth, systems have boundaries. That is, it is possible to set lines of demarcation to determine the elements included in a system of interest as well as those that are excluded. Finally, complex systems are open systems. That is, they are permeable so that forces in their environments, or contexts, will affect what goes on within the systems. In turn, open systems influence their contexts as they exchange energy, materials, and/or information with their environments.

Even this simple portrayal of an organization as a system indicates that every organization has it environment and its inputs, processes, and outputs (Figure 2.4). Systems thinking demands that analysts understand the powerful influences that driving forces in the environment have on the organization as a system and the challenges and opportunities these driving forces present to decision-makers throughout the organization. The organizations that developers' study are open systems; that is, they take in inputs—energy, materials, people, capital, and so on—from the environment. They then process these inputs and, in due time, return them to the environment in the form of outputs: goods and/or services.

Every organization has a purpose, a mission. The organization exists to carry out its mission, to do its work. Improving the work life of the people in the organization is not, as some would have us believe, the primary purpose of a business organization. Producing quality outputs for customers is the primary reason for the existence of any organization. When organizational customers do not seek an organization's outputs, it must change what it does or die.

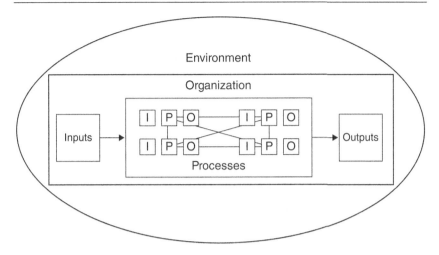

Figure 2.4   Interdependencies of Subsystems Inputs, Processes, and Outputs

Every complex business organization consists of a number of subsystems, each of which has its own internal customers. They function interdependently with all the other subsystems in achieving the whole organization's mission. Depending on particular performance issues, subsystems such as marketing, production, distribution, human resource development, and research and development may be singled out by performance improvement specialists. Thus, what is treated as a system on one occasion may be treated as a subsystem on another occasion.

All such internal subsystems—each with its own inputs, processes, and outputs—can be identified by their purposes, their missions, and their customers within the total organizational scheme. Internal and external customers alike are powerful because they determine the quality, quantity, and timeliness criteria for their acceptance of systems and subsystems outputs. Decision-makers within systems must heed the customers' criteria for the goodness of systems outputs.

Power-oriented analysts tend to simply look to top management for problems to be fixed by means of their improvement solutions. Mechanistic and human relations developers focus on fixing individual employees and managers. Systems analysts, in contrast, are aware that causes are often far removed from organizational effects. As a result, they feel compelled to struggle more with the breadth and depth of the analysis.

These systems-oriented analysts know that focusing activities and programs on the wrong targets is a waste of organizational resources. They understand the importance of examining the interdependencies between organization subsystems to identify the real sources of problems, most of which will not yield to isolated personnel development efforts.

Partial Solutions Don't Work

A software firm added new communication equipment to speed the process of answering customers who telephoned with software questions. Besides purchasing the equipment and training the product support staff to use it, the economically oriented consultants offered training in listening skills and new methods for defusing the emotion of frustrated customers. As expected, responding to customers' needs took a little less time following the development program. However, increasing sales volume meant that the customer support staff had to respond to an ever-increasing number of callers. They began hurrying each caller along. Rising customer complaints about the lack of response to their software problems prompted the vice president of sales to question the consultants about the effectiveness of their performance improvement effort.

As another example, the organizational development department of a large manufacturing company implemented a program to increase supervisors' expertise in conducting performance-based appraisal interviews. This activity was in direct response to a request from the management team. The driving force for the request was the company's president. While attending a professional conference, she had been persuaded by the urgent legal requirement to conduct unbiased performance appraisals. Simultaneously, the personnel department was carrying out management's directive to hire a consulting group to institute a new company-wide compensation system. The two situations were treated as unrelated events in this company, even though the power-oriented human resource staff was aware of the potential effects of the new compensation system on the appraisals.

To take yet another example, an employee survey identified a wide-ranging requirement for increased communication skills in a rapidly growing service organization. Because the survey did not establish that the real organizational performance issues was intergroup communication, the performance improvement staff focused on developing interpersonal skills. The analysts failed to take a systems view of their growing organization and the requirement to assist increasing numbers of interdependent work groups in learning new ways to coordinate their work efforts. And the humanistically oriented staff, working at the interpersonal skills level, had completely missed a major systems issue.

Systematic Performance Improvement Interventions

In the performance improvement field, professionals place too much emphasis on creating new tools, methods, and techniques and not enough on the importance of integrating their use with the nature of the organizations they are trying to improve. For example, the corporate person who attends any national professional conference will be offered a huge list of presenters, each claiming the merits of his or her new tool. What these presenters can't say is whether their new tool is appropriate for a specific organization, exactly where in the organization to apply it, and how to adapt it to the organization's need. That is where systems thinking becomes useful. But this approach is easier said than done. Systems thinking consistently results in a struggle to define the elements of the system, the relationships between elements, and the framing of systems or in the dilemma of where to draw the boundaries around a subsystem so that it may be analyzed. Although this effort is always a struggle and never perfect, these are not valid reasons for rejecting systems thinking.

In the end, it is clear to most people that systems theory, systematic performance diagnosis, and systematic documentation of expertise are powerful means for dealing with complex performance issues.

Systemic and Systematic Performance Improvement Process

Most theorists and practitioners agree that a systematic process should be used to carry out performance improvement efforts. They also agree that a general performance improvement process consists of five phases: analysis, design, development, implementation, and evaluation. But practitioners and theorists do not agree on the detail and rigor required of the specific steps and subprocesses that make up each of the five phases. Therefore, we want to state clearly that we take a rigorous view of the performance improvement process.

Figure 2.3 shows the performance improvement process overlaid on the major elements of the organizational system. Again, you see the core model of the organization within the environment. The environment is further delineated in terms of economic, political, and cultural forces surrounding the organization, while the organization is broken into mission and strategy, organization structure, technology, and human resources (Tichy, 1983). Performance improvement is displayed as one process within the organization. The performance improvement process interacts with the other organizational processes—such as marketing, production, distribution, and research and development.

Analysis is the first and most critical phase of the performance improvement process. In the analysis phase, developers and managers work together to achieve the critical steps of determining the organization's performance requirements and the desired performance goal or standard. In this phase, developer and manager also work together to determine whether management actions, development efforts, environmental forces, or some combination of these will affect the change in performance. In addition, they document organizational processes and their improvements along with the expertise (precisely what people are required to know and be able to do) to perform in the workplace.

We divide the analysis phase into three parts: organizational performance diagnosis, work process documentation and improvement, and work expertise documentation (review Figure 1.1). Performance diagnosis comes first. It is a problem-defining/opportunity method that takes into account the systemic, economic, and psychological nature of the organization. It results in an accurate identification of the actual and desired organization, process, team, and/or individual performances along with proposed systematic improvements to be made. Work process improvement comes second. When needed, this part documents existing processes, improves them, and identifies process-referenced work tasks. Work expertise documentation comes last. It is a systematic method of analyzing and documenting the work expertise—the detailed knowledge, skills, and attitudes required to perform on the job—as called for by the performance diagnosis.

Tools for executing the steps appropriate to diagnosing organization performance are described in Chapters 4–7. Documenting and improving work processes are covered in Chapter 8. Tools for executing the steps appropriate to documenting workplace expertise are described in Chapters 9 to 14. These latter steps include job description, task inventory, and task analysis. Task analysis defines precisely what a person is required to know and do in order to perform a particular task. Specific methods for analyzing procedural, systems, and knowledge work tasks are presented.

Beyond the analysis phase of performance improvement, the remaining phases include design, development, implementation, and evaluation. The linkage among all five phases is direct and substantive. The analysis phase, which must be completed first, defines and frames the entire performance improvement effort. The quality of the effort during the analysis phase is critical because it spills over into the substance of all the remaining phases. By contrast, the implementation phase only impacts the evaluation phase. Major errors can be made in any of the phases, but as you progress through the systematic development process, you encounter fewer opportunities to make serious process errors. What is more, errors in the later phases are less costly to repair. In contrast, fatal errors made in the analysis phase, and discovered later in the evaluation phase, can be costly to rectify.

Conclusion

Managers of complex organizations face choices about improving performance and about the avenues they will pursue in achieving their performance goals. Instead of gaining a true understanding of the performance problems, they may crudely choose to hire and fire people or to streamline the process and fire the excess workers. Eventually, in even the most humane organizations, people with obsolete know-how are discharged to allow the hiring of people who seemingly have the capacity to perform in the present system or the ability to reshape the systems. A systems-thinking person would judge these erratic organization pulsings as ineffective and inefficient. As a positive response, the remainder of this book provides the tools to systematically diagnose and document organization performance and worker expertise—the critical first steps in performance improvement.

Chapter 3

Guidelines for Analyzing Performance

Chapter Sections

- Performance Diagnosis Concepts
- Sometimes You Start in the Middle
- Conclusion

"You know it when you see it!" can be said about a smooth-running organization—or an inefficient one. It is amazing how quickly an outsider, on entering an organization, can tell you that a place is or is not functioning well. Even so, the mere detection that the ship isn't moving or that the crew is on the edge of mutiny doesn't qualify a person as a performance diagnostician. There are general concepts that support the development of qualified performance analysts and they are a precursor to the more specific tools described later in this book.

In a single day recently, two experiences demonstrate the point. The first was an experience of being a consumer of services provided by an automobile repair organization and the second was in a health care organization. Within minutes of encountering each organization, messages were everywhere. The automobile repair station, along an interstate highway, was staged with personnel who were courteous, wore clean uniforms, had a professional manner, worked as a team, and relied on a sophisticated technological backup system. The healthcare organization visited later that day could have learned a great deal from the repair station. The egotism of the staff, combined with their poor work systems and inept communication, was obvious soon after entering the door. But analysis at this level does not qualify as a performance diagnosis and will do little or nothing to improve the situation.

Performance analysis is much more. It is (1) a problem-defining method that results in an accurate identification of the actual and desired performance at the organization, process, work team, and individual levels; and (2) the specification of interventions to improve this performance in the

DOI: 10.4324/9781003518532-4

form of a performance improvement proposal. Performance analysis is not casual work. It requires intellect, experience, and effort. Clearly, bright people with a great deal of experience using appropriate tools are the best analysts. Since few of us are naturally equipped for this work, tools that can facilitate the process and direct the energy required of the effort are necessary for beginning analysts. It is important to emphasize again that the core purpose of this book is to help those starting out in the field on a path toward effective experience. Yet, the seasoned professional can also benefit from the tools described.

From a systems perspective, it does not make sense to think about isolated snapshots of performance. For example, we have seen managers set "new" performance goals that were lower than existing goals without even being aware of their backward move. Also, we have seen activities focused on narrowly conceived and trivial work performance when the same organization was experiencing crippling inefficiencies resulting from the lack of basic work expertise among large segments of its workforce. Even worse, we regularly see managers with a solution in search of a problem. This is what management cynics refer to as the "flavor of the month" approach to performance improvement—often based on management fads and celebrity CEOs. These rarely result in the improvement being sought.

Accurate performance diagnosis is the first step in improving performance. The research has consistently shown that performance improves through responsible and systemic performance improvement efforts (Campbell, Campbell, & Associates, 1988). A thorough diagnosis of performance examines key performance variables (mission/goals, system design, capacity, motivation, and/or expertise) at four distinct levels (organization, process, work team, and individual). The resulting information and its interplay are the basis for prescribing appropriate interventions for performance improvement.

The up-front performance diagnosis should result in (1) a formal proposal to management that views the situation, the proposed intervention, and the performance evaluation criteria for success; (2) specification of performance at the current and desired levels of attainment; (3) a specific performance improvement intervention for a specific audience; and (4) management's required commitment to the intervention.

Performance Diagnosis Concepts

A number of concepts direct the work of diagnosing performance in organizations, though the precise conceptual relationships will vary for each situation. They include framing the diagnosis, characteristics of the situation, organizational politics, and the idea that diagnosis is not always linear. At first glance, these concepts may appear to be well-understood information. But experience has shown that what is obvious to one person may not be obvious to another. Thus, reviewing these concepts will help reinforce the conceptual model for understanding and directing performance analyses.

Framing the Performance Diagnosis

The performance diagnostician frames the situation from a systems perspective to help determine the causes of perceived performance opportunities or problems. At the start, neither analysts nor managers will likely have an accurate analysis frame. For example, some managers will confidently assure the analyst that "first-line supervisors in the Accounting Department need more timely information for decision-making in order to make major productivity gains." In a situation with such a well-defined and limiting analysis frame, a performance issue can be clearly stated but that does not mean that the statement is accurate. Caution is required here in that the situation is so tightly framed that important related factors may well be ignored. Other managers will greet the analyst with "Help! I don't know what's going on. Everything is all messed up." The manager's reaction is often to pull back so far that there are no boundaries to his or her thinking. Such a general and ill-defined analysis frame provides little if any utility. Both diagnosticians and managers need to resist the temptation to precisely define the performance issue too early in the process. At the same time, providing no direction at all is equally problematic. Keeping the performance problem somewhat ill-defined, but with some focus, will provide the direction and looseness required to move ahead with the performance diagnosis. Finding a balance between specifying a performance issue and allowing for exploration is important and requires experience to achieve.

As part of the diagnostic process, the analyst checks, rechecks, and adjusts the boundaries of the analysis frame by asking questions, observing, and reviewing records to be sure to include relevant elements from the organizational system. Approaching a performance diagnosis with a frame that is too large or too small can be troublesome. Setting boundary frames that are too broad can result in inefficiencies in collecting excessive and unnecessary amounts of data to fill up the oversize frame. Setting too-narrow boundaries can result in ineffectiveness because inadequate data are collected, resulting in inaccurate identification of the performance opportunity/problem and its root cause. The cautious analyst checks and rechecks by asking:

- "Am I using too small of an analysis frame?" Probably, when the conclusions are too easily reached.
- "Am I using too large of an analysis frame?" Probably, when people intensely disagree about the performance issues being discussed.

- "Am I using an appropriate analysis frame?" Probably, if the critical data from the broader frame and smaller targeted frame confirm the data from the boundary you thought to be appropriate. Probably you have established an appropriate frame if more than one case of an organization, process, work team, or individual performance problem has been identified.

A major concern is how to frame the organization system or subsystem so that the true factors influencing performance are included within the analysis frame. Even experienced performance improvement professionals will sometimes err in establishing the boundaries for a performance analysis. Performance improvement interventions resulting from framing errors will generally be aimed at a symptom of performance, not performance itself. Even if the performance improvement effort appears well established, it can prove to be ineffective and costly when it is off-target.

Characteristics of the Organization, Decision-Makers, and Analyst

Threaded throughout the performance diagnosis process is the need to recognize, monitor, and respond when necessary to the unique characteristics of the organization, decision-makers, and analyst (Sleezer, 1991). The distinguishing features of these critical characteristics that affect the performance diagnosis are as follows:

- Organizational characteristics such as the internal and external environment, systemwide components that impact the situation, organizational culture and politics, and the language used to influence behavior. These subtle and abstract dimensions are rarely factors that first come to the surface in analyzing performance.
  - Decision-maker characteristics that include the expectations and level of consensus among multiple decision-makers, and their level of support for the performance improvement intervention.
  - Analyst characteristics, including his or her level of diagnostic expertise and information-gathering biases (Sleezer, 1991, pp. 357–358). Expert analysts, like experts in most fields, have more tools in their toolbox than they use in any one situation. Furthermore, experts choose the best approach and tool for a particular situation, not the tool they simply like to use.

Paying close attention to the characteristics of the organization, decision-makers, and analyst during the diagnostic process is important in obtaining a common perception of the real performance issue and proper remedy. Developing a common perception is also political in nature (described next).

In the end, the analyst and the organizational decision-makers must agree. A paradox emerges, however, because a common perception can build from a smooth sales pitch as well as from a disciplined diagnostic process. Unfortunately, support for implementing an intervention can be gained even when the intervention does not show much promise of improving performance—referring back to a compelling and motivational presentation with little to no potential for practical application. The emphasis on substantive improvement in performance differentiates this book from theories and practices that are barely, if at all, connected to performance. For example:

Quality management: ISO 9000. This approach does not actually promise to improve quality. It offers documentation tools that have the potential to improve quality (Du Pont, 1989).

Workplace learning: The adult learning perspective of workplace education and training does not promise to improve organizational or worker performance. It promises worker knowledge with "the possibility of performance change or general growth of the individual" (Nadler & Nadler, 1990, p. xxxvii).

Knowledge management: The simple idea of getting good information to the right people in a timely manner is not nearly enough. Until recently, knowledge management has not considered the fact that such efforts are deeply social in nature and must be approached by considering human and social factors (Thomas, Kellogg, & Erickson, 2001).

Thus, the eager and well-intentioned manager agrees to invest in an intervention that is supposed to make things better. The true state-of-affair is that many interventions do not deliver what they promise and can even hurt the performance of an organization. Piecemeal and nonsystemic performance improvement interventions have the potential of disrupting operations more than improving them. At a minimum, they can waste resources in terms of direct and indirect costs.

Politics of Performance Diagnosis

Organizations are human-made entities. As such, they can carry human frailties as well as human strengths. Thus, there is a human dynamic to diagnosing performance that people often characterize as the politics of the organization. These political dilemmas boil down to ego and power issues. They pose no small challenge in carrying out the diagnosis process.

Possibly the biggest deterrent to successful diagnosis is distrust of organization leaders who are viewed as unethical, uncaring, and unfair by those working in the organizations. These leaders are suspect when it comes to sharing the gains in mission-related performance that generally are converted into financial gains. Yet, top managers routinely make decisions about what is best for the organization without any diagnosis at all. When organization leaders exhibit extraordinary greed, such as William McGuire, CEO of United-Health Group, employees and stakeholders will likely withhold support and information. McGuire took $1.6 billion in stock options (beyond his extravagant salary) in just one year (Forelle & Bandler, 2006). At $58,000 a year, a nurse would have had to begin working in 500 BC up to the present day to earn the bonus money that McGuire made in a single year (Coleman, 2006). Such personal greed at the top of any organization has to impact those throughout the organization and the society in which such greed takes place. Fortunately, in this case, investors' negative reaction to this news caused a serious loss in market value for UnitedHealth at the time (Forester, 2006).

That, however, is not always the case. A review of MBAs as CEOs (Mintzberg, 2017) provided compelling evidence that the most successful business schools around the world ultimately place their most talented graduates in CEO positions. Yet, the review shows that performance is troubling. Out of 5004 CEOs from 2003 to 2013 "we find that MBA CEOs are more apt than their non-MBA counterparts to engage in short-term strategic expedients such as positive earnings management and suppression of R&D, which in turn are followed by compromised firm market valuations" (Miller & Xu, 2016, p. 298). The point here is not to review the MBA curricula, though it is well understood that it does not include a focus on performance diagnosis at any level of the organization (LeCounte, Prieto, & Phipps, 2017). The political and hierarchical nature of how to become a CEO versus how to perform as a CEO seems clear and diagnosing organizations does not seem to be a priority.

Later you will be introduced to the ethics undergirding performance improvement theory. It is important to recognize that performance improvement and the follow-up decisions related to the distribution of the gains resulting from that performance are two totally distinct categories of action. Yet, if participants believe or know that follow-up gains will be distributed unfairly, they will hesitate to participate honestly and openly in the performance diagnosis and intervention. For example, the failures around Hammer and Champy's (1993) organizational reengineering movement, which was built on flawed logic, were predictable given its total disregard for the psychological foundation of organizations (Swanson, 1993). The high rates of reengineering failures can be partially blamed on the negative consequences to many of the organizational members who were being asked to support reengineering efforts.

The politics surrounding the performance diagnosis process also explains why in so many situations the analyst is an outsider—either as a staff person from another organization division or as an external consultant. The external person can be seen as more objective with nothing to personally gain other than the truth of the situation. This is particularly true if the analyst is a gray-haired seasoned professional. The external person is less susceptible to insider egos and power tactics that would be difficult for an insider to ignore.

One of the authors executed an internal performance diagnosis in a Fortune 50 firm that was very political. The roadblock to progress and excellence was the top manager, who had been pointing his finger at his juniors. Before presenting the results of the diagnosis to the top management team, the division director of organization development suggested to soften the conclusions, and the advice was not taken. The executive in charge demanded to know where the information came from. The executive was reminded of the confidentiality agreement. He got red in the face and announced that he did not care and wanted to know the names. His request was again refused. Then, on their own, managers spoke up as sources of information, verifying the diagnosis conclusions. Within six months, the top executive was reassigned. Two years later, one of the managers called, describing the positive impact of the performance diagnosis on the organization, that they were still referring to the diagnosis, and that the integrity of the management team was at an all-time high.

On many occasions, analysts are brought in by an in-house performance improvement professional to lead a performance diagnosis that the internal person could have carried out. In these instances, it is important to be able to mediate the politics of the strong personalities in the organization so that their egos and power positions do not distort the diagnosis. To do this with integrity, analysts should have a defined process for doing their work and a set of personal ethical standards to guide their work.

Sometimes You Start in the Middle

In the next chapter, the organizational diagnosis process is presented as a flowchart. This suggests that you move from left to right and that there is a logical beginning, middle, and end. Theoretically, this is the way it should be and is the way an expert diagnostician ends up laying it out in his or her mind, even though the starting point may be in the middle or at the end.

The reality of the workplace is that the boss may confront you with any of the following starting points to a performance diagnosis:

- We don't have a problem/opportunity. We do not need your help.
- We think we have a problem/opportunity. Can you help?
- Here is the problem/opportunity. What is the solution?
- Here is the problem/opportunity, and here is the solution!

When the boss says, "Here is the problem. What is the solution?" you are plunked right into the middle of the performance diagnosis process. While the boss is indicating that the problem has already been defined, the question of the accuracy of the definition comes up. It may be accurate, but as an expert investigator, you pull back—ask a few questions, review available documents, and make some of your own observations to check it out. In doing so, you temporarily (and maybe privately) reject the problem as defined by the boss and quickly come up with your own conclusion, even if it is one that agrees with the boss, and then move on to determining an appropriate intervention. Through this loop, the analyst retains the responsibility of defining the problem.

Conclusion

Performance diagnosis is a complex, multidimensional activity. Issuing a simple survey to gather managerial or employee opinions about development options may help build common perceptions, but this approach will rarely suffice in accurately defining performance opportunities or deficiencies in worker expertise. Diagnosing organizations for the purpose of improving performance requires a substantial investment, with the realistic potential of high gains.

To this end, the following three chapters in Part II of the book organize and present the critical elements of diagnosing organizations. The last chapter in Part II focuses on data collection methods that can be used throughout the entire analysis effort. Make no mistake—analysis work starts with performance diagnosis—and analysis work is the most critical phase of performance improvement. Diagnosing performance well requires intelligence, knowledge, and experience. Experience alone is not enough. The concepts provided in this chapter are an important foundation.

Part II

Diagnosing Organization Performance

Chapter 4

The Performance Diagnosis Process

Chapter Sections

- Performance Diagnosis
- Using the Organizational Diagnosis Model
- The Health Management, Inc. Case
- Conclusion

Organization performance diagnosis converts ill-defined problems and opportunities into well-defined performance improvement proposals. Performance diagnosis is not the springboard of "knee-jerk management" or for a "sixty-second solution." Sometimes, it turns out that way—a quick fix for solving an easy performance issue—but that is not the norm. Performance diagnosis is rigorous work that yields powerful solutions for the purpose of improving performance. Careful attention must be paid to the specifics of the situation for well-done diagnosis work leading to significant performance gains (Turner, 2022).

Performance Diagnosis

Performance diagnosis can be thought of as a problem-defining or opportunity-defining method. Unfortunately, most organization leaders skip this process entirely. The most common situations are problems identified without any substantive analysis and solutions that are immediately sought to address these problems without any real understanding. This common practice results in poorly defined problems and quick-fix solutions that do not address the root causes. Following the tools described in this book results in (1) an accurate identification of the actual and desired performances at the organization, process, team, and/or individual levels, along with (2) specification of interventions to improve performance.

The general process of performance diagnosis contains five phases (see Figure 4.1) that begin with articulating the initial purpose and end with a

DOI: 10.4324/9781003518532-6

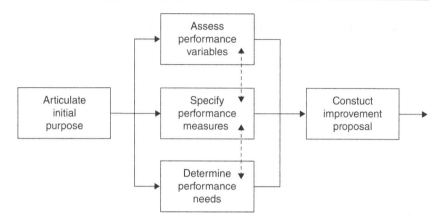

Figure 4.1 Diagnosing Performance Process

performance improvement proposal. The three phases in the middle inform each other and are not necessarily sequential. They include assessing the performance variables, specifying the performance measures, and determining the performance needs. Serious performance analysts need to find a balance between deeply understanding the real performance issues and the need to solve them as efficiently as possible. This is not an easy position to be in and experience teaches that finding such a balance usually requires a mix of expertise, tenure, and the dynamics of the situation.

The three realms—performance variables, performance measures, and performance needs—are usually pursued concurrently and as dictated by the situation. The culminating performance improvement proposal acts as a synthesis of the findings and provides the springboard for organizational approval and action. Without these three realms, proposals will generally be vague and difficult to implement (Falayi, 2019).

The following sections of this chapter detail the first four steps of the performance diagnosis process. The final organization diagnosis phase—developing the performance improvement proposal—is presented in detail in Chapter 5, complete with examples. The data collection methods that thread through all the analysis work at the organization, process, team, and individual levels are discussed in Chapter 7. These methods include interviews, questionnaires, observations, and documentation.

Initial Purpose

It is important to start the workplace performance diagnosis process by articulating the purpose of the improvement effort. The adage "If you don't know where you are going, you will likely end up someplace else"

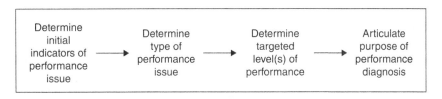

Figure 4.2 Articulate the Initial Purpose Steps

provides a useful warning. Efforts at improving performance that lack up-front clarity almost always end up being ineffective and irrelevant. The diagnostician acquires clarity by identifying four factors related to performance (Figure 4.2). Articulating the initial purpose of the performance diagnosis in this way guides the analyst through often vague and contradictory information. The steps include determining the initial indicators of a performance issue, determining the type of performance issue, determining the targeted level(s) of performance, and articulating the purpose of the performance diagnosis. Try to resist the temptation to simply accept an executive-level perspective on the problem. Instead, use the tools described in this book to get to the real performance issues and understand the data required to solve them.

Initial Indicators of the Performance Issue

The initial indicators of a performance issue will most likely come from someone who has organizational authority and who initiates the process, if only by calling attention to an issue. These initial indicators typically revolve around a critical event, a person, or a change in an external condition. They rarely include any substantive data related to the issue. Examples include production is down, there is a feeling of mutiny in the Research and Development Division, the president is not pleased with the number of e-mails crossing everybody's inboxes, the VP of International is unhappy about how the work of his group fits into the organization, or technology is advancing too fast to keep up. Recently, major changes in technology platforms are among the most common change management initiatives in today's organizations. Diagnosis is critical in making the shift in technology systems reasonable and smooth. While people in positions of authority may be able to identify this as a prevalent issue—the nature, performance requirements, timelines for conversion, and expectations are almost never specified.

Very often the initial indicators of performance issues that are reported by managers to analysts will not match the stated type or level of performance they are requesting. For example, when 50% of the production product is waste or rework—an indicator of a present and serious performance problem—this is no time to respond to a managerial request for cross-training employees for the purpose of covering for each other on upcoming summer vacations. In this example, sorting through the interviews, production records, and on-site observations will surely focus on the painful production problem, not deficiencies concerning vacation-related cross-training.

Thus, it is important to sort out the early perceptions in the diagnosis process. Early perceptions are often strongly held and often inaccurate. They are usually based on hunches, biased views or intuition—none of which make use of effective diagnosis. Your job as a diagnostician is to remain inquisitive and neutral. Remaining open expands the possibilities before reaching a conclusion. Actively thinking ahead about the substeps—(1) type of performance issue and (2) level of performance—encourages you to ask more questions and to think beyond the original perceived need.

Type of Performance Issues

Classifying the performance issues into one of three types helps separate multidimensional performance issues and assists in articulating the purpose of the organizational diagnosis. The three types of performance issues are (1) present performance problems, (2) improvements to the present performance, and (3) future performance requirements (Bjorkquist & Murphy, 1987; Buckingham, 2022; Swanson, 1982).

This practical classification scheme is essentially responsive to timing factors. Multiple performance issues exist in an organization at any one time, and they vary in terms of their immediacy. Present performance problems revolve around performance outputs that are expected and planned for but are not being reached—performance goals that are not being met. This type of performance problem—missed goals and obvious low performance—causes present pain for the organization, ineffective work system processes, and devalued feelings in workers. These conditions of high-performance improvement potential are ripe for large performance gains (Gilbert, 1996; He et al., 2021). The conditions are also ripe for blaming and secrecy among organizational personnel. The initial data sources for present performance problems tend to be basic business measures that stare you in the face through regular company performance records (Sætre & Van de Ven, 2021; Swanson, 1989).

Improvements in present performance and future performance requirements (to remain competitive) do not carry the same intensity as present performance problems. They are usually more subtle and generally can be pursued at a more leisurely pace. The initial data sources for improvements in present performance and future performance requirements tend to be trends in the marketplace, organizational practices, and survey results from employees and customers. A recent example is the tension around "back-to-the-office," "work-from-home," or some combination of the two (Marsh, 2021). Why not collect some data and gain a sense of what your workforce wants? Of course, some difficult decisions may need to be made, but to make those decision on a hunch, or a top-down, mandated approach is contrary to the concepts of this book. Using the tools we provide leads to a much better chance of addressing the range of workforce issues in expert and thoughtful ways.

Without an immediate sense of crisis, improving present performance issues within an established organization, process, team, or individual can be more rational and incremental. Also, this performance focus tends to attract more internal experts with cooperative mindsets than is true with the other two types of performance issues. Unfortunately, these conditions can also attract internal and external providers with nice-to-do interventions without a rigorous connection to performance. For example, knowledge management and quality improvement are typical projects that match up with opportunities for improving present performance (versus being a response to a present performance problem).

Future performance requirements present another twist to the situation. Sometimes future performance requirements are like those for improving the present performance, except that they are set off into the future. For example, think about a new artificial intelligence process or production system to be installed twelve months from now. When installing such a new well-defined work or technology system into an already smooth-running operation in the future, a straightforward performance improvement strategy can be established, though it still may require a great deal of effort. Yet, the future time frame must be considered since conditions will almost certainly be different at that later date. Referring to the above example of working from home or some other alternative, there are demands for future workforce performance that cannot be ignored and they carry a significant degree of uncertainty (Stuart et al., 2021). Addressing employee needs and preferences across the organization requires understanding those needs and preferences.

A more unsettling situation is preparing for a radically new and undefined future, which is where we may find ourselves today. Redesigning major organizational processes based on new technology is one example of what is occurring in many organizations. Arguably, new technology platform rollouts are one of the most common change interventions that exist today (Kinkel, Baumgartner, & Cherubinin, 2022). Adoption of new technology platforms also requires serious planning for the necessary training programs to help the workers make the transition. To go one step further, can you imagine attempting to determine the high-tech education and training needs of a sophisticated workforce based on technology that does not yet exist? This level of uncertainty creates extreme tension. In these conditions, even with the most systematic work system redesign approach, unique forces are at work as leaders struggle with conflicting views of the future. Furthermore, important characteristics among strong leaders should be taken into account when gathering, valuing, and integrating information that is provided by them. In particular, the role, status, personality, and experience characteristics of organizational experts who provide the diagnostic information for future requirements should be heeded. Roles can include new technology versus project planning expertise; status may entail knowing who is on the way up versus those on the way out; personalities can be strong and vocal, strong and nonvocal, weak and vocal, as well as weak and nonvocal; and experience could involve high versus low experience with the substance of the inquiry. Particularly in this realm of undefined futures, the role of leaders could not be more critical. The ability to demand performance—and to hold people accountable to performance expectations—regardless of role, status, personality, and experience is exceedingly rare, yet increasingly required for true attention to performance improvement (Kaplan, Sørensen, & Zakolyukina, 2022).

It seems practical, particularly for a less experienced professional or improvement team, to focus an improvement effort on only one of the three types of performance issues: (1) present performance problems, (2) improvements to the present situation, or (3) future performance requirements. Classifying the performance issues into one of the three categories helps separate the multidimensional problems in an organization and articulate the purpose of the targeted organizational diagnosis. Combining efforts to address more than one of these types at a time most likely pulls in different data, different stakeholders, and different strategies for efforts that are reasonably discrete. It would be much better to have parallel improvement projects and share data between them rather than to have them both under the same performance improvement umbrella. This idea highlights a harsh reality. It is common for a firm of 2,500 people to employ a training or change management team of about four. Thus, making it difficult to think about multiple improvement processes happening in parallel. Be selective in prioritizing performance improvement work.

Targeted Levels of Performance

Another area that should be considered in articulating the purpose of the diagnosis involves levels of performance. Four levels are identified and consistently referred to throughout the discussion of the remaining performance diagnosis phases:

- Organization
- Process

- Team
- Individual

The four levels are described as follows: The organization level "emphasizes the organization's relationship with its market and the basic 'skeleton' of the major functions that comprise the organization" (Rummler & Brache, 2012, p. 17). For the process level, the analyst must go "beyond the cross-functional boundaries that make up the organization chart [to] see the work flow—how the work gets done." At this level, "one must ensure that processes are installed to meet customer needs, that those processes work effectively and efficiently, and that the process goals and measures are driven by the customers' and the organizations' requirements" (Rummler & Brache, 2012, p. 18). The team level is the recognition of groups of workers functioning interdependently and sharing a common purpose (McLean, 2005). They are organized around an organizational process or function, with team members having some interchangeable and overlapping responsibilities. At the individual level, it is recognized that processes "are performed and managed by individuals doing various jobs" (Rummler & Brache, 2012, p. 18).

Systems theory helps us understand the four levels. For example, the cause of a company sending a customer a contract bid containing an inaccurate budget and an incomplete list of services may find its root in any or all four levels. However, the decision-maker may be falsely convinced early on that the cause is lodged at a single level or at the wrong level. For example, he or she could react in the following singular ways: "There is so much bureaucracy around there that it is a miracle anything even gets done!" or "The financial computer program has a glitch in it!" or "Our financial analysts are incompetent!"

Articulate the Initial Purpose is the first step of the performance diagnosis, followed by three steps that can be pursued simultaneously: assess performance variables, specify performance measures, and determine performance needs. While the information and decisions for each of these substeps need to be determined, practical concerns of access will control the sequence of each. In real life, they can be concurrently examined. A discussion of each follows.

Articulated Purpose of the Performance Diagnosis

Consider the example of a major online retailer. Let's say there have been shipping problems recently that have come to the attention of various senior managers. Having worked through some false leads, a clearer purpose for the diagnosis can be established. The following articulated purpose for that situation notes the performance issue, the type of performance, and the targeted levels of performance. An internal performance improvement analyst was asked to study the situation. After some investigation and careful consideration, the performance improvement analyst came to the following purpose for any further intervention.

The purpose of this performance improvement effort is to reduce "Online Retailer's" shipping returns and employee overtime in the shipping department. This is a present performance problem that has severe potential financial consequences to the company and its employees. At this point, it is difficult to determine the appropriate level(s) of performance—organizational, process, team, and/or individual—needing attention. Further analysis is required.

Performance Variables

To assess performance variables, an investigation of the five performance variables across the four performance levels should take place. Three steps are presented in Figure 4.3 to assist in understanding the dynamics of this assessment. They include scanning existing date in context of the performance variables, collecting additional data on the performance variables, and profiling any missing or flawed variables required for the desired performance.

A performance variable is a phenomenon that fundamentally contributes to systemic performance. The possible cause of performance issues usually resides within one or more of five performance variables: mission/goals, systems design, capacity, motivation, and expertise (Swanson, 1999). The first substep here is to scan the available data on the performance variables and how they presently operate in the organization being diagnosed. This requires the analyst to carry forward any existing knowledge of performance level(s), performance needs, and performance measures and to scan these data for possible connections to the five performance variables.

At this point, the diagnostician may have already determined that the performance problem is lodged at a particular performance level or combination of levels (organizational, process, team, and/or individual).

The five performance variables, matrixed with the four levels of performance (organization, process, team, and/or individual), provide a powerful template in diagnosing performance. For example, a work process may have a goal built into it that is in conflict with the mission and/or goal of the organization or the goal of the worker in the process. Often a goal of efficiency at one level comes

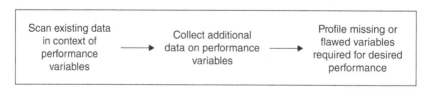

Figure 4.3 Assess Performance Variables Steps

in conflict with the goal of quality at another level. The enabling questions presented in the performance enabling matrix to help the diagnostician sort out the performance overlaps and disconnects (Figure 4.4).

This thinking matrix has great utility as a stand-alone job aid to refer to when doing an organizational diagnosis, as a common tool of reference for a group working on a diagnosis. It can serve as a note-taking tool while collecting data (with cells opened up with white space for recording notes), and as a way to report back key findings recorded in each cell.

With this thinking matrix before you, it is easier to understand the popular saying "Pit a good performer against a bad system, and the system will almost always win." How else to explain the failure of high-aptitude experts working in organizations? When the work system ties the hands of competent people behind their backs and at times punishes them for doing their best, they either quit and leave, or psychologically quit and stay on the payroll! Another example is when a well-designed work process is coupled with organizational policies and procedures that result in hiring employees lacking the capacity to perform the work. No reasonable amount of training will get the employees up to the required performance standards.

An investigation and comparison of each of the five performance variables at each of the four performance levels peels open the performance context. Thus, a process could have a capacity that is less than the capacity of an individual working in it. Or the mission/goals of individuals can be out of sync with the goals of the process in which they work, and the process goals may have little connection to the overall organizational goals. Such performance disconnects are very common. Once the variable and level disconnects are identified, they become a basis for performance improvements actions.

The initial connections of performance levels (organizational, process, team, and/or individual) to performance variables (mission/goals, work system, capacity, motivation, and/or expertise) using readily available information may be incomplete. The second step is the collection of additional data to complete or confirm the variables as they are functioning in the case under investigation. The third substep is to profile the missing or flawed variables within the matrix required for performance improvement. In the Acme International Shipping Department, for example, the following profile resulted:

Mission/goal: Both the company and individuals clearly are concerned about surviving and prospering. While these common goals need to be harmonized, the individual "survival goals" seem to be predominant at this time and negatively affecting the company. This performance concern is being addressed by the total quality management proposal that has recently been endorsed by the president.

Systems design: The shipping department is seriously understaffed, with only one of two supervisors currently on the job. The second supervisor

Performance levels

Performance variables	Organization level	Process level	Team level	Individual level
Mission/goal	Does the organization mission/goal fit the reality of the economic, political, and cultural forces?	Do the process goals enable the organization to meet organization and individual missions/goals?	Do the team goals provide congruence with the process and individual goals?	Are the professional and personal mission/goals of individuals congruent with the organization's?
System design	Does the organization system provide structure and policies supporting the desired performance?	Are processes designed in such a way to work as a system?	Do the team dynamics function in such a way to facilitate collaboration and performance?	Does the individual clear obstacles that impede his or her job performance?
Capacity	Does the organization have the leadership, capital, and infrastructure to achieve its mission/goals?	Does the process have the capacity to perform (quantity, quality, and timeliness)?	Does the team have the combined capacity to effectively and efficiently meet the performance goals?	Does the individual have the mental, physical, and emotional capacity to perform?
Motivation	Do the policies, culture, and reward systems support the desired performance?	Does the process provide the information and human factors required to maintain it?	Does the team function in a respectful and supportive manner?	Does the individual want to perform no matter what?
Expertise	Does the organization establish and maintain selection and training policies and resources?	Does the process of developing expertise meet the changing demands of changing processes?	Does the team have the team process expertise to perform?	Does the individual have the knowledge and expertise to perform?

Figure 4.4   Performance Diagnosis Matrix

has been out for five months with a major illness and will not be returning to work. In addition, informally and over time, job roles and duties in shipping have become redefined, reduced, and isolated.

Capacity: Employees are underutilized. Most shippers have the aptitude to understand the shipping system and how to complete the shipping tickets.

Motivation: Adversarial relationships between departments make it hard to admit limitations. Employees want to do a good job yet are cautious about being made scapegoats.

Expertise: Only the hospitalized supervisor has the expertise to complete order tickets. The shippers do not have a systems perspective of the company or their department. The legitimate seat cover substitution task occurs infrequently, is complex, and requires orderly problem-solving skills.

One excellent use of the performance diagnosis matrix can be to present a summary of findings. Actual key information from a diagnosis placed in each cell forms an excellent diagnosis. What we have learned from the experience was that the filled-in matrix is a very powerful tool for communicating results and gaining managerial buy-in.

Performance Measures

To specify the performance measures, the relevant output units of performance at the organizational, process, team, and/or individual levels need to be identified. It is foolhardy to talk about development, change, and performance improvement without specifying the measure of performance. A target needs to exist. It may be all-inclusive such as market share in a five-year period or loans processed per week, or narrower measures such as the number of Uber passengers served in a six-hour driving shift, or the time it takes to complete a single customer service call. Without the target clearly in mind, it is nearly impossible to think intelligently about appropriate performance improvement actions.

Three steps help clarify the dynamics of the phase of performance diagnosis in which performance measures are specified (see Figure 4.5). In specifying performance measures, the diagnostician needs to keep in mind (1) the levels-of-performance perspective (organizational, process, team, and individual), including the system outputs at each level; and add (2) a units-of-performance perspective to the picture. The units of performance can be further thought of in terms of the following features:

- Time
- Quantity

- Quality
- Cost

The original notion of the workplace performance being analyzed is usually fuzzy and in need of clarification. For example, the original perception may be that too much time is spent in meetings. If confirmed, reducing the meeting time would be the appropriate performance measure. Additional investigation may reveal that important decisions need to be made that are not being made in a timely manner because of poorly run meetings. The output could then shift to the number of decisions or the quality features of company meetings.

Time is defined here as the measurable interval between two events or the period during which some activity occurs. In the workplace, performance is commonly measured in terms of time. Reductions in performance time usually yield important financial consequences to the organizations (Swanson, 2001).

Quantity is a measure of the exact amount or number of products, services, or other outcomes that result from the worker, team, or process performance. Quantity units are relatively easy to define and monitor in the organization. Examples of such quantity units are the number of patents approved, clients served, sundaes sold, and sales earned. All four of the performance dimensions must be quantified, but the "quantity" dimension is the only one that is restricted to counting the simple, usually observable, worker or workgroup outputs (Swanson, 2001).

Quality features are the characteristics of products or services that meet agreed-on specifications. Quality features of a product or service typically revolve around design, procurement, manufacturing, marketing, sales, service, customer education, and ultimate disposition (Tribus, 1985). Quality features can be measured and estimated in value.

Costs are simply those expenditures attributed to the effort and determined according to the accounting procedures within a particular organization (Swanson, 2001). These may include fixed, variable, direct, and indirect costs.

The process of specifying performance measures within the performance diagnosis contains three steps (see Figure 4.5). First is identifying the system outputs of performance for the relevant organizational levels, if they

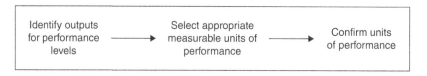

Figure 4.5 Specify Performance Measures Steps

differ. Second is to select the appropriate measurable units of performance. Finally, there needs to be a simple confirmation of the appropriateness of these units. Paying close attention to these performance measures and how they relate to the earlier concept of performance variables helps you move on to the examination of performance needs.

Performance Needs

To help you understand the dynamics of the performance needs phase of the organizational diagnosis, we have included three steps. They are to classify needs according to performance levels and taxonomy, confirm classification of performance levels and taxonomy, and specify needs in terms of performance levels and taxonomy (see Figure 4.6).

To determine performance needs, investigation of the performance issue in terms of both performance level and performance taxonomy must take place. The discussion of levels (organizational process, team, and/or individual) earlier in this chapter needs to be recalled. Remember that each level can set out profoundly different perspectives. Knowing this, combined with the taxonomy of performance, allows a deeper understanding of the performance issue in question.

As you will recall, the taxonomy of performance lays out five tiers of performance: understand, operate, troubleshoot, improve, and invent (review Figure 2.2). This taxonomy is also divided into two general categories: maintaining the system and changing the system. Since almost all organizations have to engage in both maintaining and changing their systems—and are struggling with both—they regularly get them confused. The result of undisciplined jumping from one realm to another can result in performance improvement in schizophrenia. We consistently observe organizations delivering support and resources at a lower performance level and expecting performance gains at a higher level. For example, they may provide people only enough information to understand a system and then expect them to be able to operate and even troubleshoot the system. These misjudgments on the part of organizational decision-makers are generally made without their realizing the built-in discrepancy between the performance interventions they choose and the performance expectations they desire.

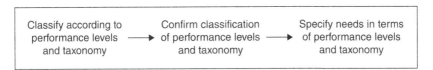

Figure 4.6 Determine Performance Needs Steps

The performance taxonomy provides a lens that helps operationalize systems theory for those working in dynamic and complex organizations. For example, a quality improvement effort to "change the system" could hit a brick wall because there is not enough workforce expertise to "maintain the existing system"—a present performance problem that must be first addressed. Thus, moving from the performance concern of change to the prerequisite issue of how to maintain may be the critical step in getting back to the concern for change.

These estimates of performance levels (organizational, process, and/or individual), connected to the performance taxonomy (understand, operate, troubleshoot, improve, and invent) must be confirmed by data and key people as these data are fed back into the diagnostic process. Once confirmed, the diagnostician can specify the needs in terms of levels of performance and appropriate taxonomy tiers.

Using the Organizational Diagnosis Model

The five-phase model of performance diagnosis (Figure 4.1) shows the major components of the diagnosis as presented throughout this chapter. Figure 4.7 visually captures all the details for each of the five major phases and records the key points. Use this figure as a complete visual summary of this chapter.

It is important to remember that not all of this model's features are used all the time. Doing so would be inefficient and impractical. The analyst, using the basic five-phase model in one situation, can confidently speed through the process when the questions, data, and synthesis of the data are readily available, clear, reliable, and valid. Thus, for one performance issue, the diagnostic model can result in a one-hour investigation. In another, it may take a team of performance diagnosticians a month.

Chapter 3 presented and discussed the reality of the boss confronting you with any of the following starting points of a performance diagnosis:

- We don't have a problem.
- We think we have a problem. Can you help?
- Here is the problem. What is the solution?
- Here is the problem, and here is the solution!

Each of these starting points locates the analyst at a different place in the diagnostic process and requires the analyst to move out accordingly in the five-step organizational diagnosis process so as to effectively and efficiently reach the last performance proposal step. Knowledge of the complete model helps ensure effectiveness. Experience is the path to efficiency.

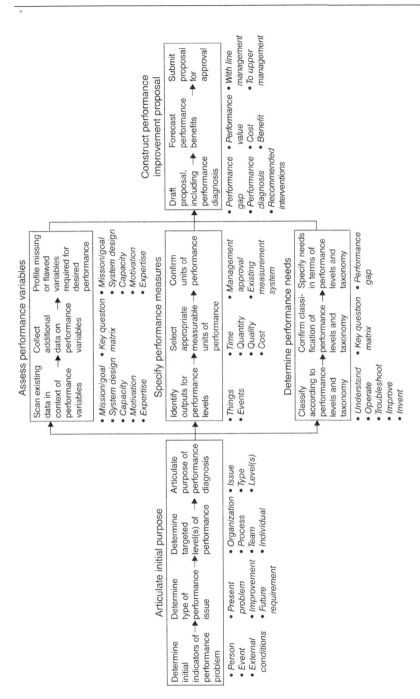

Figure 4.7 Overall Process of Diagnosing Performance

The Health Management, Inc., Case

Health Management, Inc. (HMI) is an organization that manages health-care services by bridging the gap between a number of parties, including the healthcare providers, the companies purchasing group healthcare coverage, private and government health insurance organizations, and individual patients.

HMI works in a rapidly changing, complex, and competitive industry. The core of its business is information, the analysis of information, and the speedy access to information for decision-making with the promise of high-quality healthcare at lower costs.

Performance and performance diagnosis are valued at HMI. The following case illustrates, at a general level, a performance analysis by a consultant who is asked to join the HMI team as a major innovation rolls out.

The Consultant's Starting Point

The consultant, with expertise in starting up new systems-oriented training, is called in by two HMI managers. As the conversation unfolds, the consultant is assessing the people in the room as well as HMI, while the managers are assessing him.

HMI has developed a new macro-management information system (MMIS) that will revolutionize the way it does its work. Every aspect of the business will be monitored and increasingly controlled through MMIS. The software will be completed in six months; at that time, the company will pilot-test two of the five software subsystems. The pilot test will involve training and the rollout of two MMIS subsystems.

The consultant's job is to develop high-quality, performance-based training and become a member of the rollout team. The team also includes the manager of R&D, who is responsible for MMIS, and the manager of operations, who is responsible for overall performance improvement in HMI.

From the discussion, it is clear that there has been high-level performance diagnosis at the strategic level resulting in justification for developing MMIS. The key players in this step included the CEO, the VP of R&D, and the VP of Operations, along with the executive team, which based its decision on a performance diagnosis of the healthcare industry. The consultant, in preparation for the meeting, read HMI's annual report and the appropriate industry analysis section contained in the Value Line Investment Survey, Ratings, and Reports, a stock and industry analysis service. The two sources confirmed each other.

The next performance diagnosis tier—the tactical level of delving deeper into the information system and software options—was left to the two VPs and the two key managers referred to previously.

The need for a performance diagnosis at the implementation level is the point of the consultant's entry. Systems thinking is critical to understanding the journey to this point and the diagnosis of the MMIS rollout performance issue. Recall the five components of performance diagnosis:

- Articulate the initial purpose.
- Assess the performance variables.
- Specify the performance measures.
- Determine the performance needs.
- Construct a performance improvement proposal.

Articulate the Initial Purpose

The performance improvement consultant already has a fair amount of information about the initial purpose and other diagnostic questions. For example, external conditions are driving this total effort, which revolves around MMIS, a "thing," and the start-up of MMIS, an "event." The performance issue is aimed at future MMIS performance requirements for almost all five hundred employees in the organization. MMIS is a major change in the core business process with specific expertise required at different job levels. Finally, the organization has developed an internal four-part performance scorecard that is already in place.

Determine the Performance Needs

Given this highly structured situation, it seemed important to learn more about the system requirements. The Taxonomy of Performance and its five levels helped establish the need for MMIS "understanding" the level of expertise among all five hundred employees. In addition, all employees need to know basic "operation" of the MMIS system, and all employees need to know how to "operate" at least one of the five different MMIS program subcomponents. Closer inspection will likely reveal seventeen specific tasks, with three to four tasks within each of the five MMIS components. Furthermore, about six of the specific tasks are already being used by employees in the existing system.

Another requirement is to deliver training to multiple groups at 20 sites throughout a six-state region. Furthermore, since HMI is growing rapidly, there will be a continuing need for new employee MMIS training and performance support and training.

Assess the Performance Variables

The team approach is a major clue that HMI understands that training alone will not ensure the successful start-up of MMIS. Having the MMIS expert (the operations manager) and the performance improvement consultant work together makes sense. A mock trial of these two based on the key question matrix would peel back some of the roadblocks to performance.

It is also important to collect objective data from a number of sources in context of the five performance variables (mission/goal, system design, capacity, motivation, and expertise) about the present performance and the future performance at various levels in the organization and at various locations. To do this, open-ended, in-person interviews with selected employees should be followed up by a quick but systematic employee survey.

Specify the Performance Measures

To a fault, HMI has performance measures. The new MMIS introduction is a good time to revisit the connectedness of the existing and planned measures at the organizational, process, and individual levels to see whether they are pulling in the same direction. Accurate and timely data for the purpose of making sound decisions are the recurring theme. The four-part performance scorecard being touted by the executive management team is very specific and will continue to be used as the performance measure template. Therefore, it should be carefully reviewed.

Construct a Performance Improvement Proposal

The performance proposal begins to take form from the diagnosis. It comes from everyone involved in the project, not just the consultant. The major portion of the proposal will be training that is enveloped in a management support system at rollout time. The workplace expertise required of the MMIS modules and job holders must be analyzed.

The training will necessarily be packaged in stand-alone modules that can be combined as required by job roles and by individual employees. General modules will be prepared with an eye toward media-based self-instruction. Specialized modules will be structured for group classroom training and follow-up, on-the-job training. The specific media and presentation options will be chosen based on the financial forecasts. The system rollout will include local managers as partners in its management and training delivery.

Case Study Summary Comment

The purpose of this case is to paint a picture of orderliness in the middle of a complex and high-pressure organization. When all is said and done, the rollout of MMIS must work. To do this, five hundred employees need to develop very specific workplace expertise, and their managers must create the conditions to ensure improved performance.

☑ **Checkpoint**

Figure 4.7 provides an overall visual summary of the five-step performance diagnosis process, the substeps within each, and key points within each substep. Looking at this figure, answer the following questions:

1 The articulate the initial purpose phase serves to focus the performance improvement effort. True or false?
2 The performance diagnosis matrix has two axes. They are

  a Variables and levels
  b Variables and domains
  c Levels and domains
  d Mission and expertise

3 Performance outputs

  a are an optional concern
  b are always expressed in terms of quality
  c are related to the organization mission/goal
  d cannot be easily converted into financial worth

4 Performance needs

  a are always evident
  b remain constant when thinking about the taxonomy of performance levels
  c can be thought of in terms of performance gaps
  d are illusive

5 A performance improvement proposal

  a provides a summary of the diagnosis
  b specifies an intervention
  c makes a financial forecast
  d All the above

Answers: 1. True; 2. a; 3. c; 4. c; 5. d

Conclusion

It should be easy to see that the information required to conduct a performance diagnosis is not available in a predictable manner. This is the challenge. Some critical information will be waiting for you as you begin your investigation. Other information may not exist at all and should. Some will be held captive by individuals in the organization for either political or proprietary reasons. Thus, to suggest a precise sequence to the process is not realistic. Your job is to obtain the key information as effectively and efficiently as possible and to engage as many people in the organization in the process to gain credibility and acceptance.

The data collected in the diagnostic process are analyzed as needed to move the process along to the final phase of diagnosing performance— developing the performance improvement proposal. The next two chapters discuss performance improvement proposals and data collection methods, respectively.

Chapter 5

Constructing a Performance Improvement Proposal

Chapter Sections

- Process of Constructing a Performance Improvement Proposal
- Elements of a Performance Improvement Proposal
- Process of Assessing Financial Benefits
- Sample Performance Improvement Proposal
- Conclusion

Organizational specialists in areas like product research, marketing, and sales maintain their vital contributions to the organization by developing plans of action to improve organizational performance, gaining approval for their plans, and then by carrying out the plans. Human resource development, quality improvement, reengineering, and performance technology specialists should act no differently. For this reason, an important outcome of a performance diagnosis is a formal performance improvement proposal. The proposal provides an overview of the performance gap, an analysis of the performance variables, intervention options, recommendations, and forecasted benefits. The purpose of this chapter is to help you gain management approval for your performance improvement intervention.

It is increasingly common to see the use of abbreviations and acronyms in organizations. The performance improvement proposal is sometimes referred to as a "PIP" and there are different kinds of "PIPs." Sometimes this refers to a "personal improvement plan," or a "performance improvement plan" and these cases often involve an individual employee who may be close to being let go. To be clear, the performance improvement proposal you will learn to produce in this chapter is much more comprehensive. Yes, sometimes individual performance issues can be included, but as you will see, the proposal needs to be more multifaceted.

The performance improvement proposal is the fifth and final step of the performance diagnosis process (see Figure 4.1). Chapter 4 covered the first four steps that provide the diagnostic information required for the proposal.

DOI: 10.4324/9781003518532-7

Process of Constructing a Performance Improvement Proposal

The process of constructing a performance improvement proposal includes three substeps (see Figure 5.1). The first is drafting the proposal (including the performance diagnosis), the next is forecasting the performance benefits, and then submitting the proposal for approval. The first two steps help the analyst organize the information for the purpose of creating an effective and brief proposal that can move forward in the organization.

The data for each substep comes directly out of the performance diagnosis process. Added attention in this chapter is given to forecasting the benefits from the proposed performance improvement investment.

In the performance improvement proposal phase, you should not need to generate additional information. Furthermore, the proposal should not display everything you know about the performance issue. Your job is to choose and present appropriate information for the purpose of helping the organization make a sound investment decision.

The performance improvement interventions specified in the proposal should address the performance need and goal as well as the performance variables (mission/goals, systems design, capacity, motivation, and expertise). References should be made to the organizational performance levels (organizational, process, team, and/or individual) (Brache, 2002) and the tiers of the taxonomy of performance (understand, operate, troubleshoot, improve, and invent) only if doing so enhances the clarity of the proposal. While your responses to the questions about performance variables and performance levels (see Figure 4.4) help focus the intervention selection, a working knowledge of a wide variety of improvement interventions is needed. The basic promise of improving performance pushes the diagnostician back to the performance requirements and toward appropriate interventions.

Elements of a Performance Improvement Proposal

At a minimum, a performance improvement proposal should address four major elements:

- Performance gap
- Performance diagnosis

Draft proposal, including performance diagnosis ⟶ Forecast performance benefits ⟶ Submit proposal for approval

Figure 5.1 Constructing a Performance Improvement Proposal

- Recommended interventions
- Forecasted benefits

Performance Gap

The proposal for performance improvement is founded on the premise that the program you are proposing is in response to a carefully determined performance requirement. Most improvement efforts claim to be based on up-front analysis. In practice, many programs being implemented are based on superficial analysis activity that barely scratches the surface of the systematic diagnosis of performance described in Chapter 5 (Wickens et al., 2021).

Performance improvement cannot occur in a vacuum. The central objective of accurately determining performance requirements is achieving congruence between (1) the present performance, (2) the performance goal of the organization, and (3) the performance improvement effort. Nonetheless, a majority of today's development programs, whether or not their stated purpose is to "improve performance," are unconnected to the factors necessary for achieving organizational success (Diamantidis & Chatzoglou, 2018).

Practitioners can provide greater organizational value by putting a measurable performance stake in the ground along with a promise of improvement. This will show the distance from the present performance to the performance after the approval of the proposal and implementation of the intervention.

Performance Diagnosis

A performance issue is carefully specified at the individual, process, and/or organizational level (Brache, 2002). It can be expressed in the form of performance goals or as gaps between present and desired performance. Either way, it should be central to the mission of the organization. As recommended earlier, framing the diagnosis in terms of (1) a present problem, (2) improvement, or (3) future performance is important. Your performance improvement frame needs to be communicated in the proposal.

Historically, performance diagnosis (Gilbert, 1996; Harless, 1980; Mager & Pipe, 1984) focused attention on the importance of systematically examining the cause(s) of individual-level performance problems. For example, employees fail to meet performance expectations for a number of reasons: they do not have the aptitude (capacity) to perform; they choose (motivation) not to perform; they do not have the proper tools, equipment, or environment (systems design) to perform; or performance expectations (goals) are not clearly defined in the first place. Thus, beyond lack of knowledge or skill (which is most often addressed by training), individual performance problems can be attributed to low aptitude, a lack of motivation and incentives, and a poor work environment.

Scholars and practitioners then point out that performance determinants (variables) are not totally independent and that "training competes with and interacts with better selection and enhanced motivation as strategies for improving productivity through higher individual performance" (Campbell, Campbell, & Associates, 1988, p. 178). At the end of the twentieth century, the process and team levels took center stage, with efforts at improvement being classified as (1) incremental (Harrington, 1992; Juran, 1992; Tenner & DeToro, 1997), (2) radically revised (Davenport, 1993), or (3) totally reengineered (Brache, 2002; Hammer & Champy, 1993). Modifying processes has an impact on, and interact with, the individual, team, and organizational performance levels.

The overall organization performance perspective tends to focus on (1) strategic planning (Kotter, 1990; Tichy, 1983) or (2) leadership (Kouzes & Posner, 1987; Wheatley, 1992) as the basis of performance improvement.

To reiterate, the harmony among the four performance levels—organizational, process, team, and individual—is critical for successful performance improvement efforts.

Each of these performance levels provides a means of understanding the performance issues. Yet, in terms of effective communication, we have found that using the five performance variables (mission/goal, systems design, capacity, motivation, and expertise) as the framework for presenting the analysis findings works best. This approach allows the analyst to profile, substantively and succinctly, the performance gap between what is and what should be.

Recommended Interventions

Most performance needs critical for organizational success cannot be adequately addressed by one-dimensional interventions such as adding new technology, training, or better compensation. As explained earlier, performance in the workplace is almost always multifaceted. Thus, proposed performance improvement interventions almost always need to be multidimensional. Each relevant performance variable identified in the performance diagnosis (i.e., mission/goal, systems design, capacity, motivation, and expertise) should be considered in choosing performance improvement interventions.

In nearly all cases, proposals for performance improvements important to the organization will likely include multidimensional interventions. And there will likely be a number of intervention options to choose from, again going beyond targeting individuals who are having performance issues. The selection of appropriate interventions for the required performance improvement should be made and defended on the following criteria (Swanson, 2001):

- Appropriateness to the organizational culture and tradition
- Availability of the intervention
- Perceived quality of the intervention design
- Prior effectiveness of the same or a similar intervention
- Cost of the intervention
- Expected benefit to the organization

Without these criteria, ineffective and inefficient intervention options can rise to the surface. For example, interventions focused solely on training often gains management support, because those solutions suggest performance can be improved simply by increasing workforce learning and avoids higher level managerial responsibilities. Yet, single-dimension solutions like those are usually inadequate given the appropriateness, availability, and cost criteria. Training for just a few employees, or for a task best taught in the work setting, will likely not meet the criteria.

Forecasted Benefits

The concept of benefits is an extension of performance gains. An effective performance improvement intervention will close the gap between the present level of performance (actual) and the required level of performance (goal).

Any performance can be given a value. Apart from this added value of the gains in units of performance, there are costs for obtaining a level of performance. The benefit is arrived at through the simple process of subtracting the cost from the performance value (Swanson, 2001). Performance values, costs, and benefits can be discussed in both monetary and nonmonetary terms. An analyst who can talk in monetary terms can also talk in nonmonetary terms, but the opposite is not necessarily true. We recommend a financial forecast for every performance improvement proposal, as we would for any business investment.

Process of Assessing Financial Benefits

Assessing financial benefits of performance improvement development interventions is quite easy once you have mastered the specific techniques. The purpose of this section is to overview and illustrate the process. The Basic Financial Assessment Model is as follows (Swanson, 2001):

Performance value (performance value resulting from the intervention)

Cost (cost of the intervention)
Benefit (benefit is the performance value minus the cost)

The financial question in the performance improvement proposal is: What is the forecasted financial benefit resulting from an intervention (before-the-fact assessment based on estimated financial data)?

Tram Ride Financial Benefit Case

This simple tram ride case is used here to build a conceptual understanding of the financial benefit assessment method. You are the HRD coordinator for the City Zoo. The zoo's board of directors would like to make better use of the zoo's valuable volunteers by having them conduct tram tours on weekends. The board wants ten trained volunteers, each of whom would lead two tram tours per weekend. The net income from each tour is $40. No volunteers have previously been entrusted with this job, and you must now decide between what you believe are reasonable HRD program options. Would it be economically more beneficial to the zoo to train the volunteers by having them learn about the tram tours from experienced staff on the job, or would it be more beneficial to have them use a self-instructional package?

The first option, on-the-job training, consists of trainees simply riding along with experienced operators until they are fully trained. It requires four hours of unstructured training time spread over two weekends for each trainee-volunteer. These trainee-volunteers will perform no tours on their own during the two-week training period. The second option, a self-instructional package, consists of a specially prepared map, script, and operation manual, which each of the volunteers will study for three to four hours as their first-weekend commitment to their new volunteer job. They will be fully trained at the end of the first week. The trainee-volunteers who participate in this HRD program will conduct two tram tours (on their own) during the second week.

It is not the point of this case to argue whether these two options are the best interventions for the situation or whether they will actually do the job. Assume that at the end of either program, each participating volunteer will be fully trained and able to conduct tram tours on his or her own.

Financial forecasting is proactive and a part of the performance improvement up-front analysis and proposing phases. This method helps performance improvement professionals speak to decision-makers about the forecasted estimate of the effects of an intervention on system performance and the financial consequences. Forecasts can be in the context of a particular intervention or the relative financial benefits between intervention options. Forecasting financial benefits helps influence organization investment decisions early on and helps developers be viewed as business partners—proactive and strategic.

Performance Value. From the case description, it is clear that a completed tram tour is the appropriate unit of performance and that the two HRD program options for volunteer tram operators are (1) on-the-job training and (2) a self-instructional package. In this example, the Zoo Tram can be viewed as a "business" within a business in that it is a fairly self-contained system, with zoo visitors paying an extra charge to ride the tram.

Furthermore, the goal of both HRD intervention options is the same: being able to conduct two tram tours per weekend. The average income for each tram ride is known to be $40. The City Zoo has been running tram rides for several years, and while the staff has this financial information, it is not generally known by those working directly with the Zoo Tram. It was obtained from the zoo's financial manager, who keeps records of income from various zoo operations.

A tram ride time performance graph helps visualize the forecasting situation (Figure 5.2). The unit of performance and the performance goal are on the vertical axis—two tram rides per weekend for each of the trained volunteers. The horizontal time axis illustrates the fact that the self-instructional package gets volunteers to learn what they need to know in one week and that they are then able to conduct tram rides the second week. In comparison, the on-the-job training requires two weekends of riding along with an expert tram operator; on the third weekend, they are ready to perform.

Another factor to keep in mind is the number of individual performers, groups, or systems involved. For the tram ride, a total of ten volunteers will participate in the development program. Thus, individual performer gains need to be multiplied by 10.

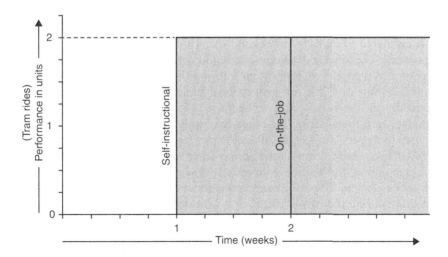

Figure 5.2 Tram Ride Time Performance Gap

The time performance graph illustrates that fact that all trainee-volunteers begin the program with zero tram expertise (zero performance). None have been exposed to the tram ride job before this occasion. Neither program option results in trainee-produced performance during their development periods. Note that an expert driver is operating the tram as the trainee-volunteer rides along. Every tram ride performed during the on-the-job training program is credited to the skilled operator, not the trainee-volunteer. There is no added performance value in having the trainee along, and, in this situation (unlike most other HRD situations), there is no anticipated reduction in the performance of the skilled operator.

The numbers will be as follows, and with each assessment method, the self-instructional package will be determined financially as being the best option.

	On-the-Job Training	Self-Instructional Package
Performance value	$0	$800
Cost	0	$300
Benefit	0	$500

The unstructured on-the-job training option has a two-week development period during which no trainees conduct tram tours. The self-instructional package option has a one-week development period during which no volunteers conduct tram tours. These times to competence are judgments made by the HRD professional based on the complexity of the subject matter to be mastered and, in this tram case, the logistics of getting trainees and expert operators together for the on-the-job option. On-the-job training was estimated to take two weeks and the self-instructional package to take one week. The longest development period between the two options is two weeks, and the units of performance during that time for both options are noted. In this case, the self-instructional package volunteers conduct two tours during the two-week assessment period. The on-the-job volunteers conduct zero tours during the two-week assessment period.

Two tours per volunteer at $40 each, times ten volunteers, would add up to $800. This is the forecasted total performance value for the self-instructional package option during the two-week assessment period. (There is a forecast of zero tours and $0 performance value for the on-the-job training option program during the two-week development period.)

Cost. Forecasting the direct financial cost of HRD interventions requires a costing template that is backed up with experience or some price data gathering. All HRD departments should have a defined process (e.g., analyze, propose, create, implement, assess; analyze, design, develop, implement, evaluate; etc.) and steps within those processes. Various cost categories re-volve around the performance improvement process. For the tram ride case, adding up the forecasted component costs for the self-instructional package resulted in a cost of $300. In comparison, there are no direct intervention costs for the unstructured on-the-job training option.

Benefit. Forecasting the financial benefits is a simple subtraction problem. The forecasted performance value minus the forecasted cost results in the forecasted financial benefit. The $800 forecasted two-week period perfor-mance gain from the self-instructional program minus the $300 forecasted cost of the program yields a forecasted $500 benefit for the two-week period. The no-cost, unstructured, on-the-job option forecasted no direct cost and no performance value during the same two-week assessment period. Please note, however, that this case involves very short-range thinking—two weeks. If the zoo is open 50 weeks of the year and if the volunteers conduct 20 tours per weekend at $40 each, the net performance value for the year for each op-tion would be close to $40,000. The only forecasted bad decision in this case would be not to recruit, develop, and use the volunteers.

The purpose of the preceding section was to give an overview of the general process of assessing financial benefits and to illustrate the assessment options through a simple tram ride case example.

Sample Performance Improvement Proposal

Proposals should be brief and to the point. Of course, backup documenta-tion should be readily available that is organized and elaborates/supports key points. A cover letter or memo for the proposal may tell a bit more about that backup information and the key people who contributed to the effort, as well as the process used to get to the proposal.

What follows are a (1) full outline for a performance improvement pro-posal (Figure 5.3), containing all of the required parts for an effective pro-posal, (2) a narrative description of an actual organization's performance issue (Figure 5.4), and (3) a complete performance improvement proposal example utilizing the outline and narrative (Figure 5.5).

Conclusion

There are two ways to communicate the results of a performance diagno-sis to the decision-makers: through face-to-face presentations and written performance improvement proposals. Both are generally required to gain organizational commitment. The presentation may be most powerful in gaining approval, while the written proposal is the contract. The written proposal is the lasting agreement and documentation of the diagnosis phase of performance improvement.

LETTERHEAD
Date:
To:
From:
RE: Performance Improvement Proposal

Performance requirements:
This section should provide details about specific costs the organization is experiencing as a result of the performance issues. Provide concrete data to illustrate the challenges. The section should be brief—no more than 5–7 sentences to provide the overview of the problem.

Performance goal:
This section provides a concise overview of the goals — these should be specific, measurable, and time bound.

Performance diagnosis:
In this section, provide a breakdown of each component of the performance challenge, covering:
- *Mission/Goal*
- *System Design*
- *Capacity*
- *Motivation*
- *Expertise*

Intervention options:
Provide a synopsis of the approach to correct the performance challenges, including:
Management Elements (in other words, staffing adjustments)
Development Elements (training, support to team members)
A Program Description (a high-level summary of the program overall)
The Evaluation for the Program's Efficacy

Figure 5.3 Outline for a Performance Improvement Proposal

The following example shows a performance improvement proposal for an engineering firm in which leaders are considering moving data from storage on local servers to a cloud-based system. The effort would require virtually all employees to change the ways they access, save and store critical data related to various infrastructure projects throughout the United States. You can see there is a technical/physical element (moving the data) and a human element (training employees to use the new system).

Figure 5.4 Description of a Performance Issue

INFRASTRUCTURE ENGINEERING Inc. LETTERHEAD
Date: month/day/year
To: S. Jackson, CEO
From: C. Kotschevar

RE: Migrating Project Documents to the Cloud – Performance Improvement Proposal

Performance requirement
Migration of project documents into a new cloud-based tool began in 2019. The migration effort was radically expanded and expedited given the former document management tool being discontinued and quarantine mandates from a pandemic. The urgency of the situation and abbreviated planning process created serious consequences. With roles were clearly defined and haphazard training -- workers are overwhelmed. Overlapping job roles, meetings out of frustration, and no clear communication channels prevail.

The lack of fully adopting the new cloud-based document management tools presents significant risks, including data security. If people refused to use it and continued storing sensitive information on local servers, critical data about municipal drinking water and wastewater infrastructure will remain unsecured and potentially in violation of federal data security regulations. Additionally, reduced access to critical project records for internal teams and external stakeholders could result in schedule delays and inefficiency. At the company level, complete migration (100%) of active project documents into the tool was required for successful operation. Exceptions cannot be granted based on the severity of risks.

Performance goal: project/team
To achieve total compliance, project level goals include (1) reducing average helpdesk response time from thirty-six hour to less than twenty-four hours (2) assignment of training modules and documentation of training completion through an online learning system and (3) creation of and adherence to a workflow that delivers pre and post migration open-houses, conducted by joint teams of migration SMEs and change management champions available to provide ongoing support for two weeks during core migration efforts.

Performance diagnosis: project/team
1. *Mission/goal:* The objective of the migration project is to provide secure access to organized project documents in a standard folder structure the is in alignment with the firm's commitment to exceptional project delivery. The speed of the implementation due to unanticipated external conditions created a project approach that compromises the ability of the project team to deliver its core objective. A recent migration pause has created space to address this issue.
2. *System design:* While the new cloud-based tool is able to accommodate most of the file types common to the engineering industry, more exceptions are discovered with each migration. Critical file types used for cost estimating and construction design are unable to operate within the tool. Technical experts are looking at customize programming efforts that may be able to resolve these conflicts.

Figure 5.5 Sample Performance Improvement Proposal for Engineering Inc. (*Continued*)

3. *Capacity:* The project team requires more individuals dedicated to training alone, who will not be utilized for migration or helpdesk support. These dedicated training team members will also need to be accountable for training content revisions and administration. More helpdesk staff with experience using the new tool are needed to decrease response times.

4. *Motivation:* The lack of trust between the technical migration team and the change management team has created an atmosphere of mutual disrespect and blame. Both teams focus energy and resources trying to hold the other accountable for poor project performance instead of completing actions to drive progress.

5. *Expertise:* The Technical Project Manager, Migration Lead, and two trainers have previous experience managing migrations into this tool for similar organizations. The majority of the change management team and trainers have little to no exposure to the new tool or similar projects.

Recommended interventions

The following interventions are recommended for improving this data migration project.

1. Create new critical success factors (CSFs) in addition to # of projects migrated. Document approval from steering committee and core team.
2. Revise roles and responsibilities to focus on achieving each of the CSFs. Document approval from the steering committee and core team.
3. Enforce a protocol to log each change management call as a helpdesk ticket (as this is already set up for reporting)
4. Create
   a. A comprehensive schedule that includes migration dates, communications, training (open house, follow up deadlines, etc.)
   b. A change management issue log that is shared with the steering committee on a weekly basis
   c. Missing workflows related (issue elevation, pre and post migration open house and follow up, etc.)
   d. Standard agendas for standing calls and corresponding attendance matrices
   e. Training modules for
      i. "Hands-on" interactive training module
      ii. Non users/leaders and follow up survey
      iii. Training module and support resources for new project set up
5. Increase visibility of advanced training/resources
6. Create a guidance document/Protocols on file management, communication, relevant systems (This item needs to be addressed at the corporate level and is in progress but would benefit from input from the ProjectWise core team)

Financial analysis

Performance Value	$85,000
Cost	$30,000
Benefit	$55,000

Figure 5.5 (Continued)

Chapter 6

Data Collection Methods

Chapter Sections

- **Approaching the Data Collection Task**
- **Interviews**
- **Questionnaires**
- **Observations**
- **Organization Records**
- **Conclusion**

Performance improvement analysts are required to collect and analyze data to diagnose organizations, document work processes, and document workplace expertise. Several general data collection methods are used throughout the overall analysis process:

- Interviews
- Questionnaires
- Observations
- Organization records

This chapter provides an overview of these four data collection methods. The intention is to provide just enough guidance to ensure sound data collection practices and to provide recommended sources for more technical assistance. Clearly, the content of this chapter could be a book by itself.

Analysts committed to improving performance require firsthand information about organizations, processes, work teams, and job performers. They must delve into the organization and its workplace issues to obtain accurate information. The task of searching and analyzing information on organization-specific performance issues is challenging, but it can be as much fun as reading a good mystery. In diagnosing and documenting organization performance and workplace expertise, analysts regularly call

DOI: 10.4324/9781003518532-8

on the four general data collection methods. Each method has appropriate uses, and each demands careful execution in searching for valid information.

Approaching the Data Collection Task

Several overriding principles should guide considerations in using the various data collection methods and tools within the analysis for improving the performance realm.

Use More than One

More than one method or source of data collection is generally required to gain enough information to understand a phenomenon. Using multiple methods and multiple perspectives increases the validity of the assessment. For example, trends in organization records may provide a target and interviews with workers may reveal the underlying causes. Similarly, interviewing managers may give a partial picture, while interviewing the workers and customers may fill in the picture.

Strengths and Weaknesses

Every data collection method has strengths and weaknesses. They are noted in the following sections of this chapter. To be overly infatuated with one data collection methodology is dangerous. For example, surveys are easy, using the Internet is easy, and together they can be very inappropriate.

Method versus Analysis Question

Let the analysis question(s) determine the method, not the data method constraining the question(s). The nature of the question to be answered should dictate the data collection method so as not to distort the question to meet the demands of the data collection method. Concerns for data collection efficiency and personal preferences for one method over another can falsely lead to using less appropriate data collection methods.

Impact of Data Collection

Getting managers to agree to and assist in collecting data has an impact on the organization. The act of data collection becomes part of the intervention. Just the fact that people in an organization care to inquire about what is going on has an impact on those asking for information, those being asked to provide information, and those not being asked to provide information. Thus, how the data collection effort is perceived is very important.

Interviews

The interview method enables analysts to gather information directly from people in the workplace or people connected in various ways to the organization and its processes in person, in groups, and by phone or video conference. Interviewing demands a high level of competence and commitment from the analyst. See Figure 6.1 for a concise summary of the technique of interviewing.

Interviewing people in the workplace is a time-consuming but useful technique for discovering what happens at the organization, process, team, and/or individual job levels. The skillful interviewer anticipates the need to establish rapport with the interviewee—not an easy task when questions of adequacy or efficiency of performance are involved. The interviewer is obliged to record accurate notes, to ask questions of people using their language, and to listen with respect.

Interviewing is done with a critical eye to the process. The following questions will assist you in keeping your interviewing on track:

- Have I done my homework?
- Am I talking to the best possible person, or would someone else be able to offer a more accurate account of the situation?
- Am I getting straight information?
- How do the responses of several people compare?
- Is something being implied but left unspoken?

Interviews yield great quantities of information that can be difficult to manage and analyze. Plan to spend twice as long writing about the interview as you did in conducting it.

Telephone or Video Conference Interviews

Interviews conducting by phone, or a video conferencing platform, require several unique steps. According to Lavarakas (1987, pp. 18–19), they involve a ten-step process:

1 Deciding on a sampling design, including the method of respondent selection with a sampling unit.
2 Developing and formatting a draft questionnaire.
3 Choosing a method to generate the pool of telephone numbers that will be used in sampling.
4 Producing a call sheet for each number that will be used in sampling.
5 Developing a draft introduction/selection sheet and fallback statements for use by interviewers.

1. Description of interview technique

The interviewer and interviewee(s) talk (alone or in small groups), and the interviewer asks questions to get information.

2. Types

A. *Structured:*   The interviewer has a predetermined list of questions arranged in some format. All interviewees are asked the same basic questions plus follow-up questions. This limits the content to some predetermined topics.

B. *Unstructured:*   The interviewer and client talk without any preset format. The interview may cover a wide range of subjects. Different people may be asked entirely different questions.

C. *Combination:*   Combining structured and unstructured is the most common method.

3. Uses

A. To establish rapport for other data gathering
B. To get details of work protocol
C. To learn about plans and projects
D. To get workers' viewpoints about procedures and processes
E. To find out about difficulties
F. To get opinions about organization, morale, supervision
G. To follow up on critical incidents

4. Key skills

A. The ability to develop questions that will get meaningful answers
B. The ability to ask open-ended questions spontaneously
C. The ability to create an atmosphere of trust—*not* defensiveness
D. The ability to take complete and accurate notes without infusing one's own ideas

5. Pros and cons

Pros	*Cons*
A. Allows study of a wide range of subjects	A. Can be expensive and time consuming
B. Source of valuable and meaningful information	B. Interviewer can create bias—that is, interject own feelings into the response
C. Allows interviewer to gain "empathy" or a feel for the situation	C. Can be hard to interpret the meaning of answers
D. Process can allow the interviewer to gain the trust of clients	D. Depends on skillful use of questions; takes practice
	E. Difficult to synthesize

Figure 6.1   Interview Technique Summary

6 Hiring interviewers and supervisors, and scheduling interviewing sessions.
7 Pilot-testing and revising survey instruments.
8 Printing final questionnaires and other forms.
9 Training interviewers and supervisors.
10 Conducting fully supervised interviews.

The same approach applies for video conferencing, which is more prevalent in organizations today than phone calls. Platforms like Zoom, Skype, or Teams allow interviewers the convenience of easily recording and transcribing the conversation. Additionally, the option to use video creates a more conversational experience for the interview subject and can help enhance their comfort and overall experience (Nehls, Smith, & Schneider, 2015).

Group Interviews

Focus groups are a popular form of group interview where a targeted group of stakeholders come together to provide information about a specific topic. The following focus group–moderating skills outlined by Krueger (1988) capture the uniqueness of this group process technique: (1) selecting the focus group location, (2) preparing mentally, (3) engaging in purposeful small talk and revealing the presentation strategy, (4) recording the group discussion, (5) pausing and probing, and (6) being ready for the unexpected. While interviews of teams are helpful for performance problems or performance improvements, the rich interaction from focus groups is particularly helpful in sorting out future performance issues.

Questionnaires

Deceptively simple, the survey questionnaire is often used as a primary data collection tool. After all, what could be easier than writing up a questionnaire and mailing it off to a hundred people or more, right? Wrong! Good questionnaires require skill to develop, and getting sufficient numbers of responses from the target population can be difficult. But done correctly, no tool is more efficient for obtaining data from a large, dispersed population. See Figure 6.2 for a concise summary of the questionnaire method.

Expert analysts use interviews as a first step for discovering the most useful content for a questionnaire. The questionnaire then offers a way to accurately evaluate the extent and the credibility of the facts and opinions gathered by interviews.

By keeping questionnaires short, you will ensure the goodwill of the respondents and will simplify the data analysis. Pilot-testing a questionnaire with a few respondents and, if necessary, rewriting questions can save you from gathering a mountain of useless data.

1. Description of questionnaire technique
The investigator has a specific set of written items that require the client to respond in some meaningful way.

2. Types
A. *Open response:*   The items are open-ended questions. The client writes essay-type answers, which are then interpreted by the investigator. The investigator must somehow code the responses and subject them to a data analysis.

B. *Forced response:*   The questionnaire items require some specific type of response such as yes or no, true or false, a checkmark placed in a box or on a scale, or a word written in a space. The investigator codes the responses according to a system and then subjects them to data analysis.

3. Uses
A. To cover large populations of people
B. To overcome problems of geographical distance
C. To measure attitudes or opinions
D. To ask about what people value or do
E. To gather descriptive data

4. Key skills
A. The ability to specify exactly what type of information is required
B. The ability to develop items that will get appropriate responses
C. The ability to do data analysis
D. The ability to lay out the questionnaire in a clear, readable way

5. Pros and cons

Pros	*Cons*
A. It's relatively easy to quantify and summarize the data gathered.	A. It's a relatively "cold" approach– that is, no personal contact.
B. Questionnaires are easy to use with large samples.	B. It may miss important issues because the questions are predetermined.
C. They are relatively inexpensive.	C. It's difficult to write good items.
D. You can obtain large amounts of data.	D. People may misread items and make inappropriate responses.
E. This method is less time-consuming than some other methods.	E. The data may be overinterpreted.
F. Statistical analysis is quick and easy with computers.	F. The response rate may be too low.
G. Questionnaires can often be used in more than one setting.	
H. They are more objective than interviews.	

Figure 6.2   Questionnaire Technique Summary

Unless you are trained in statistical analysis, you would do well to acquire expert guidance in handling all phases of the questionnaire process. Too often the result of an inept questionnaire is garbled information that is useless to the analyst and ultimately to all the people who have spent their time and energy filling out your instrument.

The questionnaire process must begin with the following questions: "What do I want to know?" and "If I get it, how will I use this information?" The process ends with "Did I discover what I wanted to know?" and "How can I use this information?" The same questions are asked for every item on the questionnaire.

Assuming you have not let all this talk of statistical analysis discourage you from sending out a simple questionnaire, ask yourself the following:

- Did I receive a sufficient number of returned questionnaires?
- What did I find out?
- Are these data useful?
- Did I discover something that I should verify through a review of performance records or through observations or interviews?
- Do these data confirm or contradict what I have learned through other means?

Organizational Culture Questionnaires

Culture surveys are an important tool for performance improvements (vs. performance problems or future performances). They provide an effective and efficient method of gathering information from employees (Sleezer & Swanson, 1992).

Surveys must be organized around clear purposes and managed in a simple and effective manner (while maintaining the reliability and validity of the data). Employee perceptions are a window into the health of the organization! A comprehensive survey covers 13 culture categories, including the following: organizational mission and goals, corporate management's leadership, department management leadership, supervisory effectiveness, working conditions, productivity, accountability, communication, interpersonal and interdepartmental relationships, job satisfaction, employee compensation, employee career development, training and development, and training options (McLean, 1988). Pulse surveys can be created to target any one or two categories at a time in a shorter, easier-to-answer format. The critical features are ensuring anonymity, having an objective third party present, and providing constructive feedback to the organization. Customized surveys to address specific strategic change efforts can be developed from selected culture categories. Baseline data can be used to compare results with those of later surveys. Open-ended responses can also be solicited and analyzed. The following is a sample "strongly agree to strongly disagree" culture survey question: "When problems occur in my job, I have the freedom to solve them."

Customer Satisfaction Questionnaires

From a performance improvement perspective, what your customers think is critical. Short of talking to every customer, customer surveys are the most direct and valid means of measuring what customers are thinking (Hayes, 1992). The input of customer requirements can shape organization goals/ processes. Customer satisfaction is a critical "scorecard" of organization achievement.

High-quality customer surveys can be used to determine customer requirements and customer satisfaction. They can be used for both external customers and internal customers. Customer surveys can answer the core questions: What do customers want? Are customers satisfied with what they receive?

Carefully designed paper-and-pencil surveys tied concisely and directly to customer requirements are the most cost-effective means of surveying customers. Surveying smaller samples, instead of entire groups, increases efficiency and minimizes customer annoyance. Subtle or ill-defined customer requirements may require face-to-face techniques, such as focus groups or critical incident techniques (Flanagan, 1954). Critical incidents are reports or descriptions of things people have done or have observed others doing. The critical incident technique can be called on for any of the four general data collection methods. Regardless of the specific data collection technique used, customer satisfaction surveys should match the important customer requirements accepted by the organization.

Observations

Thinking, planning, imagining, and estimating are abstract work behaviors and, one would think, unaccountable. People express the results of their work performances through observable actions, however, and the qualities of their actions can be observed. When practiced systematically, observing people at work will yield a great deal of qualitative and quantitative information about the work, the worker, and the work environment. See Figure 6.3 for a concise summary of the observation technique.

Observing people at work requires considerable skill. Great sensitivity and the ability to be unobtrusive are essential. To avoid altering the work process, you must become part of the flow. The unobtrusive observer is more likely to perceive errors, problems, and creative solutions than the intrusive observer.

1. Description of observation technique

The observer goes on-site and watches the work behavior of people doing the job.

2. Types

A. *Overt:*   The observer tells the worker what is going on. The worker knows what the observer is looking for. The observer may even ask the worker to do certain things in order to help with the observation. This type of observation is frequently combined with an interview during which the observer asks the worker to explain things as they are done.

B. *Covert:*   The observer doesn't tell the worker what is going on. Normally the observer is in plain view, but the worker is unaware of what actually is being observed. The observer normally doesn't communicate with the worker or interfere in any way with the work. This helps let the observer watch the natural work method in its actual sequence, without special effort.

3. Uses

A. To analyze work methods for effectiveness and efficiency
B. To corroborate employee performance with interview reports
C. To analyze conditions in the work environment
D. To find safety/housekeeping problems
E. To analyze communication patterns
F. To watch work flow
G. To locate critical incidents

4. Key skills

A. The ability to find the best people and times to observe
B. The ability to keep out of the worker's way
C. The ability to be open to new ways of doing the work
D. The ability to spot when the work is being done correctly and incorrectly
E. The ability to take accurate notes or remember the important things seen

5. Pros and cons

Pros	*Cons*
A. The observer can collect firsthand information on behavior.	A. It can be difficult to interpret what is observed, especially when the worker is solving a problem by thinking it through.
B. Observations occur while the work is actually being done—not after it's over.	B. Sampling the people and times can bias the results. (It could be a unique situation.)
C. Observations can be adapted to many situations.	C. The observer can create bias by interjecting own feelings.
D. They may reveal totally unexpected problems.	D. Follow-up is usually required to help interpret the observations.
E. They may reveal new and better methods.	E. It can be costly.
F. They are not filtered through another's words.	

Figure 6.3   Observation Technique Summary

Some activities happen more or less frequently than others, some take a longer or shorter time to complete, and some happen only at the beginning or the end of the month. Therefore, judging the length of the required observation time can be difficult. One thing is certain: the longer you observe in a setting, the more you see. Before beginning to analyze work behaviors, take care to observe long enough to be able to discriminate between those behaviors that:

- add something of value to the product or services or process (productivity);
- add nothing (waste of a team's/worker's effort or time);
- are linked and ordered in meaningful ways; or
- take away from the value of the product or service or process (mistakes, negative remarks, interfering with others at work, etc.).

Your major assets as an observer are wide-open eyes and ears, a curious and nonjudgmental nature, and the ability to discern the subtleties of human behaviors.

If you can't figure out what a particular work behavior is, ask. If the technology of the work is unfamiliar, if the nature of the work behavior is subtle, or if you encounter a controversy about how the work should be done, you will benefit by researching the work and the setting before continuing to observe.

By accurately recording events, you can test the beliefs of management and workers and even your own first impressions of the work performance. Is the behavioral protocol the same for all employees? How frequently do the observed behaviors occur? What qualities of the behavior are important? Speed? Accuracy? Decision making? Language? Do obstacles to performance exist in the work environment? What are the expected versus the actual results of the work behavior? Is the work performance rewarded, punished, or ignored? What behaviors differentiate the high performers from the low performers?

Be cautious when interpreting the data derived from observation. Consider that your presence can change the situation and affect the data collected. Were you sufficiently prepared for the observation to understand what you were observing? How accurate are your data? Were you unable to record what you saw because of a lack of time or recording skill? Is that important? Does the observed behavior fall into phases or stages? Is it cyclical?

The canard that "A picture is worth a thousand words" applies equally to analysis work. The picture in the realm of performance improvement analysis consists of the actual organization, the functioning processes, and the teams/individuals working in them. Firsthand observation provides a tier of information that cannot be obtained through talk and paper—interviews, questionnaires, and organizational records.

Organization Records

Organizations keep records of many everyday occurrences. These include employee turnover; absenteeism; grievances filed; units of performance per person, per hour, per day, per week; career growth and development plans; succession planning materials; and costs of production. Policy manuals, procedure manuals, interoffice memos, minutes of board meetings, and the like, are kept on file. Trends and cycles can often be spotted in these records. You may find clues to trouble spots that will provide useful questions for your interviews. Ordinary, everyday business records are a great source of information for the adept analyst with skills in interpreting data. For more information on the organizational records technique, see Figure 6.4.

Organization records generally reflect the consequences of a problem situation, just as they may later reflect its resolution. Thus, these records are most useful in zeroing in on present performance problems (vs. performance improvements or future performances). Caution must be taken in interpreting these data because they are generally collected for other purposes. How old are the data? How reliable were the collecting and recording methods? Be alert for aggregated information that may hide major organizational problems among innocent-looking, averaged figures. Look at the extent of variation. Having knowledge of statistical methods is useful to the careful analyst.

Once you have verified the accuracy and considered the context of the organization records, spotted trends, and identified problems, ask yourself whether any of the data seem surprising, contradictory, optimistic, pessimistic, or problematic. The data should confirm or deny the facts gained through other data collection methods.

Benchmarking is the search for the best practices that will lead to the superior performance of an organization (Camp, 1995). It is a process that integrates data obtained from all four of the general data collection methods (interviews, questionnaires, observations, and organization records). According to Camp, the ten process steps include the following:

1 Identify what is to be benchmarked.
2 Identify comparative companies.
3 Determine the data collection method and collect the data.
4 Determine the current performance gap.
5 Project future performance levels.
6 Communicate the benchmark findings and gain acceptance for them.
7 Establish functional goals.
8 Develop action plans.
9 Implement specific actions and monitor progress.
10 Recalibrate the benchmarks.

1. Description of organizational record technique

The analyst classifies, studies, and interprets the meaning of the numbers or information buried in the records.

2. Types

A. *Primary:*   The analyst gathers and studies cost, time, and productivity data or reports as a primary source of information. Information is usually classified and depicted in a way that reveals specific points of interest. This type of data analysis is normally used to locate areas of loss or trends.

B. *Secondary:*   The analyst classifies and studies data gained through interviews, observations, or questionnaires in order to design an overall picture from many separate pieces of information. This type of analysis is frequently used to consolidate information gathered from all the other methods of investigation.

3. Uses

A. To analyze areas of loss
B. To corroborate and expand work behavior protocol
C. To spot and predict trends
D. To consolidate information gathered from other investigative methods
E. To spot cyclical problems
F. To classify information into categories

4. Key skills

Note: Data analysis can require a wide variety of technical skills; this list covers a few of the basics.
A. The ability to classify or group information into categories
B. The ability to find relationships between categories or separate pieces of information
C. The ability to select and use statistical and other math techniques
D. The ability to depict data with charts and graphs
E. The ability to interpret data and make verbal explanations of their meaning

5. Pros and cons

Pros	*Cons*
A. The organizational records technique minimizes people's biases.	A. It can be difficult to locate the best data or reports.
B. Numbers tend to be believable and easy to understand.	B. The data could have been biased by those who recorded them in the first place.
C. This technique can identify accurate "baselines" against which to measure changes in performance.	C. It can be difficult to quantify some important aspects of performance.

Figure 6.4 Organization Record Technique Summary

☑ **Checkpoint**

Use the following multiple-choice items to check your understanding of the techniques for data collection. Select the best answer for each item. The answers to these questions are at the end of the test.

1 The observer does not communicate with the person being observed when ___.

    a the worker does not want to be observed.
    b the observer could get in the way.
    c observing the most natural work process is desired.
    d management objects to the observation process.

2 Observations are used to ___.

    a gather data from large populations.
    b learn about plans and goals.
    c find work environment problems.
    d spot cyclical problems.

3 The analyst has observed four workers in the department, but the manager is unimpressed with the findings because the observer ___.

    a did not ask the workers about their work.
    b failed to separate high and low performers.
    c is wrong about the count of behaviors.
    d did not observe a sufficient sample of workers.

4 The analyst should use the interview techniques to collect data if ___.

    a getting a feel for a situation is important.
    b time and money are in short supply.
    c productivity data is required.
    d determining points of consensus is important.

5 The skill that is most essential in interviewing is ___.

    a fostering trust.
    b asking questions that get meaningful answers.
    c taking complete notes.
    d all the above.

6   Because of the difficulty of designing good questions, a thoughtful analyst would _____ before sending out a hundred questionnaires.

a   carefully select the people who will receive the questionnaire.
b   establish the budget for design, printing, mailing, and data analysis.
c   plan to mail the questionnaire in two batches.
d   pilot-test it with a few respondents.

7   The exclusive use of limited-response questions may result in a questionnaire that is easy to tabulate but that fails to identify an important issue. To avoid this possibility, the analyst could ___.

a   include at least one or two open-ended questions.
b   invite respondents to write comments anywhere on the questionnaire as thoughts occur to them.
c   pilot-test the questionnaire and interview respondents.
d   all the above.

8   An analyst without the requisite statistical analysis skills is at a disadvantage because ___.

a   an outside expert must be consulted.
b   the importance of some records could be missed.
c   only certain records can be made visual by graphing.
d   interpreting and explaining data are essential.

9   Establishing the accuracy of primary records is ___.

a   difficult.
b   impossible.
c   essential.
d   assumed by the organization.

Answers: 1. c; 2. c; 3. b; 4. a; 5. d; 6. d; 7. a; 8. d; 9. c

Conclusion

The general data collection methods—interviews, questionnaires, observations, and organization records—provide an eclectic toolbox for the analyst. They are used at the levels of organization diagnosis and documentation of expertise.

Each method has strengths and weaknesses. In almost all instances, using more than one data collection method is necessary to ensure valid conclusions about the trends, factors, and causes of organization, process, team, and individual performances or the dimensions and substance of workplace expertise. There are numerous useful data collection methodology references available (Bartlett, 2005; Dillman, 2000; Forster, 1994; Nehls, Smith, & Schneider, 2015; Swanson & Holton, 2005).

Chapter 7

Documenting and Improving Work Processes

Chapter Sections

- Documenting and Improving Work Processes
- Identifying a Work Process to Be Improved
- Healthcare Insurance Sales Case
- Tips for the Analyst
- Conclusion

One major outcome of a performance diagnosis is the possible realization that a core organization process is out of control. Thus, proposing to document and improve processes can become part of the performance improvement proposal. This chapter is focused on the specifics of documenting and improving work processes.

There are many ways to analyze organizations. Some examples include analyzing organizations from the perspectives of power, politics, communication, shared meaning, and finance. While these and other perspectives are worthy, analyzing organizations from a process perspective has great utility. A process can be thought of as a systematic series of "actions" directed to some specified end.

The notion of continuously improving organization processes has become deeply ingrained in organizations through the quality movement. Although varying in approaches, all the quality improvement systems support the core ideas that processes should be identified, continuously managed, and improved. The methodologies and tools of process improvement have generally proven to be quite effective. Two problems with process improvement endeavors are that (1) they often lack controls to ensure that process improvement resources are being focused on core processes and (2) they often have weak follow-up links for specifying and developing the expertise required to function in the process. Figure 7.1 is a five-step general model of documenting and improving work processes. The step is the input and the last in the output. The three in the middle wrestle with the process itself.

DOI: 10.4324/9781003518532-9

Figure 7.1 Documenting and Improving Work Processes Steps

Documenting and Improving Work Processes

Work processes as a focal point for organizations is basic to organization understanding in the twenty-first century. Moreover, work processes are the least threatening place to start in terms of detailed analysis. Organization work processes are inanimate, not person-centered. Work processes are just there, inside the organization. They are the way things are done—good or bad, effective, or ineffective, efficient or inefficient—and have evolved over time with input from people at various levels. This cannot be overstated. By focusing on a work process, you are not calling out any individual. Work processes carry the brilliant and flawed logic of the organization, without attributing the credit to anyone. The defining benefit of process documentation by a group is that it creates shared understanding.

At the end of an effective work process documentation session, stakeholders can see how their role interacts with other people, technology, machines, and information systems. They can see where inefficiency, duplication, and bottlenecks can be eliminated, no matter their workplace language, culture, or bias. Work process documentation removes the subjective judgment about the way things should be and draws a representation of the real. It is important to remember that analysis for improving performance will invariably surface issues that organization members will try to attribute to individuals. Eliminating the blame and credit game allows people to set personality and job role agendas to the side (at minimum, to dilute them). Focusing on documenting and improving work processes is central to the challenge of improving performance. An additional benefit to the impartiality of process documentation is the power that simple visualizations have in driving informed decision-making. In some cases, people might contribute effort to a work process for many years without understanding how that process leads to or impedes organization performance. When each contributor's unique perspective is combined to create a comprehensive representation an awareness of the "big picture" is gained.

It is without question that people operate with "pictures" in their heads. In this case, it is a "picture" of the work process. As long as there are various pictures in different peoples' minds, the work process itself will remain mysterious. Documenting work processes allows for a comprehensive and accurate picture of the work to be achieved. Once this is complete, improving on the work process is much easier when everyone can see the same visual representation.

Identifying a Work Process to Be Improved

Work processes that require improvement should be identified through the organization performance diagnosis. Process performance issues can surface through that level of analysis, and recommendations for improving work processes should be highlighted in the performance improvement proposal.

While there is direct interplay among the organization, process, team, and individual levels of performance, sometimes the wrong level is targeted. For example, developing workforce expertise to work in an ineffective and inefficient work process does not make sense. Yet, this is being done in organizations all the time.

A case in contrast, while consulting with an organization at the mission and work process levels. As the process documentation began to form, it became painfully clear that the company was lacking so much basic work expertise that improving the core work processes had to wait. They needed to first get minimally acceptable output from their poor system. In this case, the project shifted to developing worker expertise for the existing work process in the short term that was followed later with major work process improvement.

Analyzing whether the present work process is effective and efficient is a critical aspect of performance improvement. While working on performance improvement efforts you may find yourself moving from one performance realm (organization, process, team, or individual) to another as the situation unfolds. This may sound unsystematic, but the reality is that this book presents a large set of professional tools that are sequenced under ideal conditions. While working in the real world, conditions vary and expert judgments about the tools and the timing of their use must be made.

Healthcare Insurance Sales Case

The case study reported here is from a major healthcare insurance company in the United States. The business goal was focused on increasing sales in a changing and competitive environment. In this case, it was determined that the core sales work process required major revision and realignment in relation to the business goal and the workforce expertise. This case clearly illustrated the need for new approaches to analyzing and building workplace expertise in a dynamic competitive environment.

The need for this major company-wide effort was fully clarified in a thorough performance improvement proposal based on the rigorous analysis method laid out in this book. The general steps of the performance diagnosis process included (1) articulating initial purpose, (2) assessing the performance variables, (3) specifying the performance measures, (4) determining the performance needs, and (5) constructing an improvement proposal (see Chapter 5).

A summary of the large up-front analysis data collection was reported back to senior management through the cells created by the performance diagnosis matrix enabling questions used in this diagnosis phase (Figure 7.2).

Performance variables	Performance levels		
	Organization level	Sales process	Individual new business manager
Mission/goal	Does the organization mission/ performance goals fit the reality of the economic, political, and cultural forces? No—Economic; No—Political; No—Cultural	Do the process goals enable organization and job level goals to be met? Partially—A process orientation is emerging	Are the work goals of individuals congruent with the organization's? Inconsistent—NBM/CM separation creates conflicting incentives
System design	Does the organization system provide structure and policies supporting the desired performance? Partially—However, clear NBM/CM separation is not possible or desirable in all sales offices	Is the process designed in a logical and systematic way? No—Poor service processes and information systems interfere with high performance	Does the job design enable the individual to perform as required by the process? Yes—However, NBM/CM separation impedes long-term productivity
Capacity	Does the organization have the leadership, capital, and infrastructure to achieve its mission/goals? No—Infrastructure is inadequate. Communication and change management from home office is poor	Does the process have the capacity to perform re quantity, quality, and time line requirements? No—Suboptimization is occurring due to inefficient and ineffective supporting processes	Does the individual have the mental, physical, and emotional capacity to perform? For normal conditions it is assumed so
Motivation	Do the policies, culture, and reward systems support the desired performance? No—Policies and culture; the compensation system supports NBM/CM separation, which impedes performance	Does the process provide the required information? Is the process motivating for the workforce? No—Supporting processes, including systems, lack integrity	Does the individual want to perform no matter what? Yes—But high performers are taxed by unrealistic sales goals, and morale is low
Expertise	Do the selection and training policies and resources enable the desired performance? Partially—No clear competency criteria has existed in the past; some training deficiencies exist	Is the expertise required by the process continuously determined and developed? No—A process orientation is just emerging	Does the individual have the knowledge, skills, and expertise to perform? Partially—Level of competency among individuals varies

Figure 7.2   Performance Diagnosis Matrix for Healthcare New Business Managers

Each cell in the analysis matrix contains a basic question with the findings summarized as a *yes, no, or partially satisfied* along with a supporting comment. This one-page summary was used to solicit management support. The data supporting these cells were used as a basis for uncovering existing system sales performance problems, opportunities, and solutions.

The major conclusion from the performance diagnosis was that the existing sales work process was incapable of meeting the strategic business goals of timeliness and quality features necessary to retain company market share. Thus, the sales work process needed to be significantly improved, the job roles in the process needed to be clarified, and the expertise required to carry out the roles within the "new" process needed to be defined and put in place.

Methods for Documenting the Present Work Process

In analyzing a work process, it is essential to understand its scope or how big it is, the process steps (what's happening and in what sequence), and which steps must happen before others can occur. The purpose of a flowchart is to create a graphic or visual representation of a work process. The process-step categories include inputs, conversions, decisions, outputs, feedback, and more. In short, a standard flowchart is an articulated and meaningful set of lines and symbols.

The end result—a process flowchart—is a clearer picture of what changes are needed. Figure 7.3 is a simple flowchart. Readily available computer software programs make flowchart documentation quite easy (e.g., SmartDraw, Microsoft Visio, Powerpoint, Lucidchart, among others).

We have some hesitation in presenting flowcharting symbols since they are dynamic, and their meanings continue to grow and change depending on who uses them. Although standards have been established, people logically deviate from these standards to suit their organization's needs. Figure 7.4 provides a sample of flowchart symbols.

The use of flowcharts provides significant benefits. For starters, it increases the understanding level of a process. Fundamentally, before any work process improvement can be performed, it must be understood in its present state. Recalling a recent work session with a management team to document their core business processes, it was difficult to get past the first few steps because most of the people in the room had such different understandings about the core work process that they worked with day in and day out. Flowcharting brings into existence a needed common understanding. By creating a picture with symbols, lines, labels—semantic and interpretive differences are overcome.

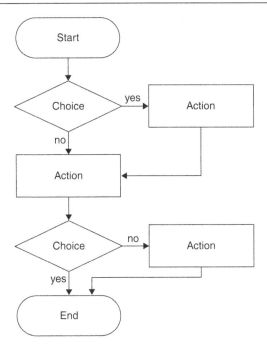

Figure 7.3 Sample Process Flowchart

Integrated Flowcharts

Integrated flowchart documentation is a systematic, structured method for describing an organizational process(es) in an integrated, graphic document format. It is an invaluable tool for performance improvement professionals. The three major elements of the integrated flowchart are (1) the steps from the work process flowchart, (2) the workers (people) engaged in the process, and (3) the worker in the lead for each process step. Check out these three elements in Figure 7.5.

Not only do these types of flowcharts show the process flow, but they also reflect which individual has responsibility for each process step. This clarity reduces workplace conflict. The flowchart information is useful when a work process has dozens of steps, when steps transcend multiple departments, and when responsibility is shared by more than one individual. Integrated flowcharts can identify which worker (job) or department is performing the greatest number of steps in the work process. The work process flow is revealed through this effort. Also, convoluted paths are identified, such as is the case when part of the work process flows back and forth too often and unnecessarily.

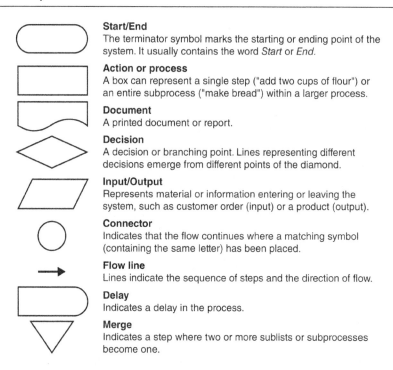

Start/End
The terminator symbol marks the starting or ending point of the system. It usually contains the word *Start* or *End.*

Action or process
A box can represent a single step ("add two cups of flour") or an entire subprocess ("make bread") within a larger process.

Document
A printed document or report.

Decision
A decision or branching point. Lines representing different decisions emerge from different points of the diamond.

Input/Output
Represents material or information entering or leaving the system, such as customer order (input) or a product (output).

Connector
Indicates that the flow continues where a matching symbol (containing the same letter) has been placed.

Flow line
Lines indicate the sequence of steps and the direction of flow.

Delay
Indicates a delay in the process.

Merge
Indicates a step where two or more sublists or subprocesses become one.

Figure 7.4 Standard Flowchart Symbols

	Implementation and account management subprocess steps	1. MGMT	2. NBM	3. PSS	4. BSC/ CM	5. BSC/ Serv	6. Pro	7. UW	8. IM/IS	9. C
						Workers and their roles in the process				
	25 Assign service representative to case *or*	⊗	X		X	X				
	26 Request case manager from BSC for the case	⊗				X				
	27 Are customer's expectations in sync with____capability to deliver product, price, and service? (If no, go to 15 and 16.)				⊗	X	X	X		X
A	**Process measure:** Number of times____capability is not in sync with customer's requirements of cost, product, or service	⊗								
	28 If yes, review presale file, proposal, and underwriting rates		X	X	⊗					
	29 Confirm internally what products were sold		⊗	X	X	X		X	X	
	30+ Advise customer of network developments and/or introduce any new service delivery		X		⊗		X			
	31 Notify implementation team of sale and engage		⊗		X				X	
•	32 **Conduct implementation meeting** (*Comment:* For management training, stress minor role of NBM.)		X		X	X	X		⊗	X
	32.1 Answer benefits question				X	X			⊗	
	32.2 Answer questions on administrative process				X	X			⊗	
	33 Send letter to customer following up on implementation process				⊗	X			X	
•	34+ **Deliver and negotiate financial contracts**				⊗					X
	35 Monitor service process	X		X	⊗					

⊗ Bold means leadership responsibility; X nonbold means contributor.
• Large, multistep activity.

+ This activity could occur anytime from this point on.
A This step should be automated.

Figure 7.5 Flowchart Steps within the Healthcare Insurance Sales Process

Integrated Flowchart for the Healthcare Insurance Case

The existing sales process in the healthcare insurance case was documented and found to be a 79-step process spread over nine job categories. The original work process data can be derived using the data collection methods outlined in Chapter 6 (interviews, questionnaires, observations, and organization records).

The resulting integrated flowchart from the multisource data—an integration of the steps within the process and the people that work in the process—brings the process and the people working in the process to the fore. As you can see in Figure 7.5, each step from the integrated flowchart is coded against all the job roles directly involved in that step. For example, three job roles are engaged in step 31. Of those, the new business manager (NBM) is primarily responsible for the oversight of this step with input from the client manager (CM). The bold X against the NBM role for step 31 indicates responsibility. A separate time-sensitive longitudinal flowchart of each of the 79 steps is also produced.

The core method of documenting the existing process was to (1) interview a select group of salespeople, sales managers, and sales support personnel (interviewees came from four regions throughout the United States); (2) create a first draft of the integrated flowchart; (3) visit multiple sales offices, and observe sales personnel and sales support personnel carrying out their work (including going on sales calls); (4) create a second draft of the integrated flowchart; and (5) send out the sales integrated flowchart to the select group for review, revision, and approval. With the interactive remote technology available for collaboration, it is easier than ever before to gather a diverse group of process participants and accurately document the steps together using interactive platforms like Miro and Mural. These types of platforms facilitate real-time collaboration, allowing team members to work together regardless of their physical location. By providing a virtual workspace where multiple users can contribute to workflow documentation simultaneously, these tools enhance the speed of communication. Compare real-time interactive documentation with the "old world" that required performance consultants to send versions of workflows to various stakeholders, collect suggested revisions, and go through several cycles of revisions before achieving consensus.

Improving the Healthcare Insurance Sales Work Process

Improving the work process is often referred to as going from an "existing" work process to a desired "improved" work process (Figures 7.6 and 7.7). The integrated flowchart of how the existing work is presently done is used as a basis for selecting a group of personnel to review and revise into an improved work process. This revision is best done in a face-to-face two-day

Workers within process	Phase 1: Integrated flowchart of a major business procedure as it exists (22-process-step example)																					
	1	2	3	4	5	6	7	8	9	10	11	12	13	14	15	16	17	18	19	20	21	22
Job 1.	X		X		X		X					X					X	X				
Job 2.			X						X		X	X			X	X						
Job 3.	X	X		X				X		X			X			X	X	X	X		X	
Job 4.		X	X		X	X												X				
Job 5.	X			X	X	X		X		X					X	X	X			X		
Job 6.			X		X			X		X			X	X			X	X	X			X

(Process activities over time)   X means contributor

Figure 7.6 Integrated Flowchart of Existing Work Process

work session of key people. Each participant had the existing flowchart prior to the meeting and was informed of the work process improvement goal. As each process step was reviewed, along with the job roles contributing to that step, improvement revisions were entertained, evaluated, and acted on by the group. In this healthcare insurance case, the 79-step process was reduced to 52 steps, and all nine job categories contributing to the existing process continued to contribute to the revised process in a modified manner. In addition, the 52 steps were clustered into subprocesses or phases: presale (24 steps), implementation and account management (25 steps), sales renewals (18 steps), and settlement (12 steps). Following the two-day work session, the revised integrated flowchart was sent to a discrete list of organization decision-makers for their final approval.

During both process documentation and future-state development meetings, if participants at different levels in the organization are co-contributing, more junior staff can feel politically unsafe by disagreeing with leaders.

Workers within process	Phase 2: Improved integrated flowchart of a major business procedure (reduced from 22 to 19 steps)																					
	1	2	3	4	5	6	7	8	9	10	11	12	13	14	15	16	17	18	19	20	21	22
Job 1.	⊗		⊗		X		⊗				X					⊗	X					
Job 2.									⊗		X			⊗	⊗	X		X	X			
Job 3.	X			X				X		⊗		⊗			X	X	⊗	⊗				
Job 4.		⊗	X		⊗	X												X				
Job 5.				⊗	X	X		⊗		X	⊗				X	⊗	X					
Job 6.			X		⊗			X					⊗	X	X			X	X	⊗		

(Process activities over time)   ⊗ means leadership responsibility; X means contributor.

Figure 7.7 Integrated Flowchart of Improved Work Process

Creating a "safe space" for recommendations and observations is important. Make it clear that accurate documentation and process improvement can only be achieved if people feel able to provide their honest perspectives without repercussion.

Tips for the Analyst

1 Determine the work process to be defined. Make sure that "scope creep" doesn't appear. This occurs when you start out to flow a certain process and then end up flowcharting the entire company! Perhaps all of us have experienced scope creep at one time or another.
2 Decide on the level of detail that's needed. This is important. Is a very broad and general-level flowchart needed? One that is extremely detailed could be equivalent to detailing systems tasks, or is there a level in the middle that is just right?
3 Determine the work process steps, their sequence, and the people involved in each step. The objective is to obtain all the steps that are thought to be taking place, the order of their occurrence, and those involved.
4 Review and revise the work process steps, their sequence, and the people involved in each step. The objective is to consider revising all the steps that are thought to be taking place, the order of their occurrence, and those involved.
5 Have the improved work process reviewed and approved by organizational decision-makers.
6 Prepare for disagreement among subject matter experts. Even high-functioning teams of can differ in their understanding of a work process. Establish an escalation path for resolution of differences.
7 Define the final approval process including identifying the final decision team.
8 Try to uncover hidden steps. When a process crosses different departments there is potential for details to be undocumented or "slip through the cracks."

Conclusion

Documenting and improving work processes can prove to be efficient and effective. A significant portion of this analysis activity is in uncharted territory for many organizations and work groups. The overall perspective of directly connecting organization performance improvement goals and work processes is logical and fruitful. Further, documenting work processes is also an activity that reveals inefficiencies investigated using the data collection methods described in the previous chapter.

Part III

Workplace Expertise Boundaries

Chapter 8

The Nature of Workplace Expertise

Chapter Sections

- Perspectives on Job and Expertise Analysis
- Dilemmas in Developing Expertise
- Workplace Expertise
- Getting to Expertise
- Conclusion

Beyond the performance diagnosis of organizations, the subsequent challenge is to document workplace expertise—what workers need to know and be able to do to succeed in their jobs. Workplace expertise is the fuel of an organization.

Expertise can be thought of as the level at which a person is able to perform within a specialized realm of human activity. True experts evolve beyond their knowledge of how to preform specific tasks and gain the ability to effectively navigate new circumstances they have never encountered before (Nichols, 2017). Their "toolbox" grows so extensive that they can reliably craft solutions to nearly any challenge related to their realm of expertise. Most of us are exposed to high levels of expertise. We can view performances by experts in almost any field we can imagine. We are surrounded by technology, art, music, lectures, books, movies, and sports exhibited by experts.

On television and the Internet we can see expert home restorers whiz through complicated procedures using tools that we have never seen before, let alone ever mastered. A local church choir may have warmth and charm, but can it stand up to the Mormon Tabernacle Choir recording being played on a high-tech digital sound system? The examples are endless. While the digital era has provided the gift of access to an endless universe of information and potential expertise, there is a dangerous dark side to this gift. Mixed in with true experts are a growing number of people who share misinformation or create content providing advice without

DOI: 10.4324/9781003518532-11

the analysis depth required to support it. It is no wonder that novices and those feigning expertise take shortcuts by skimming the internet and publishing their own views—adding to unsubstantiated claims. When business leaders pick up the language of the latest pop management book instead of learning organizational psychology or systems theory, what are the consequences? Today we have CEOs who are often unable to flowchart a simple process—like making a cup of instant coffee. Yet, they are unleashing wrath by outsourcing key elements in their companies in response to opinion journal articles (or managing with the tyranny of the bottom line). Social media sites often promote this perspective on management and leadership based on very short opinion pieces. Even social media sites that are marketed as professionally focused (such as LinkedIn) have fallen victim to masqueraders. User beware—a few sentences from a highly active social media personality do not constitute the kind of deep analysis and documentation of expertise we are focused on here.

Perspectives on Job and Expertise Analysis

It needs to be said that job analysis is not expertise analysis. A very long history surrounds the phenomenon of job analysis. That history has not had much to do with developing workplace expertise (Nichols, 2017). Torraco (1994) has criticized these perspectives as being out of touch with the contemporary workplace. Most of it has had to do with human resource management issues of recruiting, selection, compensation, legal compliance as well as studies out of industrial psychology conducted at arm's length from actual work (see Brannick & Levine, 2002). The extensive job analysis literature rarely looks at human expertise head-on and rarely, if ever, concerns itself with determining precisely what people need to know and be able to do to perform on the job. For example, John Miner's (2002) tome of 888 pages, *Organizational Behavior: Foundations, Theories, and Analyses,* has only one reference to expertise in the extensive index. So many of these professionals ignore the scholarly and practitioner literature on expertise (e.g., Ericsson & Smith, 1994; Pfeffer & Sutton, 2000).

The growing risk of losing institutional knowledge due to the highest rates of turnover and shortening tenure we have ever seen is compounded by a shrinking population of people who understand the importance of expertise (Sullivan, 2022). This trend is easy to understand based on how little today's society members value true expertise (Crawford, 2006). Not long ago, extensive vetting of experts and their opinions was required before a media company would risk their reputation by publishing false information. Now that information sharing is cheap, easy, and entirely unregulated for those with access to social media. The value of expertise is clouded by the glamour of "infotainment" and what might gain the most attention. Readers of this book are encouraged to demand more than using social media posts as the primary source when developing a view of relevant expertise. Performance improvement professionals who know how to analyze the expertise required to achieve results will be able to deliver, time and time again.

Dilemmas in Developing Expertise

Developing expertise is not an event. It is a purposeful process. As a result, organizations serious about workplace expertise face a number of dilemmas in their efforts to deal with their organization's demands for workplace expertise:

- Defining what expertise is needed
- Emphasizing general knowledge versus specific expertise
- Hiring versus developing expertise
- Nature versus nurture paths to expertise
- Considering time requirements

Defining What Expertise Is Needed

Richard Herling's (2000) classic definitional article on expertise provides disciplined thinking and definitions for performance improvement professionals. His article is summarized as follows:

Human expertise is clearly a complex, multifaceted phenomenon, but by means of an operational definition, expertise can be expressed in measurable terms.

Human expertise can be defined as displayed behavior within a specialized domain and/or related domain in the form of consistently demonstrated actions of an individual that is both optimally efficient in their execution and effective in their results.

Human competence, a related construct and component of expertise, can also be expressed in measurable terms, and defined as: displayed behavior within a specialized domain in the form of consistently demonstrated actions of an individual which are both minimally efficient in their execution and effective in their results.

The operational definition of human expertise recognizes domain-specific (1) knowledge, (2) experience, and (3) problem-solving as the core elements of human expertise. Thus, the profession gains conceptual access to one of the most powerful tools for improving performance: human expertise. (p. 21)

Workplace Expertise

Herling (2000) characterizes human expertise as a complex and multifaceted phenomenon. He defines human expertise as displayed behavior within a specialized domain and/or related domain in the form of consistently demonstrated actions of an individual which are both optimally efficient in their execution and effective in their results. Meeting and maintaining workforce expertise requirements that are connected to organization goals and core work process requirements are a fundamental challenge to organizations.

Traditional Job/Task Approach to Expertise

Organizations have for the most part embraced the job- and task-oriented approaches to defining workplace expertise and have relied on multiple analysis procedures (Brannick & Levine, 2002; Holton, 1995; Swanson, 1996a). These approaches are familiar to most human resource management professionals and are driven by federal law in many cases. Essentially, they all contain three basic steps:

1 Developing a list of tasks that are performed in a job
2 Verifying the task inventory as a valid representation of the job
3 Analyzing precisely what a person needs to know and be able to do to meet a specified performance standard for each task

Fundamentally, job analysis methodologies address work tasks as core organizers that can be grouped together to constitute a job or that can be individually detailed for greater understanding. In practice, the custom is often to use existing job structures, current work practices, and current employees as the frame with which to determine those work task requirements. The outcome is task and expertise analyses that are grounded in the present. In stable environments, this approach works. What happens, however, if jobs, work tasks, and task expertise are not stable and changing rapidly? In today's ever-changing world, job responsibilities and requirements can change and shift quickly. One response has been to schedule the task analyses within a shorter time cycle so that job analyses reflect changes in jobs. The assumption here is that traditional thinking and analysis methods are okay, but they may need to be used more aggressively.

At the other end of the thinking, some organizations take the position that jobs must be designed to be indeterminate and flexible. As a result, how do you analyze them? There are suggestions in the literature that flexible job models that allow organizations to manage competencies—not jobs—are necessary. Tolerating this ill-defined state has severe performance consequences.

Competency-Based Approach to Expertise

Competency assessment is one approach to overcome some of the limitations of traditional job analysis (Dubois, 1993; Fine & Cronshaw, 1999; Jacobs, 1989). Competencies are generally defined as some underlying characteristics of an employee that enables that person to perform the job or task. Because it is an underlying characteristic and one step removed from the tasks themselves, it is a more flexible approach that can be used to select and develop employees across multiple jobs.

Competency models generally proceed in the same fundamental steps as the job analysis model, the only difference being that tasks are analyzed for underlying general competencies as opposed to specific job-required knowledge and expertise. In some cases, job holders are simply used to create competency lists. This is particularly the case in broad occupational analysis (not job and task analysis).

Competency models and expertise models are both job based and therefore operate under the same assumptions outlined here and are subject to the same criticisms related to change. To the extent that competencies are more likely to be stable than job tasks, they are an improvement. Yet, they still fall short for all situations, particularly in the realm of defining the specific expertise (not general competencies) and the details of what is required to perform.

Emphasizing General versus Specific Expertise

Experts are good problem solvers in their domain of expertise. Good problem solvers utilize specific methods. The more general the methods used, the less expertise is involved. There are good reasons for people to study situations at a general level. Many people who study jobs and work have a goal of defining occupations and jobs at the most general level. It can be useful to describe in a general way what an executive does, versus a manager, versus a first-line supervisor. This level of analysis assures you that you are "in the ballpark." All of us have figuratively found ourselves "out of the ballpark" and know how humiliating that is. Specific levels of analysis offer protection against being wrong.

We used the tools for documenting expertise presented in this book in a Fortune 50 corporation to determine the expertise required of first-line supervisors in its manufacturing plants. By determining and documenting precisely what plant supervisors were required to know and be able to do in order to function as experts, the supporting performance improvement effort realized a 9:1 return on investment (900%) in two years. This was no academic or off-the-shelf view of good supervision—it was production-specific and company-specific.

In contrast, there was a chance to audit the results of an expensive off-the-shelf "managing people" program that had been provided to every manager in a Fortune 10 financial corporation for a ten-year period. After a lot of investigation there was no evidence that the program had any impact on the corporation. The "managing people" generalities covered in the program were interesting to the participants but did not represent what people were required to know and be able to do in order to perform on the job. In other words, the work generalities did not capture workplace expertise.

Hiring versus Developing Expertise

Many organizations are not well equipped to manage the development and maintenance of expertise in their workforce. Working under the assumption that expertise is the fuel of an organization, one reaction is to outsource expertise rather than develop it. "Hire versus develop" is a fundamental business decision that is aggravated by changing markets and changing technology (Gupta & Baksi, 2022).

Some firms decide to outsource work requiring specific expertise as they compare the costs and benefits of maintaining internal expertise. Even so, much workplace expertise is company-specific and it is impossible to hire such expertise in the open market. Imagine, too, having expertise critical to the life of an organization that is undocumented in any formal manner. Organizations wanting to survive and grow must deal purposefully with the decisions about procuring or developing as well as maintaining workplace expertise. This book includes tools that enable readers to document workplace expertise. This gives companies or clients the foundation necessary to make those complex decisions with accurate information.

Getting to Expertise

Now we're ready to discuss the tools used to document workplace expertise. These include the job description, task inventory, and task analyses. A job description defines the boundaries of a job, while a task inventory highlights the discernible parts (tasks) of a job or work process, and task analyses detail the expertise required to perform each task. A job can be described in terms of an artist's canvas. Job description is a broad-brush activity. The analyst-painter uses a finer brush and finer movements to define the expertise embodied in each task. At the most meticulous level, the details of the job emerge with an almost photographic quality. To put it in more concrete terms, the job description is painted with a four-inch-wide brush, the task inventory with a two-inch-wide brush, and the task analyses are painted with a one-sixteenth-inch-wide brush.

Consider the following job title as an example: corporate director of human resources. Most of us would agree that this is an impressive title, but what does a director of human resources really do? Let's look at the job behind this title in one company and compare it with the job behind the same title in a second company.

Company A: The director heads the corporate-wide human resource department, supervises fifteen professionals, and manages a $2 million budget.

Company B: The director heads the corporate-wide human resource department, supervises an administrative assistant, and is responsible for proposing and implementing performance improvement programs under a zero-based budgeting system.

In two quick sentences, these seemingly similar jobs are shown to be very different. Even so, there is hardly a clue as to exactly what a person is required to know and be able to do to perform in either job. These broad-brush job descriptions need to be supplemented by a finer level of detail— detail provided by a task inventory and task analyses. The task inventory will provide a list of the specific tasks the director's job entails; the three methods of analyzing tasks—procedural, systems, and knowledge—will accommodate the varying nature of the expertise expected of the director.

These general workplace expertise documentation phases just discussed are displayed as a process in Figure 8.1. In Figure 8.2, these phases are detailed according to the presentations in the following chapters. Whether you are a researcher, manager, trainer, internal auditor, industrial engineer, or consultant, many people in the organization will expect you to be able to analyze a job skillfully. Your ability to analyze and synthesize

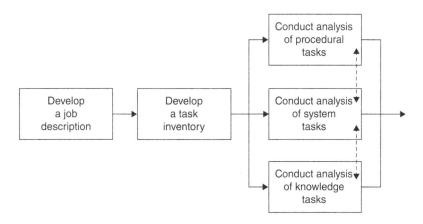

Figure 8.1 Documenting Expertise

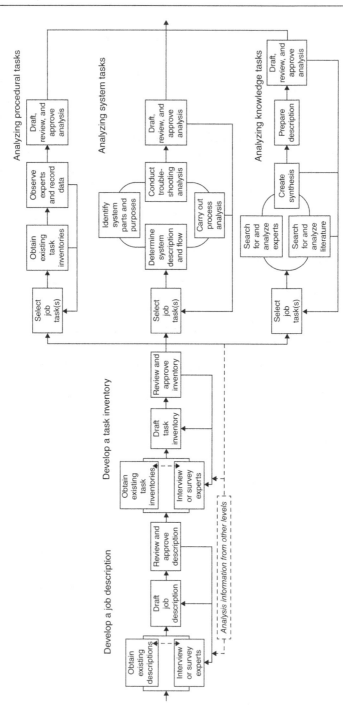

Figure 8.2   Overall Process of Documenting Workplace Expertise

will establish you as an expert capable of documenting the most complex workplace behaviors.

Chapters 9–14 present the tools for documenting workplace expertise: job description, task inventory, and the four task methods of procedural task analysis, systems task analysis, knowledge task analysis, and cross-functional task analysis). Figure 8.2 combines these five subprocesses for an overall process picture of documenting workplace expertise.

In Figure 8.3, several work factors, such as work behaviors and work interaction, are laid up against the five phases of analyzing workplace expertise. This matrix provides a comparison of the key features of the analysis of expertise presented in Chapters 9–14. Documentation forms (see the appendix) are used for each tool and underscore the important fact that each task from the task inventory is analyzed and documented with one or more of the three task analysis methods.

The final workplace expertise documents, and many of the in-process documents, should be saved in a secure and frequently backed-up filing location. These documents need to be revised and manipulated to contribute to a variety of performance improvement investments including quality improvement efforts, training materials, and various forms of certification.

Here are a couple of helpful tips: Many organizations have formatted the various documentation forms to serve analysts as they start their work, not after the fact. Also, many companies establish revision protocols on top of their original documentation process to capture improvements and changes as they occur.

Conclusion

This chapter has provided a brief introduction to the documentation of expertise in the workplace. Again, it is worth highlighting the fundamental premise that rigorous documentation of this expertise is the true source of training content and a starting point for many performance improvement efforts.

The next several chapters consider each of the task detailing tools used to document workplace expertise: job description, task inventory, and—most significant in terms of usefulness and stability—the detailing of tasks through procedure task analysis, systems task analysis, knowledge task analysis, and cross-functional task analysis.

Analysis tools

Work factors	Job description	Task inventory	Procedural task analysis	System task analysis	Knowledge task analysis
Work behaviors	• Clusters of activity	• Discrete activities	• Observable	• Partially observable	• Nonobservable
Work interactions	• Degree of variety	• Degree of variety	• Worker-materials • Worker-machine	• Worker-process	• Worker-worker • Worker-idea
Work structure	• Degree of structure	• Degree of structure	• Bound to a particular work procedure	• Bound to a particular process or system	• Many performance situations
Worker autonomy	• Worker relationships	• Task relationships	• Follows procedures	• Works within established systems	• Works within vague or fluid systems
Performance objectives	• Contributes to organization performance goals in terms of clusters of performance	• Segments job performance into discrete elements	• Follows correct procedures, leading to standard performance or results	• Uses efficient methods, leading to standard performance or results	• Uses structured knowledge, information, leading to standard performance or results
In-process products	• Existing job description • Interview notes	• Existing task inventory • Interview notes	• Task details • Sketches • Digital photos • Existing job aids	• System description and flowchart • System parts and purpose list • Process analysis chart	• Expertise data collection instrument • Collected data • Research cards from literature search • Synthesis model(s)
End product of the analysis	• 25- to 75-word narrative overview of job	• List of discrete job tasks	• Step-by-step procedure • Diagram of machine or material	• Troubleshooting analysis • In-process documents • Diagrams	• Knowledge task description (may include synthesis model) • Reference list

Figure 8.3   Features of the Six Analysis of Expertise Tools

Chapter 9

Documenting Job Descriptions

Chapter Sections

- Developing Job Descriptions for Performance
- Criteria for a Performance Improvement Focused Job Description
- Additional Examples—Shipper and National Practice Leader
- Volatile Jobs
- Conclusion

Role ambiguity and job vagueness are at an all-time high (Fernandez de Henestrosa, Sischka, & Steffgen, 2023) and this condition is anti-performance oriented. Increasingly, job descriptions include opportunities for successful applicants to have input in defining the role. While this may be an effective practice to attract the desired expert candidates, once hired, the successful applicant and manager should clarify the role according to the principles of this chapter. For the purposes of this book, a job description should be understood as a very specific document used by performance improvement professionals to help understand tasks required within a role. There are a variety of documents often called job descriptions—including those used to recruit for open positions, those used to support equity and compensation analysis, and those used to detail career growth and development. Here, our focus is on job descriptions that establish the scope of the actual responsibilities of a specific job in a specific organization. Determining the scope of job responsibilities is the basic purpose of writing a job description for performance improvement, but other reasons for writing job descriptions exist as well. Some organizations purposely mandate vague and/or open-ended job descriptions to preserve organizational flexibility for job restructuring while maintaining legal compliance. In other instances, job descriptions serve as the baseline for role leveling or compensation and equity analyses across the company, but these are not usually focused on performance improvement.

These other types of job descriptions often contain more information on job prerequisites than on actual job responsibilities. For this reason,

DOI: 10.4324/9781003518532-12

they have limited value in establishing precisely what a person is required to know and be able to do—to perform a specific job (expertise). Here are two examples of job descriptions used for hiring and legal purposes (not for performance improvement):

Data entry manager: Supervises the operation of data entry operators; oversees the recording of a variety of alpha/numeric data onto storage media; requires a minimum of two years' data entry experience; and some supervisory experience is preferred.

Pharmacist: Fills prescriptions; must have very strong formulary knowledge, and requires pharmacy degree.

In contrast, job descriptions written for the purpose of performance improvement are specific and well-defined. They embrace the full scope of work that the job holder actually does, not the prerequisites. As such, it is critical to differentiate performance improvement job descriptions from those used to recruit for open roles. Performance-focused job descriptions forgo the surrounding culture content aimed at attracting applicants.

Developing Job Descriptions for Performance

The process of documenting job descriptions requires some reflection on the available and true sources of expertise (Figure 9.1). The starting point is the criteria for job descriptions. This is followed by two data-gathering steps that can occur simultaneously or sequentially, depending on the specific circumstances.

One of these steps is to obtain existing job descriptions within the organization or from external sources, such as professional references, associations, any of the myriad job posting platforms available today, and other organizations. The second step is to interview experts—people who have a deep understanding of the job. Usually, this includes job incumbents,

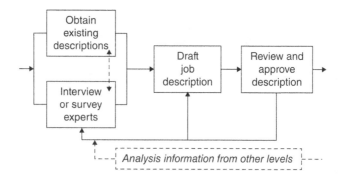

Figure 9.1 Developing a Job Description

managers/supervisors of job incumbents, and coworkers. These interviews are usually fairly brief and often result in discrepancies that ultimately get resolved at a later time. In many organizations, the support of a total rewards or compensation and benefits team is helpful. Their access to historical documentation, cross-referenceable descriptions, and level-appropriate parameters can be leveraged in this stage.

It is important to note that job descriptions are ultimately validated through the more detailed task inventory and analysis of each of the tasks. The angst about the validity of job analyses (Sanchez & Levine, 2000) does not come from those involved in documenting precisely what people need to know and be able to do on their jobs. Rather, it comes from human resource generalists and organizational psychology researchers trying to create general analyses of jobs.

The next step in the process—drafting the job description—begins to solidify the job description. Rarely will a draft escape criticism and revision during the review step that follows. While the expert job incumbent and that person's manager/supervisor should be involved in the review, the manager is the most appropriate one to approve the final job description. This approval can always be open for a later review, revision, and approval. In fact, the job description, as with the other levels of analysis, should be revised when additional information challenges its accuracy or completeness. Such information is obtained at the more detailed analysis levels of the job.

The following is an acceptable job description. Read it carefully and note the level of detail used. After this, we will look at the criteria for good job descriptions and task inventories and then at the methods for producing them:

Job description
Job or program: vinyl laminator
Location: Custom Kitchens, Inc.
Department: Lamination Department
Analyst: D. Parker
Effective date: (month/date/year)
Cancels earlier version: None
Dated: (month/date/year or "None")
Approved by: (name/signature)

The job of vinyl laminator involves laminate job planning, ordering, and installing vinyl laminate sheeting to a variety of surfaces including countertops, doors, and panels with hot and cold adhesives. The work is conducted on-site and in-plant. It is a skilled job requiring detailed planning, high craftsmanship, and the use of a variety of computer-operated power and hand tools to meet customer requirements and quality standards.

Criteria for a Performance Improvement Focused Job Description

Remember that the job description shows the boundaries of the job and that the analyst uses a big brush and large strokes. The four criteria for good job descriptions focus on the title, scope, form, and length of the description. They are as follows:

Title: a succinct combination of words capturing the overall job function—more than one word and, depending on the role level, often less than four.
Scope: embraces the totality of the job and communicates this by labeling two to seven job functions or clusters of work activity.
Form: written in complete sentences—usually one paragraph and sometimes two.
Length: a range of 25–75 words.

Writing an acceptable title for a job is usually fairly easy. Making it too general is a common error, however. For example, the title supervisor is too broad; first-line supervisor is better. To take another example, computer operator is too general and should be avoided in favor of a more specific title like SPSS software consultant.

Scope is the most difficult criterion to satisfy. The idea of clustering job functions, rather than listing tasks, requires further discussion. The analyst identifies logical clusters among a detailed listing of work activities. For instance, it is easy to list a number of tasks carried out by a restaurant server, such as these:

- Preparing tables
- Taking food orders
- Delivering food orders

But what is it that cuts across, or clusters, these individual tasks? Such behaviors as being friendly, courteous, alert to empty coffee cups, and attentive to customer needs may at a minimum be clustered under the words attentive to customer needs. Knowing the menu and handling basic billing mathematics could be identified as other functions or clusters for this job. Of course, the job of a server will be very different in a fast-food establishment compared to a fine-dining restaurant. These types of differences should be reflected clearly in the job descriptions.

The form and length criteria are easily understood and should be adhered to. Errors such as making lists rather than writing sentences, or including too much information, are the result of analyst's not paying attention to the criteria. Self-discipline in writing a good job description now will pay dividends later by providing an accurate framework for specifying the details of the job.

The following is an example of a poor job description. Check it against the four criteria and look for deficiencies.

Job Description

Job or program: Supervisor
Location: Headquarters and Middletown
Analyst: L. D'Annunzio
Effective date: (month/date/year)
Cancels earlier version: (month/date/year or "None")
Approved by: (name/signature)

The supervisor is in oversees bottom-line productivity of a work group. More than any other member of the management team, this individual is responsible for translating company goals into reality by meeting production quotas.

The following is an example of a good job description for you to check against the four criteria:

Job Description

Job or program: Electronics production supervisor
Location: Headquarters and Middletown
Department: Companywide
Analyst: A. Sheu
Effective date: (month/day/year)
Cancels sheet dated: (month/day/year or "None")
Approved by: (signature)

The supervisor is responsible for effective and efficient accomplishment of work within their respective realm of electronics production authority. The supervisor understands, supports, and delivers the sequential management functions of planning, organizing, staffing, directing, and controlling. On a day-to-day basis, the supervisor engages in problem analysis, decision-making, and communication activities.

The problem analysis, decision-making, and communication activities are primarily focused on the customer's requirements and quality standards.

You can easily see that these two job descriptions for supervisor differ. At first glance, some people might have judged the first description to be acceptable, although it meets none of the criteria of a good job description.

Additional Examples—Shipper and National Practice Leader

Two additional examples should further clarify the nature and scope of performance-focused job descriptions. The first is a job description for the role of "shipper" for an online retailer company. The second is for a technical leadership position in an environmental engineering company.

Shipper Job Description

Job or program:	Warehouse shipper
Location:	St. Paul, Minn.
Department:	Shipping Department
Analyst:	F. Parker
Effective date:	(month/date/year)
Cancels sheet dated:	(month/date/year or "None")
Approved by:	(signature)

The warehouse shipper is responsible for accurately selecting, packing, and loading products for shipment in response to customer orders. Within the "Online Retailer" system of sales, production, distribution, and inventory control, the shipper uses systems data to process and ship customer orders. The warehouse shipper also monitors and maintains efficient shipping operations.

It should be easy to see that different levels of jobs necessarily involve different kinds of responsibilities and thus, the range of work will differ. Senior level leadership positions require job descriptions because they create boundaries for the role and define expectations. It is common for leadership roles to remain dangerously vague. The intent may be to give trusted professionals leeway to craft the role as they see fit. While the work at these levels is usually wider in scope, job descriptions set the foundation for understanding the major roles and responsibilities—ultimately leading to expertise. Leadership roles are critical for executing on company performance goals. When those roles are vague and disconnected from goals, a significant opportunity to influence results, is missed. The following job description is a good example:

Technical Leader Job Description

Job or program:	National practice leader—engineering
Location:	All
Department:	Technical Practices
Analyst:	J. Bishop
Effective date:	(month/date/year)
Cancels sheet dated:	(month/date/year)
Approved by:	(signature)

The national practice leader (NPL) sets the vision and strategy for their practice while ensuring alignment with company goals of revenue growth and operational efficiency. The NPL is responsible for increasing market share nationally, developing talent, and delivering high-quality solutions to support technical differentiation from competitors NPLs select and supervise a team of six specialty leaders that reflect key areas of the organization's most needed technical talent and growth potential.

Volatile Jobs

Organizations and jobs in organizations are more fluid than ever. In fact, jobs are often more fluid than the tasks that make up an individual job. With continuing organizational restructuring, "stable" jobs come and go. At the same time, the tasks more often remain and are reshuffled into new or restructured jobs. The impact of post-pandemic conditions and the continuation of disruptive trends in the labor market has resulted in more organizations, both public and private, considering unconventional staffing solutions.

Unfortunately, job descriptions in organizations have become increasingly ill-defined. In some cases, job descriptions explicitly include an invitation for nonexpert employees to partially define the role. This practice should signal a problem—we have a job, but we don't really understand what this person is expected to do. This practice is also fundamentally at odds with improving performance. Historically, job descriptions were partly the way an organization was vertically defined—jobs having been connected to organizational functions. Today, we take a systems and process view of the organization. The horizontal process view dictates worker tasks pragmatically be clustered into jobs. If the trend towards a more flexible workforce continues, rigor around the clarity of performance-focused job descriptions is a growing necessity.

☑ **Checkpoint**

Take about five minutes to write a job description of either your present job or a past job. If you prefer, use the job description form provided in the appendix, and write a job description that meets the four criteria of title, scope, form, and length. Because you will be making a task inventory next, limit the length of your job description to 25–75 words and the scope to 2–7 functions or clusters of work activity. Check your job description against the criteria and the good examples to see whether it meets the criteria.

Conclusion

Job descriptions for the purpose of documenting expertise and improving performance must be written in a manner that diligently seeks to define what people actually do in their jobs. This type of description should not be focused on hiring prerequisites such as prior education and work experience. The identification of job functions at the job description level begins to paint a picture of expertise. The follow-up inventory of tasks that comprise the job and the detailed analysis of each of the tasks more fully complete the picture. Once this detailed and more complete information is obtained, it may suggest revisions to the job description to make it more effective at driving desired performance results.

Recall the unacceptable pharmacist job description presented earlier: "Fills prescriptions. Must have very strong formulary knowledge. Requires pharmacy degree." If you detailed what a drugstore pharmacist actually does on the job, he or she most likely spends a good part of the job communicating and counseling with customers. The pharmacist example, written for hiring and legal purposes, completely missed this important aspect of the actual work.

The next chapter describes the process for producing task inventories—an identification and listing of all the tasks that make up the job.

Chapter 10

Developing Task Inventories

Chapter Sections

- Creating a Task Inventory
- Criteria for a Good Task Inventory
- Task Inventory: National Practice Leader—Engineering
- Tips for the Analyst
- Conclusion

Most jobs consist of a variety of discrete activities or tasks. Even jobs that first appear to be one-dimensional usually become more complex on closer inspection. Take, for example, the job of a violinist. At first glance, this job appears to be one-dimensional: playing the violin. A closer look, however, yields a list of discrete tasks such as violin maintenance, music procurement, performance scheduling, practicing, and performing. A task inventory is a list of the discrete activities—such as those just listed—that make up a specific job in a specific organization.

Being able to create an accurate task inventory list is the focus of this chapter. Later chapters cover methods for documenting precisely what a person needs to know and do to perform each of the tasks. For most people who talk and write about task analysis, they do not go any deeper than creating a task inventory—this chapter. Fine and Cronshaw (1999) believe that "the fundamental challenge of job analysis is to describe and define the dimensions of the work activity being evaluated" (p. 169). We take the position that the job dimensions—or inventory of tasks—provide a very important conceptual organizer for understanding a job, but the follow-up detailing of the tasks provides the substance for performance improvement. The task detailing also gives the ultimate validation of the task inventory, rather than statistical manipulations of perception and secondary data (Sanchez & Levine, 2000).

DOI: 10.4324/9781003518532-13

Creating a Task Inventory

The task inventory process has four steps (Figure 10.1). It starts with two data collection steps: obtaining existing task inventories and interviewing experts. Drafting the task inventory is the third step and having it reviewed and approved is the last step.

The data-gathering advice given to you for job descriptions in the previous chapter applies equally to producing the task inventory. Also, the data for both the job description and the task inventory can be collected at the same time. Again, as with job descriptions, the important steps of drafting and then reviewing and approving the task inventory are presented. The task inventory documentation form, or a digital version, records the final product of the process. The print version is found in the appendix.

As each task is individually detailed later, the insights derived from that more detailed analysis will likely suggest revisions to the task inventory and possibly the job description.

Criteria for a Good Task Inventory

The four criteria for a good task inventory pertain both to the inventory as a whole and to each task statement in the inventory. The criteria are as follows:

Comprehensive: All work activity fits into one of the inventoried tasks.
Intermediate: A task unit of work activity is intermediate in specificity between that of the job cluster or function and that of a step-by-step procedure or detailed aspect of the job.

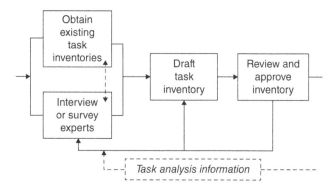

Figure 10.1 Developing a Task Inventory

Discrete: Each task is distinguishable from the others and has a definite beginning and ending.

Active: Each task statement contains an action verb and the object of the action.

Describing tasks so that they meet the first three criteria—being comprehensive, intermediate, and discrete—is like cutting out a toddler's jigsaw puzzle. The goal is to cut the work into fairly big pieces that do not overlap but that logically fit together to form a complete picture. The size of the units and the pattern of the pieces will vary from analyst to analyst. The size of the units of work specified at the task inventory level may also vary between companies or departments, within companies or between work groups. Take, for example, the nuclear power industry. Here you will find that the technical production people classify job tasks in much smaller units than do their counterparts on the management side. We recognize that analysts are not always comfortable with this variability; common sense should be the arbiter. And remember, once you move on and detail each task (i.e., when you know more about the work), you can revise the task inventory.

The fourth criterion, emphasizing the active nature of the task, connects the work behavior to the object of the work. For a task inventory item, the word supervises is too large in scope. Furthermore, it does not meet the active criterion of naming the action and the object being acted on. "Supervises employees" satisfies the requirement of indicating the action and the object. This item still may not be discrete enough, however. For example, such tasks as "supervises sales personnel" and "supervises office personnel" most likely will require different work activities and therefore should be listed separately. "Repairing machinery" is appropriate language for a job cluster in a job description, but it is not specific enough to be useful at the task inventory level. "Repairing production-robot grippers" and "replacing milling machine cutting tools" both meet the criteria for a task inventory statement.

Including too much detail in the task statement can also be a problem. The details of job skills should not appear in a task inventory. The full range of specificity is as follows:

"Repair machinery" is too general for a task inventory statement, though good for a job description.

"Repair production-robot grippers" is just right for a task inventory statement.

"Repair production-robot pneumatic tub #2" is too specific for a task inventory statement but would be fine as part of a task detail.

☑ Checkpoint

Now it is your turn to judge the following statements. Place a "T" next to the items that meet the four criteria of a reasonable task inventory statement. Some of the items are too general; they belong in a job description. Some are too specific; they are procedural steps.

_____ 1. Sign purchase orders.
_____ 2. Image enhances a set of photos.
_____ 3. Repair machinery.
_____ 4. Order backup supplies.
_____ 5. Direct department work flow.
_____ 6. Obtain stock price quotation.
_____ 7. Remove a molded part from its mold.
_____ 8. Ring up a sale on a cash register.
_____ 9. Analyze and report data.
___ 10. Patch an automobile muffler.
___ 11. Print pictures from a file of digital images.
___ 12. Conduct a market analysis.
___ 13. Return customer calls.
___ 14. Schedule worker vacations.
___ 15. Check final product quality against standards.

Let's work through your answers one by one. Naturally, we recognize that some important situational information is missing that could cause one reader to answer task, another to answer job, and still another to answer task detail (a small step of performing a task), all for the same item. For example, signing a purchase order is, in most work, a small procedural step. (Purchasing floor maintenance equipment could reasonably be labeled a task statement; signing purchase orders, a procedural step.) Yet signing purchase orders in a particular purchasing job that entails a complex process of purchase approvals could be elevated to the task level. A situation of this nature would rarely occur, but you find this out for sure by going through the analysis with an expert job holder. Here are our answers:

Activity	Reasonable First and Second Choice Answers
1. Sign purchase orders.	Task detail, task
2. Image enhance a set of photos.	Task, task detail
3. Repair machinery.	Job, task

4. Order backup supplies.	Task, task detail
5. Direct department workflow.	Task, job
6. Obtain stock price quotation.	Task detail, task
7. Remove a molder part from its mold.	Task detail, task
8. Ring up a sale on a cash register.	Task detail, task
9. Analyze and report data.	Task, job
10. Patch an automobile muffler.	Task, task detail
11. Print pictures from a file of digital images.	Task, task detail
12. Conduct a market analysis.	Task, job
13. Return customer calls.	Task detail, task
14. Schedule worker vacations.	Task, task detail
15. Check final product quality against standards.	Task, job

Now, how do you produce a task inventory? There are two approaches, which we will call bottom-up and top-down. The bottom-up approach requires extensive observation and study of the activities and detailed knowledge required of a worker. The analyst gathers the details and clusters them based on natural breaks or separate categories of activity. The clusters are then labeled and turned into task statements. In the top-down approach, the analyst starts with an existing or newly written job description and then interviews the job holders and their supervisors. The analyst asks questions about the nature of the work, the kinds of activities required, and the amount of time spent on each. Asking how time is spent on the job helps the job holder consider all the tasks, not just the most obvious ones. This method of self-reporting produces a fairly accurate task inventory with a minimal investment of time. Gathering the details of a specific work behavior by observing the performer at work results in a much greater level of understanding of the task than does eliciting details through interviews. New clusters of details and new perceptions of tasks will likely be identified through observation. Therefore, a task inventory produced in the top-down manner will usually be revised after the detailed task analysis is performed.

Task Inventory

Job or program: Vinyl laminator
Location: Custom Kitchens, Inc.
Department: Lamination Department

Analyst: A. Rinehart
Effective date: (month/day/year)
Cancels sheet dated: (month/day/year or "None")
Approved by: (signature)

Tasks

1 Develop work order plans.
2 Estimate and order materials.
3 Set up work site.
4 Cut laminates to size.
5 Apply laminates.
6 Apply adhesives.
7 Trim laminates.
8 Inspect and protect finished products.
9 Clean-up work area.

This example is a task inventory for a fairly specific job. It is meant to illustrate that a job description (Chapter 9) is next broken down into specific tasks. As the level of the job increases in complexity and vertically in any organization, usually, so does the scope of the work the job covers. Think about specific functional jobs versus general management jobs. It should be easy to understand that the range and scope of responsibilities—and therefore the tasks required—will differ.

Task Inventory: National Practice Leader—Engineering

When thinking about more complex jobs and increasing ranges of responsibility, tasks can be grouped into general areas. Here is another example of a task inventory for a more advanced position. The job description for the job title "National Practice Leader—Engineering" was provided in Chapter 9. The task inventory provided below groups more specific tasks under more general tasks of oversight (Figure 10.2).

Each task from the task inventory is to be detailed later and documented with one or more of the task-detailing tools: procedural task analysis (see Chapter 11), system task analysis (see Chapter 12), knowledge task analysis (see Chapter 13), or cross-functional task analysis (see Chapter 14). Procedural tasks are made up of people–thing work behaviors that are highly observable and step-by-step. Systems tasks are made up of

Title: National practice leader–engineering
Location: Any
Department: Technical practices
Analyst: J. Bishop
Effective date: (month/day/year)
Cancels page dated: (month/day/year or "None")
Approved by: (signature)

TASK INVENTORY

Title: National practice leader–engineering
Location: Any
Department: Technical practices

TASK	TASK ANALYSIS PLAN
Practice leadership	
1. Set the vision and communicate the technical practice strategy	System/Knowledge
2. Drive practice-wide use of the practice portal	Knowledge
3. Ensure active communication and collaboration as an active leader	Knowledge
4. Support and leverage strategic company innovations	Knowledge
5. Oversee budget and team performance	Procedure/Knowledge
Project delivery	
6. Serve as main point of contact with area/regional practice leaders	Procedure
7. Coordinate with regional practice leaders to ensure application of standards during project delivery	Knowledge
8. Ensure consistent application of national technical standards including process and design guidelines	Knowledge
Client development and sales	
9. Inform annual business and strategic planning within the business units	System/Knowledge
10. Inform technical strategy on key pursuits with local client service managers	Knowledge
11. Research competition in terms of strategic direction of their technical focus, staff, strengths and weaknesses	Procedure

Figure 10.2   Task Inventory for a National Practice Leader—Engineering (*Continued*)

12. Collaborate with business units and build capacity by recruiting best-fit candidates	Knowledge
Technical standards	
13. Oversee implementation of Quality Fundamentals and Subject Matter Specialists (SMS) governance	System/Knowledge
Talent development	
14. Develop a training plan for SMS advancement within the practice	System/Knowledge
15. Lead implementation and adjudication of SMS governance, systems and plans for talent development	System/Knowledge
16. Lead enterprise recruiting for staffing the practice	
17. Collaborate with business unit leaders to identify performance objectives	Knowledge
Brand and industry leadership	
18. Champion strategic national conferences, presentation strategies, and selection of technical attendees	Knowledge
19. Support local conferences, workshops and other means of visibility in strategic geographies	Knowledge
20. Stay current with technology and market trends—inform annual State of the Industry Report	Knowledge

Figure 10.2 (Continued)

interlocking dimensions of work tasks around people–hardware systems or people–knowledge systems that are not usually observable. Knowledge tasks are made up of work behaviors requiring more general methods, concepts, and theories as they relate to people–idea and people–people work behaviors. You will become more familiar with these three classifications after reading Chapters 11–14.

Identification of the appropriate task-detailing tool(s) for each task should become part of the task inventory. For example, the first task—"Prepare seat cover order"—is best analyzed using the procedural task analysis method and should be coded as such. Please review the appropriate task analysis coding for the shipper job tasks on the following task inventory. Very rarely is a job made up of tasks that are all one type. The job of shipper has seven tasks—four procedural, one systems, and two knowledge.

One more important point is that some tasks can be cross-functional. While the first three shipper tasks are sequential, "Monitor and troubleshoot shipping operations" (task 4) cuts across all the other tasks. In a similar way,

"Perform as shipping team member" (task 6) cuts across all the tasks. The analyst makes the decision as to whether the work behaviors are embedded with tasks or whether they are pervasive enough to justify their own status as a task. Chapter 14 provides descriptions and examples of tasks that cut across organizational functions and they usually involve multiple jobs.

☑ **Checkpoint**

In Chapter 10, you wrote your own job description. Now, using the method of self-reporting, construct a task inventory for your job. If you like, you can use the task inventory form in the appendix. Because you will need this task inventory to do an exercise in a later chapter, it is important that you complete it and that it meets the four criteria of being (1) comprehensive, (2) intermediate, (3) discrete, and (4) active. In this instance, you are both the analyst and the subject expert.

On the job, there will be two of you. The next step is to evaluate your task inventory using the four criteria. Rate your success in complying with each criterion, and write four statements about how your task inventory performance measured up.

Job Title: _____

Task inventory criteria	*Success*	*Comments*
Comprehensive?	____	Yes
All work activity fits into one of the	____	No
inventoried tasks?		
Intermediate?	____	All
The task unit or work activity is interme-	____	Some
diate in specificity between that of the	____	None
job cluster or function and that of		
a step-by-step procedure or detailed		
aspect of the job.		
Discrete?	____	All
Each task is distinguishable from the	____	Some
others and has a definite beginning	____	None
and ending.		
Active?	____	All
Each task statement has an action	____	Some
verb and the object of the action.	____	None

Chances are, if you experienced difficulty in meeting one of the criteria, it was the core activity or intermediate criterion. Finding the right level of specificity takes practice. The concept of task detailing versus task identification will be further clarified in the next chapter. After you learn more about detailed task analysis in Chapters 13–15, you can come back to this point and revise your task inventory as needed.

Tips for the Analyst

Thus far, work expertise has been documented at two levels: job description and task inventory. But when a job is simple and the tasks are limited, it may be reasonable to include the task inventory in an expanded job description, rather than to produce two separate documents. When the job is complex, it may be reasonable to use the clusters of work activities to organize the job tasks. For example, the second example provided above for the "National Practice Leader—Engineering" is a task inventory for a team leader in an environmental engineering company. Here you see specific work tasks listed under organizers such as project planning and project execution.

Should the analyst use the job descriptions and task inventories that already exist in the organization? Be sure to procure these documents. You will find them filed in the human resources, training, or industrial engineering departments. Be sure to question the relevance of these documents to your task. Are they current or are they outdated? For what purpose were they produced? Hiring? Training? Who wrote them? The incumbent? The supervisor? An analyst? Are they accurate? You may discover that these job descriptions fit the criteria for job descriptions and task inventories and that they may be used as is. More likely, you will find that they are outdated and were written for purposes of hiring or compensation.

At least two people become involved in producing the job description and task inventory. These are the analyst and the subject expert. The most likely subject experts are the job holders and their direct supervisors. Your interviews with these people can be complemented with existing job descriptions, task inventories, job performance aids, and training manuals.

While subject experts are a critical resource in producing quality general work analyses, the skill of the analyst in asking the right questions—the "dumb" questions, the leading questions, and the insightful questions—is equally important. Experts, by definition, are so competent that they use their subconscious minds to perform work behaviors. At the conscious level, they can't necessarily recall the detailed work that they take for granted.

Supervisors can be either more or less aware of the details of the work than are those they supervise. The skilled analyst brings to the analysis task clear criteria, an inquisitive mind, and a willingness to seek the knowledge of the subject experts—a good combination for documenting work expertise.

Conclusion

Task inventories have enormous utility for performance improvement professionals. They are critical in bridging between the organizational, process, team, and individual levels of performance. Tasks are fundamentally connected to organizational and process-level performance requirements. Even so, jobs are most often designed in terms of how the tasks fit one another rather than how the tasks relate to the organization. An option was to create a task inventory to reference the work tasks to organizational processes instead of jobs. Organizations are increasingly using process and functional workflows rather than jobs as major organizers. Also, knowing that people work in teams to oversee cross-functional processes suggests that cross-functional tasks are an important consideration. Chapter 14 shows how this is done.

The next four chapters will show you how to use task-detailing documentation tools. These more focused tools are used to detail and document what a person precisely needs to know and be able to do to perform specific job tasks. Three task analysis detailing tools are presented: procedure task analysis, system task analysis, and knowledge task analysis. Cross-job function tasks are unique in that multiple job holders collaborate on specific tasks while making unique contributions. All task documentation tools are not always needed to analyze each task. Most tasks can be analyzed by using just one. Some require more. In general, each work task will require one of the three task-detailing tools. In the next chapter, we describe the process for documenting procedure tasks.

Part IV

Tools for Documenting Workplace Expertise

Detailing Procedure Tasks

Procedure task analysis is a method of documenting "people–thing" type workplace expertise in terms of precisely what people are required to know and be able to do to perform the task. The goal of any procedure task analysis is to document the steps required to complete the task at a level of detail that any novice could follow. A procedure task analysis essentially provides directions—think of Lego sets or a recent furniture purchase that requires assembly. The manual you receive, either with your Lego set or furniture is essentially a procedure task analysis. The following small example demonstrates the important principles, elements, and uses of procedure task analysis.

You Can't Go Wrong

A small group of employees are being instructed on a new software application. As they gather around a computer terminal, the factory representative quickly moves from step to step. As she moves screen to screen, "easy as pie"—so it seems. Forgetting to note and emphasize her routine of clicking the lower right "save" icon resulted in total software utilization failure among the learners. The incredibly easy step is mandatory, and the subject matter expert did the "save" step at a subconscious level—forgetting to inform the neophytes.

DOI: 10.4324/9781003518532-15

Elements of Procedure Task Analysis

A significant portion of the knowledge and skill required to perform in the workplace is procedural; that is, the work involves people–thing interactions such as operating equipment, using tools, filling out forms, and handling goods. However, procedure-laden work has been declining over the past decades and most developed countries have increasingly become "knowledge economies" that seem to require less procedure work. In many cases, rote procedure work has been outsourced to developing countries as labor costs have shifted. Developed economies now feature computers as the dominant "work tools," yet there is still a significant and critical role for procedural task analysis to play. Activities like boxing parcel packages, entering data, processing customer orders, changing engine oil—among many others—are extremely relevant in even the most developed workplaces. It is easy to dismiss the utility of procedure task analysis as many might say "we just don't do that kind of work anymore." Yet, we would argue that almost any current work task involves some procedure component, and it is important that it is done correctly.

Procedure task analysis is the method to use for documenting work performed in a series of steps and substeps. Because all the steps to complete a task are documented, a procedure analysis document for a single task can run for several pages. If all the job tasks on an inventory for a specific job are 'people–thing' interactions, a procedure task analysis should be developed for each task. If 15 such tasks were listed for a job, 15 separate documents should be created.

Developing a procedure task analysis typically requires two people: the subject expert and the analyst. An alternative is to teach the procedure task analysis process to subject experts so they can document their own tasks—thus serving as the subject expert and the analyst. This can save a lot of time even considering the upfront training and editing required.

Another expectation in detailing procedure tasks is that subject experts perform the work during the analysis. Even if an analyst is relying on him or herself as a subject expert, the analyst should do the work as he or she documents it. Simply talking about the work without performing, it is likely to result in a failed outcome. Being accurate and complete is critical. Without directly observing the work as it is taking place, the analyst is likely to leave important steps or pieces of information out of the analysis.

The analyst should record the precise details of the work task: the type and size of the wrench, the direction to turn the nut, how far, and so on. Getting ready to do a procedure task analysis is easy—we recommend a notepad and pencil along with the digital tools we all carry with us (computers, smartphones, etc.). Pictures, videos, and screen recordings are particularly helpful in procedure task analyses. Remember, the goal is to document the task in detail and in its entirety. For now, it is useful to look at the process of procedure task analysis and the documentation form used to record the analysis.

Process of Analyzing Procedure Tasks

The process of documenting procedure tasks is portrayed in Figure 11.1. The process requires attention to detail: (1) judging the appropriateness of procedure analysis to the job task, (2) honoring the criteria, (3) obtaining existing task analysis documents from inside or outside the organization, (4) observing expert(s) performing the task while recording data, and (5) drafting a task analysis document for review and approval.

The final version of a procedure task analysis is recorded in a special format on electronic or paper forms. The procedure task analysis document is a multipage form, with the first page containing administrative, safety, and other essential information, along with the initial procedural steps necessary to perform the task.

The second page is a continuation sheet that is used repeatedly until all the details of the procedure have been recorded. Figure 11.2 is an example of the first page of the procedure analysis for the analyst's job task of developing a procedure analysis.

Heading

The top section of the first page of the form (see Figure 11.2) contains some of the who, what, when, and where reference information that becomes more valuable as time passes and the analyst's memory fades. It also contains the information needed to maintain complete and up-to-date files. In this instance, the form is simply page "1 of 1." In most instances, it would be reasonable to use many pages in detailing a single task.

The specific analysis location is important in that the work systems in one site could be unique. The fact that the work was analyzed in the

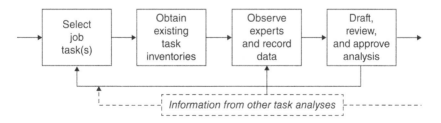

Figure 11.1 Analyzing Procedure Tasks

Procedural task analysis

Job or Program __Procedural Task Analysis__	Page _1_ of _1_
Location ___Tyler, TX___	Effective Date ___M/D/Y___
Department __Human Resources__	Cancels Sheet Dated __None__
Analyst ___R. A. Swanson___	Approved By ___Aland Rinehart___

Task The task name, taken from the task inventory

Performance standard
  The end-result work performance standard for this task

Safety and other cautions
  Safety precautions (e.g., wear safety glasses, care for fragile equipment, etc.)

Major headings	Subheadings	Sequential steps in performing the work	Notes*
1.		Short statements on the performance of a task—begin with action words	C–M
2.		Put these in the 1st-order heading column. Begin writing in the column to shape an outline form	C–M
	A.	Second order headings are key points, or explanations, which further describe the step	C–M
	B.	These 2nd-order headings begin just right of the column	C–E
	C.	If you use "A," you must use "B"	C–E
3.		Notes column: To identify a learning domain or a particularly difficult task or "skill"	C–D
	A.	Dominant learning domain: cognitive, affective, or psychomotor	C–D
	B.	Learning difficulty: easy, moderate, or difficult	C–M

*Learning domain: C = cognitive; A = affective; P = psychomotor
  Learning difficulty: E = easy; M = moderate; D = difficult

Figure 11.2 Example of First Page of Procedure Task Analysis Form

Minneapolis, Philadelphia, or London office could be essential information; in some companies, the department name is also important. For current reference and for a historical perspective, the job or program for which the analysis is being conducted should be recorded. This is important because any analysis work is colored by the purpose for which it is done. For example, the technical know-how required of salespeople will differ from that required of the service-and-repair people who deal with the same product. The substance of the organization's diagnosis and the resulting performance improvement proposal should have already made these performance requirement differences clear. In addition, the taxonomy of performance (see Figure 2.2) helps the analyst think about the nature of the expertise required of the procedural task being documented (e.g., understand, operate, or troubleshoot).

In addition to the effective date that the procedure analysis is completed and approved, the replaced document dated line indicates that this is an updated version of the procedure. Finally, recording the names on the *Analyst* and *Approved by* lines enhances accountability and future communications.

The next section of the first page, *Task*, is the place to write a single task name and number from the task inventory (see Chapter 10). The identical number and words used to specify the task in the inventory should be repeated here.

Next is the section for recording the performance standard for this task. The performance standard for the task indicates the expected performance outcomes in terms of quantity, quality, and/or time. The performance standard can come from several sources. First, a workplace standard may already be in place to assess this work. An existing performance standard may be specified at the task level or as part of the job-level standards. If it exists, use it. Otherwise, it is best to establish the performance standard after the task has been detailed. Once a task has been detailed, the performance standard will be revealed as part of the analysis.

The final section at the top of the form offers space for recording cautionary items about safety and other essential points that should be highlighted. "Must wear safety glasses" and "Use heat-resistant gloves" are a few examples of items that could be entered here.

Sequential Steps

The sequential steps for a procedure are written in the form of short statements describing the actual performance of a task. Each statement begins with an action word like turn, listen, fill, set, or compare. Here is a sample statement for setting air pressure on a production machine: "Set forming pressure to 30 to 35 pounds per square inch (psi)."

Procedural information is usually broken down into headings and sub-headings. For example, setting forming pressure requires several discrete activities. In this instance, subheadings would be as follows:

a Depress the "inflate form" button and hold.
b Set forming pressure to 30–35 pounds per square inch (psi).
c Release the "inflate form" button.

The notes column on the procedure task analysis form allows space for recording vital information about the learning domain and the estimated difficulty of learning each procedural detail. Almost any work performance involves a mix of cognitive (intellectual), affective (attitudinal), and psychomotor (sensory) domains. Procedure work rarely relies on just a single domain. Yet, one of the three domains is usually dominant. The question to ask is this:

Are the differences between workers who are expert and those who are beginners primarily the result of knowing or not knowing something, having or not having certain attitudes, or being able or unable to make fine sensory discriminations?

The answer will sometimes be surprising. Consider the following examples:

Cognitive Learning Domain

Think about a data entry expert or coder. Sometimes this employee knows a given data input system or coding language better than anyone else. Often, these involve proprietary software programs or complicated spreadsheets. These workers either know or do not know something required to complete the task. Anyone with reasonable psychomotor control could (with practice and instruction) understand the various data fields, what data to enter, how often it needs to be updated, or other. At a basic level, this kind of expert knows how to perform a procedure, fill in the correct fields, write effective code, push the parts in place, turn the adjusting knobs, trip the start lever, turn the finished part, and so on. The worker's cognitive ability to remember many sequential steps in detail allows for speed in this procedure. This activity is mostly cognitive and should be coded C.

Psychomotor Learning Domain

Other activities may include using fine discrimination with any of the senses of sight, smell, taste, hearing, and touch. In another instance, a skilled carpenter moves rapidly through a series of assembly and adjustment procedures—all of which appear to be psychomotor behaviors but in fact are not. An expert carpenter casually rubs a hand over a finely finished piece of wood to be used in the construction of a cabinet. The carpenter decides to stop and redo the work. You, in the role of the analyst, ask what the carpenter is doing. You rub your hand over the same piece of wood and feel nothing unusual. A little knowledge and the ability to make some fine sensory discrimination, developed over years of experience, are at work here. The highly tuned attention to senses on the hand and significant experience in this realm are the differences between you and the expert.

Affective Learning Domain

Caring about a required task activity is more subtle to discern than the cognitive or psychomotor realms. The simple question is: Can the person carry out the activity when they are being observed? If they can, but do not, this would be considered the affective domain. We had workers enrolled in refresher training report to us that nobody ever informed them as to why it was so important to carefully execute a particular task activity. Once they knew, they changed their behavior in the follow-up. In another example, workers who were careless carrying out steps did not know that poor execution had a major impact on the business. In so many instances around affect, sharing information about task step importance is critical.

Combining Learning Domains

Procedural tasks often combine or involve multiple learning domains. Many procedural tasks require cognitive, psychomotor, and/or affective aspects throughout the completion of the task (which should be indicated for each step in the task analysis).

On the last flight you took, once you boarded the airplane and were approved to depart, there was a ground crew working behind the scenes. They were working before and during your entire boarding process to make sure all the correct procedures were followed, and all the correct baggage was properly loaded onto the plane. The entire ground crew were following specific procedures aligned with safety, accuracy, and efficiency. Those crew members were following directed procedures and processes (and sometimes they differ from airport to airport). These are highly psychomotor tasks, which involve knowing and following the procedures and yet being able to adjust to issues that may arise in the moment. For example, if a passenger bag falls off the loading belt, action must be taken. Alternatively, a crew member may be following standard, prescribed procedures and suddenly smell or hear something out of the ordinary—particularly if the individual has been working in this environment for a length of time. The crew member will signal to others that something could be wrong. It could be the odor of jet fuel, the sound of a broken cargo loader or something else. These tasks are usually broken down into separate, multiple procedural parts of the process to load an airplane and push it back onto the tarmac. These activities often involve rote memorization of the procedures required to accomplish the task and the flexibility to adjust to interruptions along the way. These kinds of tasks rely on the ability to immediately adjust, based on expertise, and, therefore, can involve multiple learning domains.

Pilots are another good example. It may be tempting to think that pilots operate entirely on their specific expertise and knowledge that cannot be documented. However, make no mistake, pilots have extensive lists of procedure checklists to meet before they can even start the engines to get the airplane off the ground and get you on your way. Yet, in the air, encountering air turbulence requires decision making which extends the expertise into other realms of task expertise (detailed in Chapters 12–14). Both brief examples demonstrate that any procedural task can involve multiple learning domains.

By asking questions about how one would perform the work improperly or by trying to do the task yourself—or both – you can determine the learning domain. Deciding how difficult a step is to learn is another matter. Be sure to make such judgments while you are close to the work. Use the ratings E (easy), M (moderate), or D (difficult). Having this information will help at a later time when you are trying to understand why workers are either bored or stuck in the learning/working process and how you should respond. If you are a trainer, you may decide to offer additional practice time during training for difficult-to-learn tasks. If you are a manager, you may want to redesign a boring task to make the work more challenging. But for now, the analyst's responsibility is to rate each sequential step in terms of learning domain and learning difficulty.

It is important that you note the level of detail. Variations among procedure analyses usually are found in the amount of detail cited in the sequential steps. Most beginning analysts do not include enough detail. A second area of significant difference will usually appear in the notes column, with the analyst misclassifying cognitive work as psychomotor work. Take heart! Experience will reduce these differences as you become a more expert analyst. The above examples should provide a starting point.

Sketches, photographs, and existing diagrams of relevant equipment are critical additions to most procedure analyses. A sketchpad, smartphone camera, and screenshots are essential elements of the analyst's support equipment.

☑ **Checkpoint**

While you may not be ready to do a procedure task analysis, you should be able to begin. To test your skills, complete the analysis and documentation of the "scheduling a Zoom meeting" task by asking a youngster (odds are that they can complete this task faster than you), or someone newly recruited to your organization to complete the task. Time them. This work task activity is an immediate follow-up to see if your level of analysis detail is appropriate and if a novice or new employee can complete the task within the specified performance standards. Even better, if your organization uses a different online meeting platform, follow the example and create a basic procedural task analysis using that platform. Test it. Can a colleague accomplish the task and meet the stated performance requirements? If so, you have the appropriate level of detail. If not, try again—you need to be more specific. Remember that the procedural analysis criteria include the following:

1 Writing short statements of the performance
2 Beginning with action words
3 Using headings and subheadings
4 Identifying the learning domain and the level of learning difficulty for each step

---

Procedure Task Analysis Example: Initial Set-up of Monoprice 3D Printer

3D Printer Services, Inc. has eight locations across the United States that provides 3D printer consultation, prototyping, and production services for manufacturers. The Prototype Departments in each 3D Printer, Inc. location are receiving new Monoprice 3D Printers to carry out some of their work. Most laboratory equipment embraces the generic procedural tasks of (1) initial set-up, (2) project set-up, (3) operation, and (4) shutdown procedures.

This simple procedure analysis example of the initial set-up of the Monoprice 3D printer illustrates the elements of procedure task analyses. Again, the goal of any procedure task analysis is that you should be able to present the analyzed steps to anyone and they should be able to carry out the steps to accomplish the task according to the performance standard. Check out the following figures.

Procedure Task Analysis -- Initial Setup of Monoprice 3D Printer

Job or Program: Monoprice 3D Printer Operation
Location: 3D Printer Services – all locations
Department: Digital Services
Analyst: D. Parker
Effective Date: Month/Date/Year
Cancels: N/A
Approved By: L. D'Annunzio

Task: Initial Setup - Monoprice 3D Printer

Performance Standard:
Given the receipt of a new Monoprice 3D Printer, the contents will be unpacked, inventoried, assembled, and initially tested in a two-hour period.

Safety and other Cautions:
1 Handle the precision 3D printer carefully.
2 Keep operator hands away from heated elements.

Major Headings	Subheadings	Sequential Steps in Performing the Work	Notes
1 Unbox 3D Printer			
	A	Place shipping carton on stable workbench.	C-E
	B	Cut carton sealing tape carefully with box knife.	P-E
	C	Remove carton contents and place them on workbench.	P-E
	D	Carefully remove foam shipping block holding print head	P-M

2 Inventory 3D Printer Parts

A	3D printer.	C-E
B	Power supply.	C-E
C	Filament spool bracket.	C-E
D	Filament spool sample.	C-E
E	Memory card.	C-E
F	Print bed scraper.	C-E

3 Assemble 3D Printer

A	Latch the filament spool bracket into position.	P-M

B	Plug in power supply to 3D Printer.	C-E
C	Install the filament spool and then thread the filament through the extruder head.	P/A-M

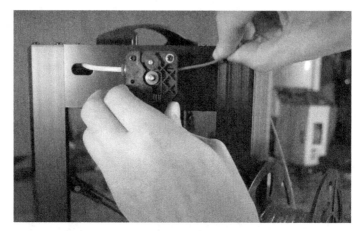

4 Initial test of 3D Printer
  A   Press the red "Move" button to confirm
            printer head movement.   C-E

  B   Press the "Power" on button to preheat
            the extruder (keep hands away from
            heated extruder and hot extruded
            filament.   C/A-E
  C   Press "Feed "on button to test filament
            feed thru extruder.   C/P-M
  D   With A,B,C success, turn off & unplug
            the 3D printer.   C-E
5 Store 3D Printer and documents
  A   Locate a logical and safe place to store
            the 3D Printer.   A/C-M
  B   Secure a container for 3D printer
            accessories and supplies.   C/A-M
  C   Label the container "Monoprice
            3D Printer.   P-E

Procedure Task Analysis – Schedule a Zoom Meeting

Job or Program: Account Representative
Location: San Francisco, CA
Department: Digital Services
Analyst: W. Muenyi
Effective Date: xx/xx/xxxx
Cancels: N/A
Approved By: I. Sheu

Performance Standard:
Trainee should be able to satisfactorily schedule a zoom meeting in 5 minutes or less.

Safety and other Cautions:
None.

Procedural Steps in Scheduling a Zoom Call:

1 Open your preferred web browser by clicking on the appropriate icon in your computer's menu bar (Safari, Google Chrome, etc...). -- C
2 Navigate to www.zoom.com by typing www.zoom.com in the web browser's search field. -- C
3 Sign into your zoom account – C-P
   a Enter your username and password. -- P
4 Once logged into your zoom account, click the icon labelled "Schedule": -- C

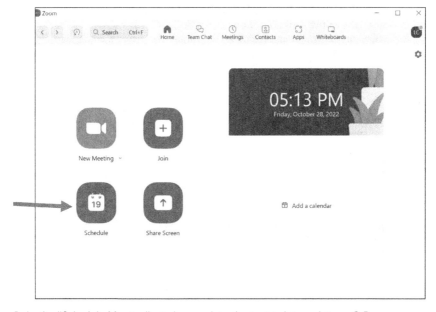

5 In the "Schedule Meeting" window, update the topic, date and time: C-P
   a Type a description for your meeting (Technology update meeting, Applicant review meeting, etc...). – C-P
   b Select the appropriate date and time for the meeting. – C-P

c Select the appropriate time zone for the meeting. – C-P

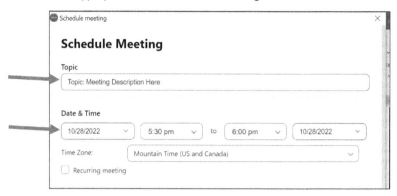

6 Click "Save" at the bottom of the window: -- C

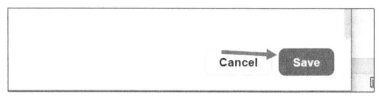

7 Upon saving your meeting, you can find a link to the lower right side of your computer screen that indicates "Copy Invitation". -- C
   a Clicking on this link opens a window that shows the meeting details, including a link to join the meeting at the appropriate time. -- C
   b Clicking on the "Copy Invitation" link automatically copies the meeting details. – C-P

8 Once you have copied the meeting invitation, switch to your preferred e-mail program and compose a new message. Input the intended recipients and meeting invitees in the "To" field. – C-P
9 Compose your e-mail invitation for the meeting. – C-A
10 Paste the link to the zoom meeting by either (Windows = holding the CTRL key + the v key, Mac = holding the command key + the v key). – C-P
11 Send your e-mail – all recipients will now have a link to your meeting at the selected time and date. -- C
       There are several other optional features that can be set from the "Schedule Meeting" window. They include:
12 Password – use this feature if the meeting needs to be secure. -- C
   a Select a password (if you select this option, the password will be included in the meeting invitation as described above in step 8). – C-P

13 Video settings – these can be updated based on the needs for the meeting. Options include automatically turning all video conferencing off or automatically requiring video conferencing from all participants. – C-P
14 Audio settings – like video settings, these should be configured based on the meeting needs. Again, options include automatically turning all audio conferencing off or automatically requiring audio conferencing from all participants. – C-P
15 Waiting room -- There is also a "waiting room" option. Selecting this option means that once your video meeting starts, you will have to admit each participant into the meeting. – C-P

Meeting ID	938 8669 8002		
Security	✕ Passcode ✓ Waiting Room		
	✕ Require authentication to join		
Invite Link	https://zoom.us/j/93886698002		☝ Copy Invitation
Video	Host	On	

Tips for the Analyst

Procedural analysis is a fairly direct method of analyzing work expertise. In most cases, what you see is what you record. Careful observers usually do a good job of documenting procedural tasks, but that is not enough. Those analysts who question skillfully, as well as observe, will most likely succeed. Be aware that the casual behavior of an expert may fool even the most careful observer. The skilled analyst gently probes for what the worker is doing and why. Whenever safe and appropriate, the expert analyst will ask, "May I try doing that?"

Conclusion

Procedure task analysis, which focuses on people–thing work expertise, is used to describe usual work behaviors under normal conditions. But abnormal conditions are certain to arise at least some of the time. What happens when a production worker experiences production problems? If the machine breaks, the maintenance crew will handle the problem. If the machine lacks the capacity to produce the number of items, management will handle the situation. If the machine is emitting abnormal dial messages or odors all is not well. In this case, consulting a procedure analysis for normal operation will not be particularly helpful. The user is facing a systems problem, not a procedure problem.

People–system workplace expertise requires that the user understand the processes involved in the system and be able to troubleshoot the system. People–thing work systems that are broken down or are in trouble require understanding the systems processes and how to troubleshoot failing systems. This is dealt with in the next chapter. System task analysis is an essential skill of the performance analyst because he or she needs to know how to document work expertise that involving systems.

Chapter 12

Detailing System Tasks

Chapter Sections

- Process of Analyzing System Tasks
- System Description
- System Parts and Purposes
- Process Analysis
- Troubleshooting Analysis
- Purchase Order System Case Study: The Voilà Company
- Monitoring and Troubleshooting Shipping Operations: The Voilà Company
- Tips for the Analyst
- Conclusion

Our 21st-century world—including the systems designed by people and the objects made by people—are increasingly complicated. The complexity of our work systems, both technical and information based, can stop us in our tracks. Procedure tasks no longer prevail in the workplace. Rather, it is now dominated by work systems and system work tasks that have become increasingly intricate and abstract. Even everyday nonwork systems can illustrate this point.

A 13-year-old boy owns two bicycles. One bike is a 20-inch, one-speed, fat-tired model that has been with him since age five and a hand-me-down from his uncle. The other is a 27-inch, 15-speed, lightweight model he bought two years ago.

The old 20-inch bike, bulky and simple in design, has been regularly disassembled and reassembled by its owner for a variety of reasons ranging from major overhauls and repainting to taking it apart just for the fun of it. This bike has very few parts—as a system, you can almost see how every part fits together and works. Thus, maintaining this system has posed few problems to the young owner.

The 15-speed bike, on the other hand, has never once been disassembled, despite its sitting disabled for long periods of time. The caliper brakes, the two

DOI: 10.4324/9781003518532-16

shifting systems, and all those gears and idlers—the multiple subsystems—have proved to be too intimidating to its owner.

A car is another familiar example, although more complicated than a bike. Tasks that used to be relatively simple have also become far more difficult due to the increasing use of computer control systems.

Time has changed the world in which we live. We used to believe that we could understand the systems in our world and had things under control. But now, with dynamic technologies all around us, we need extra help in coping with the knowledge systems and technology systems with which we are required to interact. And to be a fully functioning worker, the systems that surround us cannot be set aside or ignored. More often than we realize, the interdependence between the components of even a simple work system can escape experienced workers and result in a system that is out of control, causing waste.

Consider this example. The president of a small service firm was puzzled. Several subscribers to the firm's professional digital newsletter emailed her directly—a few even called—to complain that they had failed to receive their issue of the newsletter. Canceled deposits and letters of acknowledgment from the firm's subscription operator confirmed their subscriber status. The president talked to the subscription operator, who was worrying about her continued employment with the firm. The operator had checked her records, found the orders and the computer input records, and concluded that she had entered everything correctly. After all, most of the subscribers were getting their newsletters. To those subscribers who complained, the operator sent her apologies and her assurance that their names would be reentered into the subscriber system.

Meanwhile, the newsletter manager was frustrated over the situation. He contemplated letting the subscription operator go, but he was afraid of an even greater mess if someone else took over. He couldn't coach her, because he did not know all the components of her job (much less how they should be executed systematically for optimal effectiveness and efficiency). Neither he nor the operator understood the firm's newsletter work system, much less how to improve it.

The systems aspects of the duties of the knowledge worker, as much as in the goods-producing sector, have increased in complexity. Financial networks, personnel systems, prescribed decision-making methods, and communication systems in large and dispersed multinational organizations can make work tasks more difficult to comprehend. When errors and inefficiencies occur or when information systems fail, management is often tempted to fire people or to add a tier of supervisory and quality control staff, rather than figure out how the entire system works, how it can malfunction, or how it is being misunderstood. Because work systems, and the nature of work itself, have changed so drastically, we face a basic problem: how do we keep our costly work systems up and running, let alone improve them? The consequences of not doing so are huge and can usually be expressed in terms of large financial losses. Clearly, people are required to learn and understand the systemic aspects of their work tasks more thoroughly and more quickly than they have in the past.

Procedural task analysis methods are inadequate for describing many of the essential systemic work tasks required of many employees. The need exists for a task-detailing method that specifically focuses on the job tasks required to function within work systems and also to keep work systems running effectively and efficiently.

As we saw in Chapter 11, the results of procedure task analyses are sequential task details—detailed step-by-step information for normal operating procedures under normal conditions. Abnormal and unique situations demand more. The expertise that workers must have in order to respond effectively to abnormal conditions is often left to their resourcefulness. As a result, many workers input data, make financial decisions, or run a machine purely from a procedural perspective—unaware of how their actions may affect other aspects of the system of which the procedural job tasks are just one part. They never know what is really going on inside the overall system in which they participate.

To cope, organization managers should be requiring the same workers to have a much deeper understanding of their entire work system and to take charge whenever processes within the system are not operating normally. Even more problematic are the situations where experienced workers fail to diagnose the inoperative, inefficient, or failing system that they work in, simply because they lack system expertise. Systemic tasks, including diagnosing and troubleshooting systems, are critical activities for keeping organizations productive.

Where does a person begin to deal with a failure in a complex system? What tools does an analyst have to document system-troubleshooting expertise? Even more challenging, in the absence of an expert, how are the details required of system tasks related to existing and new systems determined?

Process of Analyzing System Tasks

Analysis of system tasks is one of three methods that constitute a complete toolbox for detailing the expertise required of job tasks. The other methods are the analysis of procedure tasks—for step-by-step, people–thing-focused expertise (see Chapter 11), the analysis of people–system-focused expertise (this chapter), the analysis of knowledge tasks that embrace expertise focused on people–idea interactions and people–people interactions (see Chapter 13). In addition, multidimension task and cross-function tasks are acknowledged (Chapter 14).

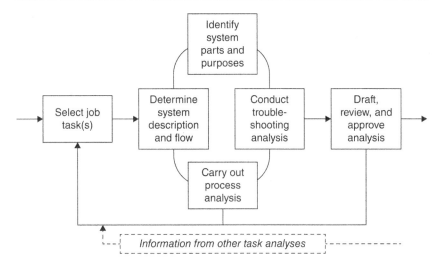

Figure 12.1 Analyzing System Tasks

In this chapter, the process of analyzing overall work systems, processes, and system tasks will be described. This is the expertise required to understand and troubleshoot workplace information-based and/or hardware systems. Several examples and explanations are provided to help you understand the method.

First, let's walk through the steps of analyzing system tasks (see Figure 12.1). These steps result in components of the final system task analysis and include (1) system description, (2) system parts and purposes, (3) system process analysis, and (4) system troubleshooting analysis.

System Description

The system description involves naming the work system or system task being detailed, specifying the purpose and spine of the work system or system task being analyzed, establishing a task performance standard for the system task, and graphically presenting the flow of the system task.

Naming the System

The name given to the work system or system task begins to focus the analysis effort. In providing a name, it is useful to think about the scope distinction between a system and a process, even though it does come down to semantics. A system is a unified, purposeful whole consisting of "interdependent components" or parts. A process is a systematic series of "actions" directed to some specified end. A system is conceptually equal to or larger than a process, and in most instances, a system has several processes (subsystems).

Any organization can be viewed as an entire system containing one or more subsystems, or processes, each of which may have a number of sub-processes. The concept of system is generally thought to be broader than the concept of process, and it is used that way in this book.

Experts interacting with a large system almost always require system task expertise and knowledge task expertise so as to be able to do their jobs effectively. In contrast, experts interacting with subsystems or processes within a larger organizational system may only require their subsystem task expertise plus procedural task expertise to do their jobs effectively. Overall, jobs that have been predominantly procedural task or knowledge task focused in the past increasingly require systems task-focused expertise as part of their job.

Thus, naming the system task or work system being analyzed is important. For example, the system scope can vary greatly for the following systems tasks: distribution, hiring truck drivers, dispatching, and inventory records. Each is either a system or subsystem within any organization that processes orders and ships products and can be classified as follows:

Distribution system	System
Truck driver hiring system	Process (subsystem of distribution system)
Seat cover dispatching system	Process (subsystem of distribution system)
Seat cover inventory system	System (transcends production, sales, and distribution)

System Purpose and Spine

The system purpose and spine are connected. Both are clear and simple. One is expressed in words, and the other is a graphic. They can be created at the same time. Both deal with the system's input, process, and output.

The system spine is a simplified diagram of the overall work system or system task where the three major components of a general system are named: input, process, and output. You start by identifying the output of the system in creating the purpose and spine of the system. For a university department faculty team, the output could be university degrees granted. For a core team leader in an R&D department of a high-tech medical device firm, the output could be mitigated or averted project risk. In this R&D example, the system task, system purpose/description, and system spine would be as follows:

System/Task name:	Manage product development risk
System purpose/ description	A system for aiding core team leaders in making decisions meant to mitigate the inherent risks in developing products such that the probability or impact of those risks is decreased
System spine:	Input → Process(es) → Output Need to Identify, analyze, Mitigated mitigate risk control, and project risk report

You can isolate the spine by asking, "What is the major or core output of the system?" For example, the output of any delivery system is a product or service delivered to a specified destination at a specified time. To create a system flow diagram, the analyst may either interview or accompany the delivery person to the final destination, noting the basic activities that take place prior and during final delivery, such as logging in with a dispatcher, signing off at the warehouse, recording data on route, carrying out the required activities at the customer site, signing off for receipt of product or service, and so on. Each of these steps may then be expanded on, such as details of the on-route recording of speed, mileage, fuel levels, and vehicle maintenance needs.

Let's take a very simple and familiar hardware work system—the incandescent lightbulb—as an example. Given such a system, the first question to ask is "What is the primary output?" In the case of the incandescent bulb, it is light. A second output of the incandescent bulb is heat. In fact, you may have used heat lamps with bulbs specifically designed to produce heat, with light being the secondary, wasted output. In our example, the primary output is light.

What do you think the major input is? Some people might have replied, "Gas." Certainly, gas could be the source of energy at an electrical power production plant, but it is not the ready source of energy for the incandescent lightbulb system. Electricity is the major input.

If you were analyzing an electrical power production system, gas could easily be an input. Because systems interact with other systems, and small systems can be nested within larger systems, drawing boundaries around the system that you are dealing with is crucial. Otherwise, you will find yourself analyzing information that exceeds the expertise required to perform the work—and you will frustrate everybody by doing so. An appropriate system with its subsystems is defined by the performance demands on the worker determined in the organizational diagnosis and the system task being analyzed.

For example, the person who diagnoses and replaces failing or broken bulbs in building maintenance or in product research does not need to know about the larger power production system that includes coal as the input. Just knowing that electricity is the primary input to the incandescent lightbulb system is enough.

Now, what about the process within the incandescent light system? How is electricity, the input, transformed into light? The process stage of any system includes both transmission and conversion. In this case, the transmission is accomplished by the electron flow through wires, and the conversion is accomplished because of the resistance to the electrons flowing through a filament that heats up, glows, and gives off light—the output.

System Performance Standard

Next is the section for recording the performance standard for the system task. As an example, the performance standard for any shipper's task, could involve a task—"Monitor and troubleshoot shipping operations." The performance standard could be as follows:

Shippers will be the first to recognize and report operations that are failing (within 12 hours or less) and be proactive members of operations troubleshooting teams. The result will be increased uptime, order fulfillment, and fewer returns.

As noted in the procedure task analysis chapter, the performance standard can come from several sources. First, there may already be an established workplace standard that is used to assess this work. An existing performance standard may be specified at the task level or as part of the job-level standards. If it exists, use it. In this instance, it did not exist. The work process was improved (changed) to include this new job task. In this case, it is appropriate to establish the performance standard after the task has been detailed. Once a task has been detailed, the performance standard will be revealed as part of the analysis.

System Flow

While the core input, process, and output are called the spine of the work system or system task, attached to the spine are the subsystems that more fully portray the complexity of the operating system. Subsystems or sub-processes are added to the spine to create the system flow.

In the system flow, the system process is broken down into its components, and the information or the materials—from input, through the process, and to output—are traced through the system. A system flow diagram provides an understanding of the system and its elements. Systems theory tells us that there are three basic interconnected components to any system: input(s), process(es), and output(s):

INPUT → PROCESS → OUTPUT

It is a view of the system being detailed from the required vantage point of the work task. Remember, although most complex systems are made up of several subsystems or processes, it is important to begin by defining the spine of the system under study.

The following checkpoint uses the automobile as a familiar example to illustrate important points about the system flow.

☑ **Checkpoint**

Let's work through another example of systems flow, the automobile. In Figure 12.2, the major elements that make up the spine of the system are labeled. Remember to start with the output and then go to the input. Do the process last.

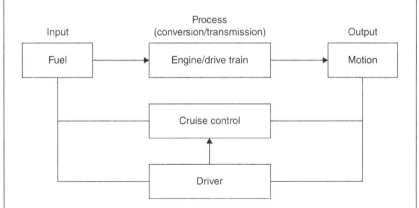

Figure 12.2 Automobile System Spine with Driver and Cruise Control Subsystems

The automobile is a wonderful, familiar, and complex system. It has many subsystems, some of which have little or nothing to do with the intended output of motion. We identified fuel as the major input, with the conversion portion of the process being the engine and the transmission portion of the process being the drive train.

A stereo sound system as a subsystem of the automobile would be an absurd place to start figuring out the complex automobile system. The automobile does, however, have several subsystems that directly affect the major output of motion. One of these is the control system. The major controller of the automobile system is the "driver." Choose and label the appropriate empty boxes in the spine of the automobile system (Figure 12.2) as driver and cruise control.

The basic systems components of input, process, and output are useful in identifying the spine of a complex system. By adding each of the subsystems, one can illustrate the complexity of the operation and the control components of the system. Familiarity with standard flowcharting symbols is useful but not mandatory. These symbols are shown in Figure 7.3 in Chapter 7. Using them allows the analyst to communicate in a standard and easily understood visual language.

Answer: Cruise control (upper box) and driver (lower box) _____

Systems Parts and Purposes

A more detailed understanding of the system is provided when identifying the system parts and purposes. This seemingly mundane step of analyzing work systems or system tasks is straightforward if a sociotechnical view is taken. That is, be sure to include the people operating and troubleshooting the information and hardware systems. Sociotechnical systems by default involve the interactions between humans and technology systems (Cummings & Worley, 2016).

For example, is the customer a part of the system or not? Not having the customer and customer service support personnel in a computer-based purchasing system designed to serve people around the country would be foolish. It might be equally foolish to insert people within the system who are not actively engaged in the system operation. Including extraneous people would unnecessarily clutter the system.

As for accurate terminology, do you call it the hopper or the bin? Talk to the employee who was told by his supervisor to clean out the bin (the size of a small house) when she really meant to clean out the hopper (the size of a desk), and he will tell you about the importance of terminology! Accurate terminology is an important outcome of all three types of task analysis. Tangible aspects of a system such as parts, data sets, documents, customers, workers, managers, and the like, should be named and their purpose described.

The reality is that two workers in the same work system don't often see the same things, don't call parts of the system by the same name, and may not view the parts as having the same purpose. When these conditions exist within system tasks, confusion can reign. For example, does a strategic plan mean the same thing to each member of the senior management team? Does monitoring the work mean the same thing to all stakeholders?

To further illustrate, here are four of 21 parts and purposes for the "Manage product development risk" system task that is part of the leader job that has been mentioned earlier:

Part	Purpose
Product development project	A written project document with a set of objectives for developing a new product
Project Investment board	A cross-functional board made up of senior management that is responsible for making project management decisions and allocating resources to projects
Risk log	A list of product development project risks generated by the risk identification team
Action item	An item or task that someone is responsible for completing

The product of a parts-and-purposes analysis is a summary list of the correct names and use(s) of the tangible parts of the work system, including data with which people interact. This provides knowledge that will be used later in the troubleshooting analysis. A rule of thumb for creating a parts-and-purposes analysis is to include every system element with which the worker interacts directly or indirectly. Shortcutting the number of system elements that the worker might interact with here is problematic—it is important to be comprehensive. A list of system parts and purposes for the employee benefits designer will differ from a list intended for the benefits claim processor. The designer will use items (e.g., tax law codes) of which the processor might only be aware. Obviously, some overlapping of items would occur on the two lists, but the claim processor's parts-and-purposes analysis might be longer (due to more numerous process steps), while the designers would reflect a more conceptual process.

The system parts-and-purposes form provides an accurate list of, and explanations for, all the process elements with which a worker interacts. Doing such an analysis for any system offers an excellent opportunity to name the system parts correctly. The use of inconsistent terminology often causes confusion and frustration in the workplace among beginners and old-timers alike. For example, confusion results from references on the shop floor to a fuel cap one time, a gas cap another time, and a tank cap still another. The workplace is filled with inefficiencies resulting from miscommunication, often caused by the use of varying terminology. Here is your opportunity to straighten out some of the language in your workplace.

Previously, we referred to subject experts as sources of knowledge. In analyzing system tasks, you will again want to use subject experts. In addition to relying on the subject experts in the organization, you will want to utilize expert knowledge from other sources, such as external consultants, original manufacturers of equipment, manuals, and technical information sheets/internet documents.

Specialty books or websites that provide detailed information are particularly helpful in preparing the system flow diagram and conducting the parts-and-purpose analysis information and hardware systems. The authors may have already analyzed the process and explained the operation and handling of the components, thus saving you a great deal of time.

That old saying that knowledge is power begins to take on added meaning once a system flow diagram and a system parts-and-purposes analysis are completed. These two sets of information form the foundation for understanding system work tasks. So far, we have discussed the broad understanding that results from system flow analysis and the essential knowledge that results from system parts-and-purposes analysis. These two analyses are important but insufficient to provide the level of understanding needed to work with a complex system.

Process Analysis

Process analysis is aimed at analyzing the system, or process, in operation. That is, you analyze how it is supposed to work or function. It is forward-looking, with the idea that this is how the smooth-running system is intended to work—how all the elements fit and flow.

Variables

Process variables such as people, materials, equipment, method, and the process environment are identified in terms of their specifications, indicators, decision points, decision-makers, controls, and effects on the process. Process variables are simply those human or hardware elements that can change—for example, timing, temperature, accuracy, knowledge, decisions, and satisfaction. Behind each possible variance is a metric such as product quality, service quality, temperature, number in attendance, proposal completeness, and so on.

Actions that need to be performed regularly in managing the system, such as taking process measurements and communicating with suppliers for just-in-time delivery, are also identified by process analysis. This information is usually recorded on a process analysis form.

Specifications, Indicators, and Controls

Process analysis helps document the connections between the system and its various parts. In a perfectly logical system, the process variables (people, materials, equipment, method, and/or environment), their attributes, and their interconnections become apparent and display critical contributions to the system's effectiveness and efficiency. As you might expect, process analysis also has the potential of identifying disconnects, unwanted variation, overlaps, and unnecessary complexity that may have been designed into or grown into the system. The end result—a process flowchart—is a clearer picture of what changes are needed. Chapter 7 illustrates a simple flowchart (Figure 7.7) with sample symbols used to document system tasks. Software programs make flowcharting quite easy. Remember, the key to flowcharting is consistency.

Troubleshooting Analysis

Based on the system task description, system flow, system parts and purposes, and process analysis, a network of the problems that could be encountered in the work system is specified. The troubleshooting options to these problems are organized into a troubleshooting analysis.

Troubleshooting analysis, the last step in analyzing system tasks, yields the flow of diagnostic knowledge needed to respond to a sluggish, failing, or inoperative system. In that sense, it yields backward logic starting with the problem. In this final component, the system flow, parts-and-purposes, and process analysis are called on and synthesized to complete the understanding of how to troubleshoot the failed or failing system.

The troubleshooting analysis forms (see the Appendix) may appear to be more complex than they really are. The two earlier steps, system flow and system parts and purposes, are necessary to equip the analyst with deep understanding needed to advance to the troubleshooting.

Problems

Remember that process analysis is forward-looking and troubleshooting analysis is backward-looking. Process analysis explains the practical operational expertise of the system in a graphic manner. Troubleshooting analysis calls on the practical understanding of a fully operational system and uses it to think intelligently about a failed or failing system. Having the process expertise is a prerequisite to the troubleshooting expertise that allows the worker to keep the system running or get it functioning again.

Neglecting even simple troubleshooting tasks can cause performance problems in the workplace, with the consequence being serious economic losses. For example, we have seen expert salespeople purposefully troubleshoot in the middle of a major sales transaction that was failing. They ended up saving the sale (and their big commission). In a similar vein, I have seen production workers trained in troubleshooting react and recover failing food production operations to end up saving the company large losses in production and downtime.

Causes and Corrective Actions

Once potential process problems have been identified, their causes and corrective actions can be specified. They should be entered on the troubleshooting analysis form. How they are listed on the form will vary. Low-cost solutions should have priority. Low cost is calculated in terms of amount of worker time, system downtime, and materials. Clearly, the desired solutions are those requiring as little of those three elements as possible. High-probability solutions have the next priority. High-probability solutions are apparent when a problem has only a few probable causes or when one solution to that problem has been successful in the past. Troubleshooting actions should therefore be listed in the following order:

1 Low cost, high probability
2 Low cost, low probability
3 High cost, high probability
4 High cost, low probability

The generally recommended order of troubleshooting is to focus first on low-cost and then on high-probability corrective actions. In fact, low-cost, low-probability corrective actions should be examined before high-probability, high-cost actions. For example, most of us have seen the home appliance troubleshooting charts that ask you first to check whether your appliance is plugged in. The minute needed to investigate this low-cost, low-probability option could save many costly headaches. When we are confronted with a problem, most of us want to jump intuitively to the answer. The system worker's knee-jerk answer can cause serious problems in the workplace. This is especially true when the costs of certain actions are high. The value of analyzing system work tasks should be clear.

☑ **Checkpoint**

Match the term on the right that best fits each of the following elements in systems task analysis.

____ 1. System	a. Spine description
____ 2. System flow	b. Backward analysis
____ 3. System parts and purposes	c. Elements
____ 4. Process analysis	d. Forward analysis
____ 5. Troubleshooting analysis	e. Name

Answers: 1. e; 2. a 3. c; 4. d; 5. b

Purchase Order System Case Study: The Voilà Company

The following is an analysis of the purchase order system within the Voilà Company. By way of an introduction, the output was determined to be an approval to purchase (Figure 12.3). The input is not a blank purchase order form but rather an employee's need for materials or services. The purchase order process includes both conversion and transmission. Taking the determined need and recording it on a purchase order form is the conversion; forwarding the purchase order to an approval authority is the transmission.

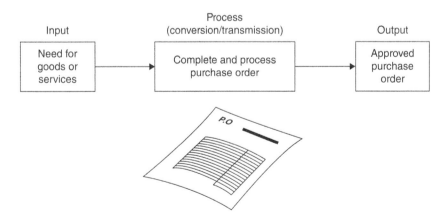

Figure 12.3 Spine of the Voilà Purchase Order System

Take the time now to review the organizational charts and the system task analysis forms, letting them speak for themselves (Figure 12.4).

One variable for an acceptable purchase order system could be a request for quotations. The specification then could be: If an item costs $1,000 or more, it must go out for quotations. This specification could be displayed on the process analysis form.

Within the existing process, the purchase cost variable requires quotations for purchases at or above $1,000. Any item costing more than $1,000 must be sent out for quotations. There is no special consequence for the plus deviation—that is, having a number of items valued at more than $1,000 on such a purchase order. However, any one item on a purchase order with a minus deviation—that is, having a value of less than $1,000—combined with other items over $1,000 would have process consequences. One consequence is the eight weeks required to complete the quotation process. Purchasing a single item of less than $1,000 takes only one day.

A second, positive minus deviation consequence is a potentially lower purchase price resulting from sending items that cost less than $1,000 out for quotation. The initial indicator is the estimated price from catalogs or from preliminary pricing per telephone request. The control is the person initiating the purchase order. Knowing the conditions, specifications, indicators, controls, and effects of deviations is the key to process control and troubleshooting.

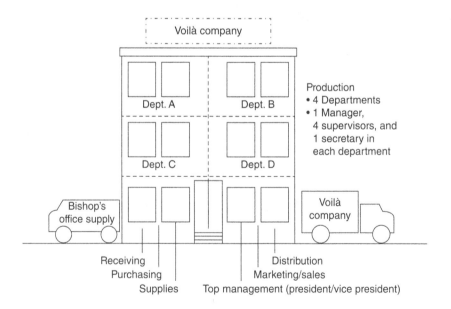

Figure 12.4a–f Voilà Company (Continued)

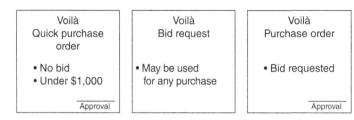

All Voilà company salaried employees can initiate purchase orders.

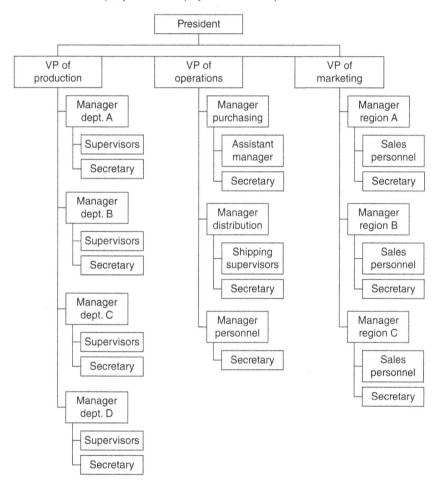

Figure 12.4b (Continued)

Systems description and flow

Job or Program __**Purchase Orders**__	Page _1_ of _1_
Location __**Voilà Company**__	Effective Date __**M/D/Y**__
Department __**Company-wide**__	Cancels Page Dated __**None**__
Analyst __**W. Blum**__	Approved By __**Jagr Rinehart**__

System purpose description
   A paper-based information system for employee to purchase needed work
   goods/services and for the company to obtain the best prices while retaining
   accurate company records.

System spine

Input Need for goods or services	→	Process(ES) Complete and process purchase order	→	Output Approved purchase order

Subsystem/Process flowchart

Figure 12.4c (Continued)

Process analysis

Job or Program **Purchase Orders**   Page __1__ of __1__
Location **Voilà Company**   Effective Date **M/D/Y**
Department **Company-wide**   Cancels Page Dated **None**
Analyst **W. Blum**   Approved By **Jagr Rinehart**

Variable	Specification	Indicator	Control	Effect of		Other information
				Plus deviation	Minus deviation	
Purchase order over $1,000	Total cost of goods/services (including taxes) $1,000 or more	Figure on bottom line of purchase order	Purchasing agent	Put out on bid	Reject quick PO	
Purchase order under $1,000	Total cost of goods/services (including taxes) less than $1,000	Figure on bottom line of purchase order	Purchasing agent	Reject quick PO	• 1 day to procure PO • Potential high cost to company for goods/services	
Bid or not bid under	Total cost of goods/services (including taxes) less than $1,000	Figure on bottom line of purchase order	Salaried employee requesting purchase	• Purchasing agent asks salaried employee if they want to bid • Potential lower costs to company	• 8 week process PO • Increased handling costs to company if put on bid	
Request for bids	Total cost of goods/services (including taxes)	Over $1,000 or request from salaried employee	Purchasing agent	Given estimated cost, send out on bid	If no estimated cost, no bid	

Figure 12.4d (Continued)

Systems parts and purposes

Job or Program __**Purchase Orders**__	Page __1__ of __1__
Location __**Voilà Company**__	Effective Date __**M/D/Y**__
Department __**Company-wide**__	Cancels Page Dated __**None**__
Analyst __**W. Blum**__	Approved By __**Jagr Rinehart**__

Part Use correct nomenclature	Purposes Explain what the part does. Also explain how it works, if not obvious.
Voilà purchase order	• Company form that specifies the vendor, goods/services, conditions, and cost of a purchase. Must be used for all company purchases of $1,000 or more, and may be used for smaller purchases
Voilà quick purchase order	• Company form that specifies the vendor, goods/services, conditions, and cost of a purchase. Can be used for purchases under $1,000
Voilà bid request	• Company form that requests a supplier's price for goods/services purchase
Salaried employees	• Company employees paid for services on an annual salary basis. Includes president, vice presidents, managers, supervisors, and secretaries
Purchasing agent	• Salaried employee responsible for approving all purchases and initiating all purchase bids. Reports directly to the VP of Operations and Finance

Figure 12.4e (Continued)

An item requiring a quotation takes eight weeks to purchase. In comparison, a nonquotation item takes one day to purchase. Work in an organization can stop because of a lack of supplies, and thus a nonresponsive purchasing system could create havoc with almost any operation. This circumstance can be averted if a nonquotation purchase order option is used instead of the quotation option. The one-day versus eight-week variation in purchase order processing is revealed to everyone through a process analysis. The one benefit of a potentially lower price with quotation is weighed against the shorter turnaround time. Troubleshooting analysis showed how this system would stop if the wrong purchase order procedure were used.

Troubleshooting analysis

Job or Program __Purchase Orders__		Page _1_ of _1_
Location ___Voilà Company___	Effective Date ___M/D/Y___	
Department ___Company-wide___	Cancels Page Dated ___None___	
Analyst ___W. Blum___	Approved By ___Jagr Rinehart___	

Problem	Cause	Corrective action
Too long to get PO approval	• Using bid PO on items $1,000 or less	• Only use bid PO when required
	• Minimum of two bids not received in a timely fashion	• Increase the number of bid requests
Paying too high prices for goods	• Not obtaining bids on $1,000 or less items	• Put $1,000 items on a bid instead of "Quick PO"
	• Not much range in bids received	• Increase number of bid requests

Figure 12.4f (Continued)

☑ **Checkpoint**

The following is a summary of the steps involved in analyzing system and system tasks. Answer the following questions: the answers provided should help you check your understanding of this detailing method.

From the example that follows, match the correct definitions and examples on the right to the system task analysis steps by placing the flow and letters A, B, C, or D by the steps (see Table 12.1).

Table 12.1 Analyzing System Tasks

System Task Analysis Step	Definition	Example
Step 1. System description and flow	Summary list of the correct names and use(s) of the component parts of the system	If this, then that
Step 2. System parts and purposes	Flow of diagnostic knowledge and purposes needed to respond to a failing or inoperative system	Control command; returns program tutoring segment

(Continued)

Table 12.1 (Continued)

System Task Analysis Step	Definition	Example
Step 3. Process analysis	Analysis of the system in operation including variables, specifications, and effects of their responses	Process vs. product
Step 4. Trouble-shooting	Breakdown of the system process into its components, tracing the information or materials from input to output	If this, then this, this, or that

Answers: Definition example Step 1. Systems description and flow D C; Step 2. Systems parts and purposes A B; Step 3. Process analysis C A; Step 4. Troubleshooting analysis B D.

Monitoring and Troubleshooting Shipping Operations: The Voilà Company

Another example of a systems task analysis involves the job a shipper. In this case the shipper is responsible for processing seat cover orders—although it could be anything you might order from any online retailer—soap, deodorant, a rug, a lamp, etc. In the end, the task might simply be described as "Process seat cover order." Figure 12.5 provides the full analysis of that task.

Tips for the Analyst

Detailing system tasks focuses on information-based system and hardware system work and is used to describe complex human expertise under abnormal conditions. Like other analysis methods, detailing system tasks provides its share of revelations. In system tasks, what appears to be obvious often ends up not being true in that the expertise is not directly observable. This is why system task analysis is needed.

The subtleties of working with systems generally prove to be difficult for both the worker and the analyst. The goal of the system task analysis is to

Systems description and flow

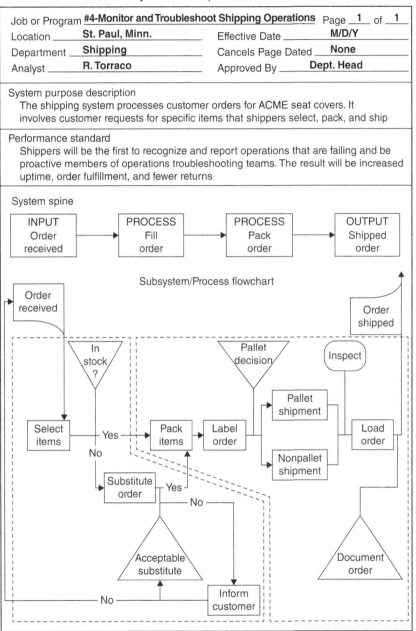

Job or Program **#4-Monitor and Troubleshoot Shipping Operations** Page __1__ of __1__

Location _____ **St. Paul, Minn.** _____   Effective Date _____ **M/D/Y** _____

Department __ **Shipping** _____   Cancels Page Dated __ **None** __

Analyst _____ **R. Torraco** _____   Approved By _____ **Dept. Head** _____

System purpose description
The shipping system processes customer orders for ACME seat covers. It involves customer requests for specific items that shippers select, pack, and ship

Performance standard
Shippers will be the first to recognize and report operations that are failing and be proactive members of operations troubleshooting teams. The result will be increased uptime, order fulfillment, and fewer returns

System spine

| INPUT | PROCESS | PROCESS | OUTPUT |
| Order received | Fill order | Pack order | Shipped order |

Subsystem/Process flowchart

Figure 12.5a–d Analysis of Shipper's System Task *(Continued)*

Systems parts and purposes

Job or Program __Shipper__   Page _1_ of _1_
Location ___St. Paul, Minn.___   Effective Date _____M/D/Y_____
Task _#4-Monitor and Troubleshoot Shipping Operations_
Department __Shipping__   Cancels Page Dated __None__
Analyst ____R. Torraco____   Approved By ____Dept. Head____

Part Use correct nomenclature	Purposes Explain what the part does. Also explain how it works, if not obvious.
Seat covers	The primary product manufactured and distributed by ACME. Referred to as *parts,* there are over 130 different seat covers offered for sale
Order ticket	The document generated by the Order Handling Department in response to customer requests for products that specifies all the data necessary to process and invoice a seat cover order
Parts bin	Large containers within which seat covers of the same part number are stored in inventory. Each part number has its own parts bin
Shipping container	Reusable, reinforced cardboard containers in which parts are shipped to customer
Conveyor belt	An automated system linking all levels and sectors of the warehouse used for the internal transport of shipping containers. Conveyor belt movement is manually started and stopped by the shipper
Flatbed cart	A manually loaded, four-wheeled vehicle used by the shipper to internally transport shipping containers within the warehouse
Shipping pallet	A portable, wooden platform for storing, moving, and shipping ACME products
Shipping mode	The method of shipment used to transport ACME products to customers. There are three shipment modes: *ground transport, air transport,* and *international air.* The mode of shipment is determined by the customer's distance from the ACME distribution point
Delivery carrier	The transportation company used to transport ACME product to customers. In addition to ACME, approved delivery carriers include UPS, DHL, and U.S. Express
Distribution director	Person responsible for the policies and direction of the distribution function in ACME
Shipping supervisor	Person responsible for overseeing total shipping process
Shipper	Person responsible for processing customer orders
Shipping clerk	Person responsible for maintaining shipping department records
Customer	Person and/or organization ordering seat covers

Figure 12.5b (Continued)

Process analysis

Job or Program __Shipper__
Location __St. Paul, Minn.__
Task __#4-Monitor and Troubleshoot Shipping Operations__
Department __Shipping__
Analyst __R. Torraco__

Effective Date _____ Page _1_ of _1_ M/D/Y
Cancels Page Dated __None__
Approved By __Dept. Head__

Variable	Specification	Indicator	Control	Effect of		Other information
				Plus deviation	Minus deviation	
Inventory status of part(s)	In stock or out of stock	Computerized display of inventory status; Presence of part(s) on warehouse shelf	Level of production of part(s), and Level of customer demand for part(s)	Excess parts in inventory	No parts in inventory	
Customer acceptance of substituted parts	Approval or disapproval of substitution	Communication with customer	Substitute parts or expedite production of parts originally ordered	N/A	Terminate processing of substituted parts	
Speed of shipment delivery	*Priority* shipment is delivered within 24 hours of order; Standard shipment is delivered within 2–3 days of order	Speed shipment selected by customer (see *delivery speed* indicated on order)	Shipper selects proper mode of shipment to meet specified delivery time	N/A	Parts delivered late	

Figure 12.5c (Continued)

Troubleshooting analysis

Job or Program	**Shipper**		Page **1** of **1**
Location	**St. Paul, Minn.**	Effective Date	**M/D/Y**
Task	**#4-Monitor and Troubleshoot Shipping Operations**		
Department	**Shipping**	Cancels Page Dated	**None**
Analyst	**R. Torraco**	Approved By	**Dept. Head**

Performance standard

Shippers will be the first to recognize and report operations that are failing and be proactive members of operations troubleshooting teams. The result will be increased uptime, order fulfillment, and fewer returns.

Problem	Cause	Corrective action
Parts not in stock	Production of parts inadequate to meet demand	Increase production of out-of stock parts
	Parts misplaced in inventory	Ensure that parts are properly stored according to ACME inventory system
Incorrect parts information on order ticket	Order ticket improperly coded	Ensure that requests for parts are confirmed with customer and coded with correct ACME part number
Incomplete parts information on order ticket	Parts information not obtained or coded by order handling department	Ensure that requests for parts are confirmed with customer. Complete *order ticket* with all information necessary for processing order
Incorrect parts information on order ticket	Change of address of current customer	Confirm customer name, account number and address with each order
	Customer account does not match customer	Confirm customer name, account number and address with each order
	Incomplete customer information on file	Do not initiate order processing without *customer status approval* from ACME sales office
Delay in shipment departure	Proper *shipment mode* unavailable	Contract for delivery through an alternate mode of shipment
	Parts for complete order unavailable	Fill order with originally specified or substituted parts
Delay of shipment en route	Mechanical breakdown	Ensure delivery carriers meet shipping contract obligations
	Order shipped to incorrect address	Ensure correct customer information on *order ticket*

Figure 12.5d (Continued)

improve the work system or enhance employee expertise so that workers will no longer be unsure of their role within the system. Following a full work system/system task analysis, what initially appeared to be a confusing and complex set of work behavior issues can become a simple set of procedural statements or a detailed process flowchart.

Having to operate both within a smooth operating system and under abnormal conditions adds dimensions to any job. These dimensions need to appear on the original job description and task inventory. System task analysis does not always result in adding more tasks to the task inventory form, however. In fact, the opposite can at times be true.

Conclusion

The process of analyzing system tasks has introduced you to a set of unique documentation tools—system description and flow, system parts and purposes, process analysis, and troubleshooting analysis.

While the tools have been used here to detail what a person needs to know and be able to do to perform part of a job—a system task—the method can be applied to any work system. Thus, these tools also have great utility for analyzing the process performance level of organization diagnosis (Chapter 6). How about a system analysis of the global market or the industry in which your company operates? Or one of the organizations in which your department operates? Or one of the processes that links workers to workers and workers to customers? System task analysis can help develop a more accurate picture and understanding of the selected system, the connections among subsystems, and the expertise required of those connections including the handoffs from one expert worker to another.

The next chapter describes the process of analyzing knowledge tasks, a method for detailing knowledge work expertise—people-to-idea interactions and people-to-people interactions. This third tool provides you additional expertise for analyzing and detailing job tasks. As you will see—as we move forward, sometimes tasks may require multiple task analyses—in different types. The advice we strongly recommend to you is to use these tools to understand workplace expertise. In other words, use these tools to capture workplace expertise—do not try to categorize everything you see in the workplace as a single kind of task. The next chapter shows you how knowledge work can be captured in its essence and sometimes revealing an overlap with system task analysis findings.

Chapter 13

Detailing Knowledge Tasks

Chapter Sections

- Process of Analyzing Knowledge Tasks
- Planning a Knowledge Task Analysis
- Task or Subject Matter
- Synthesis and Knowledge Task Description
- The Expertise and Literature Search-and-Analysis Paths
- Case of the Manager under Pressure
- Analyzing and Synthesizing the Data
- Synthesis Models
- Case Example: Knowledge Task of Responding to Sexual Harassment
- Case Example: Knowledge Task of Performing as a Shipping Team Member
- Tips for the Analyst
- Conclusion

Thus far, we have described work behaviors that have been mostly visible. The analyst has been able to follow the logic of these work behaviors by observing and questioning workers about prescribed step-by-step procedures or by studying the various information or hardware systems with which employees work. But not all work expertise is overtly observable, and not every worker knows exactly how, when, or why certain work behaviors are more effective than others. These tasks can be categorized as knowledge work. As developing economies have increasingly transitioned towards knowledge work, this chapter is critically important. More so than ever, knowledge tasks define the economies of developed countries and the importance of recognizing how to capture knowledge expertise has never been greater.

Coaching fellow workers, analyzing equipment requirements, planning projects, handling grievances—these are complex knowledge work tasks in which the individuals doing the work most often develop expertise on their own. Although some work behaviors may be observed (e.g., seeing workers scratching their heads as they think), and the results of this

DOI: 10.4324/9781003518532-17

knowledge work may be observed (subordinates walking away angry or satisfied, projects failing or succeeding), most of the work of thinking, analyzing, and deciding is not visible. The knowledge task analysis method addresses such nonvisible work expertise that centers on people–idea and people–people workplace expertise.

Why the requirement to analyze such abstract and ill-defined work behaviors? Before answering this question, let's ask a few more: Are certain investors, salespeople, decision-makers, and supervisors better at what they do than others who perform similar tasks? What are the differences between the expert and the not-so-expert performers? Would knowing these differences be beneficial in hiring, developing, and utilizing people; in job design or organizational design; and in research and strategic planning? You bet it would!

The following incident is an example of what can happen as the result of superficial task analyses.

Memorandum

To: All Department Heads From: The Boss
Subject: Training
I am pleased to announce that Dr. Consultant will be presenting a workshop on "Handling Turnover Problems." We will meet in the Holly Hotel on the 20th. As previously agreed, your department may send one representative. Send me the name of your representative by the 15th.

Manager: Hey, Hank. Look at this memo. The boss is spending big bucks on having another consultant come to town. Who shall we send this time?
Supervisor: Joe has been keeping his nose to the grindstone lately. Let him go if he wants to. Or you could send Jane. She likes to get out and meet people. She thinks it's good for her career.

Question: What work performance is lacking in this department that will be improved by Joe's or Jane's attending this workshop?
Answer: We don't know, and the manager doesn't know, either.

Many managers are beginning to recognize the limitations of short-term, shortsighted organizational development, management development, and employee training. Knowledge task analysis gives us the means to identify the substance of critical knowledge work expertise and to develop understandings that may affect performance on the job and, thus, productivity.

Process of Analyzing Knowledge Tasks

First, let's review the steps in analyzing a knowledge task, as shown in Figure 13.1, that culminate with an approved knowledge task description.

You begin by simply selecting a knowledge task or subject area of expertise that was identified through a performance diagnosis and specified as a work task on a task inventory. Your knowledge task is not procedural, nor does it involve a regularly performed systems work task. Your subject is an area of knowledge, which, if mastered, would contribute to or enhance worker expertise within the job. In one job, having knowledge of the chemistry of XYZ Company paints would improve performance. In another job, knowing the latest technology in composite materials is a requirement. In still another job, having knowledge of meeting management for building team consensus or international financial investment decision-making might be required. Any knowledge task is a candidate for analysis if success in the workplace hinges on the workers' having expertise in that realm, as determined to be required in the performance diagnosis.

This chapter, describing the process of analyzing knowledge tasks, provides examples of the major components of a knowledge task analysis. It concludes with two detailed examples that connect to other examples we have used throughout this book.

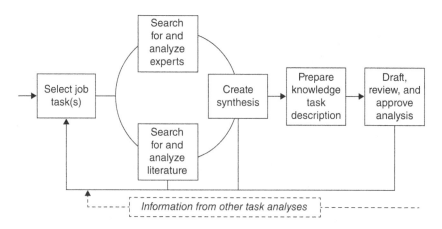

Figure 13.1 Analyzing Knowledge Tasks

Performance Standard

The knowledge task performance standard is recorded on the culminating knowledge task description form. The other knowledge task forms are in-process working documents. As with procedural and system tasks, the timing and ready source of the performance standard will vary. First, there may already be an established workplace standard used to assess this work. An existing performance standard may be specified at the task level or as part of the job-level standards. If it exists, use it. In many cases, it does not exist. The work process was improved (changed) to include this new job task. In the case of a shipping company, it is appropriate to establish the performance standard prior to the detailing of a task such as "Perform as a shipping team member." It might read as follows: "When confronted with difficult substitution problems, shipping process problems, or shortfalls in daily production, shippers will work in teams to remedy the problems using the Plan-Do-Check-Act Cycle." It is particularly interesting to note that in this example the core Shipping Department performance measures are not specifically attributable to one person and one task. The intervention proposed includes multiple jobs and tasks (more on this in the next chapter).

Following Two Paths

Having selected the knowledge task from the task inventory, you proceed with the investigation along two paths: (1) the search for and analysis of expertise among experts in the workplace; (2) the search for and analysis of knowledge in the literature by theorists, researchers, and other experts on the subject. Pursuing the investigation through experts in the organization alone will likely give you a biased and incomplete view of the knowledge task—you will be able to describe practices and constraints but will gain little understanding of the scope of the subject or of the many available alternatives. Moreover, pursuing the investigation through a literature search alone will leave the realities of the workplace out of the knowledge task analysis. Together, though, they can create a more complete picture.

In the workplace, as part of the search of knowledge worker expertise, you can study effective and ineffective workers to gain insight into the critical theories, methods, or technical knowledge connected to successful job performance. By interviewing people and presenting questionnaires, by observing the work environment and the results of particular realms of expertise, and by reviewing performance records, you assess the knowledge and expertise components of task expertise. Your goal is a complete picture of the performance area under investigation.

In the literature search path of investigation, the search-and-analysis leads you to printed materials on the subject. Reference manuals, multi-journal indexes, computer searches, the Internet, technologies like Chat GPT (though care must be taken) and bibliographies—these are your tools when searching for specific information in the literature.

You may pursue the two paths of investigation—expertise and literature—either concurrently or consecutively. You examine and analyze the expertise data collected and all the reference notes from the literature search for completeness and relevance. We have found that it is critical to put the key points of each source in your own words, not the words of the author. Next, you perform a synthesis of all the data collected. Using one or more of eight knowledge synthesis tools to be described later in this chapter, you organize, combine, and conceptualize the data into a simplified knowledge or performance model that shows the relationships among the detailed aspects of the task subject matter.

Knowledge Task Expertise Description

The final step in the knowledge task analysis method is to produce a well-organized written description of information about the subject that captures the workplace expertise of the high-performing worker. The expertise description may be in the form of either a narrative or a detailed outline. It should contain all the substantive content needed to perform properly at work, plus a list of the analyst's primary information sources.

Let's look at how one analyst planned to conduct a knowledge work analysis.

Planning a Knowledge Task Analysis

Christina Sheu, Director of Personnel Services, was given a particularly difficult assignment. James, Vice President of Human Resources at Reese Manufacturing, has informed her that three women have complained about being harassed at Reese and that this is at least two incidents too many. Martinez wants to know the legal definition of sexual harassment, whether it is a problem for women in the company, and what other companies are doing about the problem. Fortunately, Sheu is well qualified to handle the assignment. Because she has completed several such analyses in the past, she is familiar with the process of working through all the steps. This time, though, she decides to work a bit smarter—she will plan the project first. The following is her plan of action, which she may change or add to as she continues with her analysis.

Plan for Analyzing a Knowledge Task

Job: All Management Personnel, Reese. Inc.
Date: (month/day/year)
Analyst: C. Sheu

Task or Subject Matter

Defining sexual harassment and managing sexual harassment grievances
Search for and analyze experts
Interview J. Martinez, review complaint records, consult a lawyer, and distribute an anonymous response questionnaire to a sample of employees. Analyze the who, what, where, how, where, and how employees are and are not being mistreated at Reese.
Search for and analyze the literature
Identify articles, locate references, and obtain federal and state regulations. Create a database of important facts; incorporate historical, legal, cultural, and economic aspects, including definitions.
Create synthesis
Select and use at least two of the synthesis methods: one for understanding the elements and one for process understanding.
Prepare knowledge task description
Write up the details of sexual harassment in outline form for defining and understanding sexual harassment in the workplace. Include process documentation and full citations of sources.

Task or Subject Matter Identification

This step is easy. Sheu and Martinez have already conducted a performance diagnosis. The final performance proposal established the performance requirement of (1) company compliance with sexual harassment laws and (2) managers being able to follow the sexual harassment grievance process. The first performance issue required a company policy, a process, and communication at the understanding level to all employees. The second performance issue resulted in a new task for all managers in the company and the required expertise in implementing the process.

Expertise Search

For this step, Sheu knows she can interview people, observe people at work, distribute questionnaires, and search company records. She decides to do everything but observe experts at work. She figures that the expertise she is studying will often not be done openly. Because interviewing and observing are time-consuming, she will limit them to only a few key experts. Other methods she could include in her plan are talking to many people, watching people in their work environment, conducting a group interview, and so forth.

Expertise Analysis

Sheu knows from experience that this step often involves pulling her information together to see where the holes are and where else she needs to look. Other methods she can include in her plan are tossing out the extraneous data, sorting the information into useful categories, checking the information gathered from one group of people against that gathered from their supervisors, looking for contradictions, and the like.

Literature Search

In Sheu's computer files are copies of articles from the publications Human Resource Management and Human Resource Development Quarterly on the topic of sexual harassment. She keeps extensive files on current topics and is known for being able to come up with articles when others need them. When her needs go beyond her personal resources, she uses the services of the public library. She could also decide to review the reference list at the end of an article, ask the information tech to make a computer search for appropriate articles, or call the local US government information office, among other alternatives.

Literature Analysis

Years of experience have taught Sheu to keep reference notes in her computer. Notes can be grouped, sequenced, or cut in many different ways to reveal patterns of information. She will write ideas by these reference notes in her own words. This forces her to analyze the material as she reads it. She pays attention to who was quoted most often and to the material that shows up on many reference lists.

Synthesis and Knowledge Task Description

This part of Sheu's plan will be finalized when she is further along in her search. In a folder on her desk, she keeps a variety of paper forms that will help her in her synthesis and subject matter description steps.

Such plans have a way of changing as the analyst proceeds through the task. Nevertheless, creating a plan is a critical first step. Sheu visualizes carrying out her plan while she does her behavior and literature searches. She will change her plan as she discovers new possibilities for analyzing the subject matter assigned to her.

☑ **Checkpoint**

In Chapters 9 and 10, you wrote your own job description and created a task inventory. If any of the tasks requires you to interact with people or manipulate ideas or understand an unclear system in your organization, such a task qualifies as an area of expertise suitable for a knowledge task analysis. Take a few minutes to develop a plan for analyzing just one of the knowledge tasks on your task inventory.

The Expertise and Literature Search-and-Analysis Paths

Analysts who want firsthand information about people and performance must make an expertise search. They must go into the world of work to get accurate information. The task of searching and analyzing information on work behavior in an organization is a demanding one, but it can be as much fun as reading a good mystery. In analyzing knowledge tasks, the four most used search techniques are interviews, questionnaires, observations, and organizational records. Each technique has its appropriate uses, and each demands competence in searching for and analyzing information. These are the same four data collection techniques used in diagnosing workplace performance, covered in depth in Chapter 7.

No analyst worth their salt would stop a knowledge task analysis after gathering expertise data. It is equally important for you to learn from the literature what other theorists and expert practitioners have thought about or done in such situations. What behaviors, concepts, models, and rules have people found to be effective or ineffective in similar circumstances? What criteria and measuring rods have other experts used? What are some feasible alternatives? It is time for you to begin to search the literature on the knowledge task you are investigating.

Case of the Manager under Pressure

Finn Parker was notified that he must improve productivity in the Computer Hardware Division by 10% next year. Just last month he accepted, on behalf of his employees, the best division award for overall improvement of operations. But, with their competitors giving them a run for their money, the division must improve even more. At a special meeting that afternoon, one of his staff members said she had just heard her friend in another part of the company rave about a brilliant consultant who espoused situational leadership as a method for improving productivity.

She volunteered to make a literature search of the subject. She sat down at her laptop and called up a simple online search. First, she entered the keyword productivity and found 3,000,400 entries from online resources that mentioned the word productivity as the core content. She entered the term leadership next and found nearly 15,000,400 entries. She combined the two terms and queried the database again. Fewer than 7,000 entries mentioned productivity and leadership together. This was still unmanageable, so she restricted the search to 2023 and found 93 results. Aha! This was becoming a more manageable project. Finally, she asked for entries with the combined terms productivity and leadership that added either situation or situational as a modifier. Beyond the search results, she decided that further searching should be made in the peer-reviewed literature.

As she had access to a university library system, she then consulted the, Business Source Complete database. Explored might be a better word. Under productivity, she discovered references to articles titled "Managing Productivity in Organizations," "Productivity Planning and Measuring the Results," "Productivity Myths," and "After the Grid and Situationism: A Systems View." Under leadership she found articles titled "Leadership Style Training: A Myth," "Situational Leadership Theory: A Review," and "The Myth of Leadership Style Training and Planning Organizational Change." She expected to find several relevant articles among these. Perhaps she would find information that corroborated the consultant's claim. Either way, it promised to be an interesting search.

Using an Online Keyword Search

Efficiency in a literature search in this age of computer-based indexes depends on narrowing your subject matter to a few keywords, just as the analyst did in the preceding example. With such wide-ranging access to information on the Internet, narrowing the results can be an extremely difficult task. The search began by asking for a count of citations containing the term productivity or leadership, then productivity and leadership, and then productivity with situational as the modifier for leadership. In the last instance, the search located a reasonable number of citations to consider.

If the searching results in only a few articles, one book, or one-chapter additional investigation is required as the limited results will rarely present a diversity of opinions or ideas on a subject. The analyst can consider searching several additional indexes and databases next, however usually a paid subscription is required.

Using the Peer-Reviewed Indexes and Databases

Many companies and all universities subscribe to paid-access databases. These databases focus on the academic peer-reviewed research articles on essentially all topics. The following are some of the indexes and resources available in most large public or university libraries relevant to business and industry: Academic Search Ultimate, Business Source Complete, Google Scholar, *Wall Street Journal*, and Wharton Research Data Services.

Should you make a general online computer search or a search of paid-access databases? The decision is yours and may depend on your access, but we recommend that you consider doing both if you can.

Often overlooked by the new analyst are some fine opportunities to take advantage of the work done by previous researchers. Annotated bibliographies and references cited at the end of books or scholarly articles offer a wealth of resources. Reference manuals and professional handbooks will help pinpoint the topic encapsulated within the larger context—a big-picture view that an analyst sometimes ignores when pursuing detailed information about a subject.

Now aren't you curious about what you will find when you do an actual computer search on your chosen subject? Perhaps you are curious about the results of an exploratory trip through general online searches. This activity requires that you invest more time than money, but we assure you that you will be richly rewarded.

Analyzing and Synthesizing the Data

Twelve articles, four books, one video training program, and two monographs—how does anyone begin to analyze this detailed material? Perhaps you already have your own method for absorbing and classifying information.

Analyzing the Data

The following method is recommended: First, review each resource for its relevance to your subject, its timeliness, and the accuracy and usefulness of the ideas it contains. One strategy for being efficient is to review the abstracts in the cases of scholarly articles, and the introduction sections in the cases of books or more practitioner-oriented materials. Discard any resource that does not fit your needs. If you need more material, go back to the indexes and search again, though in this Information age you will likely find far more than you need and the most difficult part is deciding which sources are most relevant to your situation. Second, read the materials you have gathered and think about what you have read. What useful or important ideas, approaches, or findings did the material contain? Third, write notes about what you have read in your own words. On copies of articles, write the important ideas in the margins. Argue with the author. Ask questions and look for the answers.

Expert analysts have learned that merely highlighting the text or copying the author's words on note cards—or any other method of parroting information—does not facilitate analysis. Such tactics only add clutter and confusion to the work of analysis. The exception to this rule, of course, is your need to collect particularly relevant quotations. These you will copy into a computer-based bibliographic reference system.

At the end of your literature search, you will have a collection of important ideas, a historical perspective or context for the subject matter, an awareness of what is relevant (and what is not), and some notion of how the information may be applied effectively to accomplish the job task.

A thorough search for and analysis of expertise, plus an equally thorough search for and analysis of literature, will yield great quantities of material on cards, papers, computers, and in the memory of the analyst. What can be done with such a collection of detail to make it useful? The step of combining the results of the behavioral search with the results of the literature search is next.

Synthesizing the Data

Analysis is taking apart and examining pieces of collected data. Synthesis is pulling the pieces together again and simplifying and organizing them in a meaningful way. Synthesis is an essential step in integrating and understanding the subject matter of knowledge tasks. Just as a kite cannot be flown as a collection of pieces—tail, string, frame, and fabric—so subject matter cannot be used when it is in the form of a collection of bits of information. It is up to you, the analyst, to integrate and shape the detailed facts and impressions you have collected into usable, meaningful wholes.

Some analysts do this synthesis step easily, almost unconsciously. Others find themselves juggling vast quantities of unrelated data, which either remain up in the air or come crashing down in messy heaps. Eventually, these amateur analysts simply choose to select a few manageable pieces of the data and discard the rest. Such arbitrary choosing inevitably results in their leaving out some crucial information. The goal, then, is to include in a synthesis all of the material that is important and useful. This is not a simple step, but expert synthesizing can be learned.

Expert synthesizers were studied to determine how they approach their tasks of turning collections of information into meaningful wholes (Swanson, 1981). Even though they had trouble describing their mental processes precisely, these experts asserted that they always begin to synthesize with a rich store of information. They gather their data, they analyze it, and then they work with it. Using systematic patterns of thinking, they combine, argue with, select, compose, relate, summarize, organize, conceptualize, simplify, arrange, and fit the information into a synthesis. They find a synthesis that is logical, encompasses the data, and holds meaning for themselves and others. Some prefer using a single favorite synthesis technique; others use a variety of techniques.

Abraham Maslow probably did not set out to create his famous hierarchy of needs. He studied people and thought about them and their motivations. The notions of levels of need and of decreasing instances of need fit his data well. Violà, a hierarchy! Such a synthesis process is not magical. Synthesis models are created by disciplined minds.

Synthesis Models

A synthesis model is a structure, in words or in a document, used to organize and communicate a large amount of information—facts, ideas, impression, attitudes, or opinions—about a subject. The synthesis may be one-, two-, or three-dimensional. Because you are reading this book, I assume that you read organization-oriented publications and participate in business training seminars. Undoubtedly, you regularly encounter synthesis models. Herzberg's theory X and theory Y styles of management and Covey's seven habits of highly effective people are synthesis models. With their models, these authors have provided us with unique frameworks within which to simplify, organize, and portray great quantities of information about the subject of management. But one synthesis model will not fit all situations. You will benefit from having a variety of synthesis models at hand.

Eight Types of Synthesis Models

Expert information synthesizers describe eight synthesis techniques:

- Reflection
- Two-axis matrix
- Three-axis matrix
- Flowchart
- Events network
- Dichotomy
- Argumentation
- Graphic models

Of these, only reflection does not lend itself to capturing the synthesis on a worksheet or in a document.

Reflection. All eight synthesis methods involve reflective thinking, but here I emphasize reflection as a distinct method for considering a subject matter with the goal of seeing it in its "right" relations. The products of reflective thinking are likely to be a metaphor, a cartoon, a narrative—something that somehow "says it all." Some examples are simple; some are complicated.

Analysts who use reflection as a synthesis method have found their favorite places and times to think. Some walk; some stare out the window; some go to their favorite café and have a cup of coffee. Some think better in the morning; others at night. These reflective thinkers juggle their data until a pattern, an obvious truth, a powerful metaphor, a set of factors, or a detailed formula takes shape in their minds. When they are in control of the condition under which they think, they are also in control of the quality of their thinking.

Two-Axis Matrix. If analysts have a favorite method of synthesis, it is the two-axis matrix. The usefulness of this method is affirmed by the frequency with which it appears. If we were to pass laws against using the two-axis matrix, both business and education would grind along at a much slower pace. Figure 13.2 provides an example of a two-axis matrix that helps organize and classify the complex concept of exploitation.

When creating a two-axis matrix, you express one set of variables as a row of descriptive terms on the horizontal axis and the second set as a row of terms on the vertical axis. Where the two axes cross, cells common to two of the variables are formed. Individual cells may be filled with information or may be void. Either condition should hold some significance for the analyst. A void that should be filled is a clear signal that an important piece of data is missing.

If you think a two-axis matrix could be used to synthesize your data, use it. Run a trial two-axis matrix synthesis of the subject matter data you have collected. One analyst we know uses the two-axis matrix to organize the content of each piece of research literature he has collected. He simply writes all the titles on one axis and classifies the items of information covered in all the publications on the other axis. Then he checks off the cells by content and information source. The pattern of checks in the matrix cells provides a synthesis of the subject matter.

Three-Axis Matrix. To most of us, the three-axis matrix is not as familiar as the two-axis matrix. It is not flat like the two-axis matrix but cube-shaped—a three-dimensional object. The third axis is most often used to express a set of abstract variables such as judgment of quality, intervals of time, or types of things. Given the large quantity of individual cells produced by even the simplest of these models, it should be clear that the

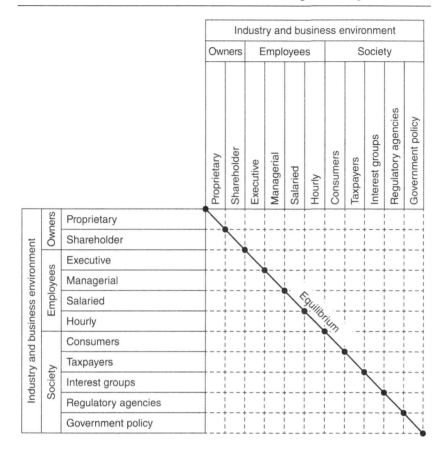

Figure 13.2 Two-Axis Matrix Showing Equilibrium Among Potential Exploitative Relationships in Industry and Business

three-axis matrix is a powerful tool for breaking down and reconnecting a very complex subject. Figure 13.3 shows a three-axis matrix used to organize the important area of human resources. Such a model could be used to think about the elements of an organizational human resource function.

The three-axis matrix can be a highly effective synthesis tool. If you find that working with three-axis matrices is easy for you, be aware that some people are not visually oriented and may have difficulty in mentally slicing this type of matrix into a series of two-axis matrices.

Flowchart. Flowcharting provides a method for organizing and synthesizing information that contains input-process–output items, decision points, direction of flow, documentation or preparation steps, and confluence and divergence. Some experts and many systems are process-oriented. If your subject matter data contain inputs and outputs, try to identify the

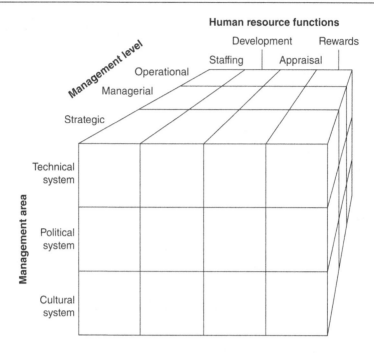

Figure 13.3 Three-Axis Matrix Depicting a Human Resource Management Cube

process elements that belong between them. Figure 13.4 displays a synthesis model of a grievance process for handling incidents of sexual harassment in a firm. It clearly shows who is responsible for what, the requirements for documentation, and the result of not resolving the grievance. Be aware that using a flowchart can create overlap between knowledge tasks and systems tasks. Depending on the level of detail desired in the flowchart, the previous chapter provides additional guidance on documenting a system as a flow-chart (more on combining task analyses in the next chapter).

Many subjects that do not appear to lend themselves easily to process-oriented thinking might benefit from such a synthesis. An analyst in a fast-food chain looked at the satisfied customers (outputs) and the hungry custom-ers (inputs). He used the metaphor of the flow of transactions from the hungry customer to the satisfied customer to synthesize the idea of solving customer problems.

Common flowcharting symbols are available in Figure 13.4 for you to copy and use. Flowcharting is especially useful for mentally and visually walking through present and future organizational processes or for identify-ing blocks. Synthesis models of critical processes can lead to better policies and improved decision-making in organizations.

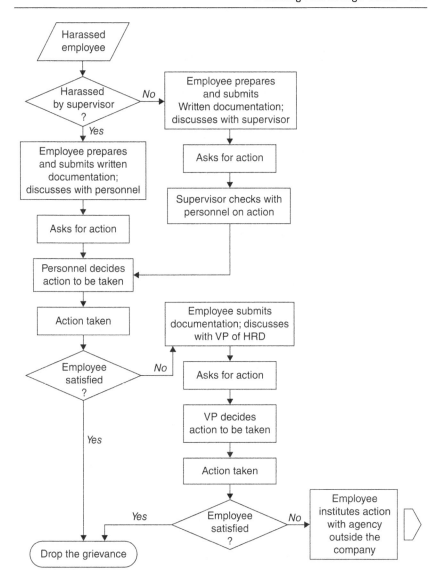

Figure 13.4 Flowchart Model

Events Network. Time-bound synthesis models that combine all the critical activities and events aimed at the achievement of goals have proven their value to planners, managers, and consultants. Events networks are systems oriented. They will help you take into account all the activity paths and events by which work toward an organizational goal is accomplished.

Often such synthesis models are used to describe what should be, rather than what is. More than a few subject matter analysts have used events networks to synthesize the masses of information needed for understanding and curing problematic systems. Figure 13.5 shows a simple events network that helped solve a major organizational problem. It seems that the subscribers deleted were the ones who had just been entered in the records. Certainly, this was no way to run a business, but no one had made the system visible. Events networks can be made as complicated and precise as necessary. Some will require a huge expanse of fine print to show the lapse of time and the depth and breadth of activities undertaken to reach a goal. Others are computerized and help calculate the total time and coordination efforts needed for large projects.

Dichotomy. One way to approach ambiguous pieces of information is to fit the data into two mutually exclusive groups or camps of contradictory issues. Argyris (1993) used this synthesis method when he subsumed management practice into two categories, espoused theory and theory in use. He used the model to show managers the contradictions between what they said and what they did.

To work with a diffuse subject area, divide the data into two parts: good or bad, yes or no, this or that. Such dichotomies help clarify unclear, undefined subjects. Difficult or ambiguous subjects, such as older workers, become more clearly defined when they are synthesized with a dichotomy model (see Figure 13.6).

Although a dichotomy can be constructed on a sheet of paper folded in half, it can be useful to create a basic form aligned with Figure 13.6. The form will be a reminder for you to use this straightforward but powerful synthesis method.

Argumentation. On the one hand, some subject matter does not lend itself to argumentation because of the irresolvable nature of the facts. Religion and politics are two cases in point. On the other hand, some seemingly irresolvable issues do lend themselves to reason and dialogue. Argumentation is a synthesis method aimed at resolving two or more theses or positions. The question "How many angels can dance on the head of a pin?" is not resolvable. But finding an answer to the question "What is the main societal condition that leads to sexual harassment?" may be possible. For purposes of illustration, we have attempted to do just this (see Figure 13.7).

Like the dichotomy technique, the argumentation method explores two opposing facets of an issue. Argumentation requires that you pose a best-possible hypothesis and its supporting logic. You then disengage from this first hypothesis and propose a counterhypothesis. The intellectual attack provides the basis for modifying and refining the original hypothesis. The process ends with a resolution to the argument. Classical debate is a prime example of argumentation. The parties to a debate must attack their own

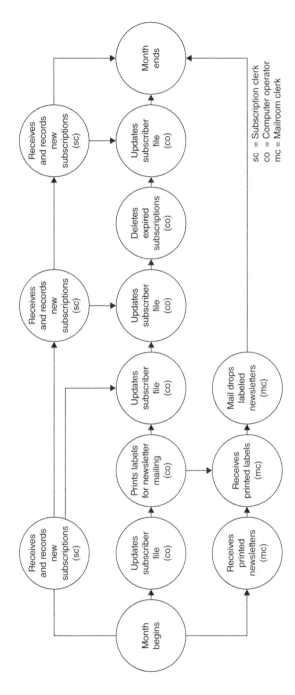

Figure 13.5 Events Network Used in Resolving and Organizational Problem

Facts related to the older worker	Facts related to the firm
Background facts—older worker	**Common employer beliefs**
• Over half of all employed Americans want to work past 65	• Age is a deterrent to productivity
• Older workers remain unemployed longer than others	• Jobs are not important to the older worker
• Chronological age is not an indicator of mental or physiological aging	• Advance in age correlated with diminishing value on the Job
• Only half of US workers are covered by a pension plan	• Older workers are rigid, inflexible, and unable to compete mentally
• Earnings account for 25% of money income of elderly	• Difficult to train older workers
• Life expectancy and financial need will keep people in the workforce longer	**Common blocks to older workers**
• The job-seeking skills of older workers are often outdated	• Benefits are frozen at age sixty-five
• Career planning programs are increasingly available	• Early retirement is encouraged by greater benefits at an earlier age
• Fewer older workers will pay into pension plans and more will draw from them (optional)	• Fixed work hours and days limit freedom to do other things
	• Older workers' experience and skills are not valued
Older worker qualities	• Must retire older workers to make room for younger workers
• Superior attendance record	**Advantages to the firm that employs older workers**
• Low accident record	• Older worker by tradition cooperates with coworkers
• Higher job satisfaction	• Reliable work habits
• Eager to learn new skills	• Experience can help firm
• Ability to learn continues into old age	• Older workers have less turnover
	• Not so concerned about advancement
Reasons older workers continue to work	• Loyalty to the job and the firm
• Financial; not making it on retirement income	• Older worker may pay in, rather than draw on benefits (optional)
• Add meaning and purpose to life	• Equal or better productivity rates
• Greater social contacts	
• Identity is tied to work	
• Look forward to longer life and better health	
• Use their education	

Figure 13.6 Dichotomy Example Involving Older Workers

arguments intellectually before those arguments are torn apart by their opponents.

Again, a simple document with headings is all that is needed to complete an argumentation. Argumentation may be an appropriate synthesis tool for your knowledge task.

Argumentation

Subject: **Sexual harassment**

Analyst:

Major hypothesis: Sexual harassment is a variety of behaviors practiced by the male members of our culture against the female members of our culture

Supporting facts and assumptions: The many instances of sexual harassment against women can be found in books and in print and broadcast media daily. The practice has harmed and will continue to harm women because policies in the workplace, the law, and the Constitution do not disallow such behaviors

Counterhypothesis: Sexual harassment is sometimes used against the male members of our culture

Supporting facts and assumptions: It is true that many men have reported incidents of being harmed by sexual harassment that was perpetrated by both men and women. This practice would seem to contradict the contention that sexual harassment is the result of a cultural bent against women

Resolution: The real issue is one of power. Men and women need to raise each other's awareness and to counter past and current views of persons as property, as objects to serve at the pleasure of those in greater power. Whenever women and men collectively organize and demand respect for their persons and their self-esteem and then work to aim all persons in society toward courtesy and fairness, sexual harassment will no longer be an acceptable behavior for anyone, no matter how powerful

---

Figure 13.7   Example of Argumentation Dealing with Sexual Harassment

Graphic Models. Organization charts, product life cycle diagrams, maps—these can be circular, spiral, triangular, treelike, wheel-shaped, and more. The sky is the limit when it comes to graphic models. When analysts capture the subject matter in a particularly fitting graphic model, it is easily understood. Such models have an appealing, visual quality that stays with even the most casual viewer. The taxonomy of performance (Figure 2.2) exemplifies the simple, visual, inclusive qualities of a memorable graphic synthesis model. For the analyst who thinks visually, the triangle could have come first to the mind's eye or through doodling on paper. Linear graphic models are particularly useful for depicting the steps or phases of a process. I created simple linear models to organize and synthesize the subject matter of this book. The difference between a linear model and a flowchart model is important. While the flowchart includes decision points, the linear model does not. In the linear model, no step is missed or skipped. All steps are experiences. Linear models can be used to capture the thinking processes of expert performers such as loan officers.

When you must create a synthesis model showing the qualities, quantities, and directions of interactions between people or machines, a graphic interaction model is appropriate. The transactional nature of much of organizational life lends itself to the use of heavy and light, dotted or dashed arrows—whatever will help synthesize the meaning of the transactions.

The form for graphic modeling can simply be a blank page with sample illustrations in the frame. This form can be easily constructed to remind you to unleash your creative faculties whenever you synthesize a subject matter graphically. Aim to make the "thousand words" of your graphic models say something important about your subject.

Caution: Although the diversity of graphic modeling offers great freedom to the subject matter analyst, far too many graphic synthesis models confuse rather than clarify. Just because a graphic model works well for you does not mean that it will work for others. Therefore, the model should not always be carried forward to the knowledge task description step.

Which Synthesis Model?

You have collected information, analyzed it, and synthesized it. The final step in the process of analyzing knowledge tasks is writing the knowledge task description, an orderly presentation of all the important, job-relevant information on a given subject. You may or may not decide to include your synthesis model in the knowledge task description. In any event, this model serves a useful purpose as the organizing framework for presenting the information. Figure 13.8 contains a knowledge task analysis of sexual harassment—a knowledge expertise description based on several synthesis models.

For credibility, the knowledge task description ends with a list of references and other sources of information that were used in the final description—not every article or book you have read. The last page of the same subject matter description lists the resources used. Some analysts prefer to develop their knowledge task descriptions in full sentences, while others prefer an outline format. A useful description will be complete, meaningfully organized, relevant to the job, and accurate. The keyword is organized. The information in a subject matter description is logically arranged and accessible. It can be used for guiding performance research, writing a report to management, or providing content for a training program.

Case Examples: Knowledge Task of Responding to Sexual Harassment

To follow through with the example we provided earlier in this chapter, here are the corresponding elements for Gradous's knowledge task of "Responding to Sexual Harassment":

Knowledge task description

Job or Program **Sexual Harassment Policies and Responses** Page **1** of **5**

Location _____**St. Paul**_____ Effective Date _____**M/D/Y**_____

Department _____**Company-wide**_____ Cancels Page Dated _____**N/A**_____

Analyst _____**D. Gradous**_____ Approved By _____**F. Parker**_____

Task: **Responding to sexual harassment**

Performance standard

To ensure legal compliance on the part of the company and to install knowledge policies and procedures for discouraging and handling sexual harassment

1. Sexual harassment is defined in several ways
   A. It takes the form of jokes, innuendos, remarks, references to women's anatomy, whistles, catcalls, or deliberately eyeing a woman up and down.
   B. Men don't perceive sexual harassment the same as women do, perhaps because of their cultural conditioning, their denial, or their lack of awareness of women's issues
   C. The *Harvard Business Review* survey of 1980 revealed that:
      1. Women may expect differential and less supportive treatment in the workplace—the men will stick together and cover for one another.
      2. Men blame the women, saying that women provoke harassment by their actions or their manner of dress
      3. Managers tend to ignore or to deny that any incidents of harassment have occurred within areas for which they are responsible; they may warn or otherwise protect the offender, whom they value as one of the team
   D. The Equal Employment Opportunity Commission has issued guidelines for executive action about sexual harassment. Sexual harassment is
      1. "A prohibited personnel practice when it results in discrimination or action against an employee on the basis of conduct not related to performance."
      2. "Deliberate or repeated unsolicited verbal comments, gestures, or physical actions of a sexual nature that are unwelcome. Within the federal government, a supervisor who uses implicit or explicit coercive sexual behavior to control, influence, or affect the career, salary, or job of an employee is engaged in sexual harassment." (federal policy 1979)
      3. Unwanted behavior on the part of one person toward another, generally taking place out of public view
      4. Unwelcome conduct of a sexual nature in the work environment that threatens one's person or one's position in the organization
      5. Ranges from looks or verbal innuendos to explicit sexual demands linked to performance evaluation and keeping one's job
      6. Verbal threats or abusive comments, leers, and nonaccidental touching.
      7. Jokes, obscenities, and double entendres about women and directed at women workers
      8. Regulations requiring women to wear provocative costumes at work and not making the same requirement of men
      9. Behavior that demeans, confuses, embarrasses, and intimidates
      10. Any sexually oriented practice that undermines a person's job performance or threatens economic livelihood

Figure 13.8a–e Example of a Knowledge Task Description Focusing on Sexual Harassment (*Continued*)

Knowledge task description

Job or Program **Sexual Harassment Policies and Responses** Page **2** of **5**	
Location _____ **St. Paul** _____	Effective Date _____ **M/D/Y** _____
Department _____ **Company-wide** _____	Cancels Page Dated _____ **N/A** _____
Analyst _____ **D. Gradous** _____	Approved By _____ **F. Parker** _____

E. Sexual harassment is not:
  1. Mutual sexual behavior between consenting adults who happen to work in the same organization. (Such behavior between persons of unequal status is open to the question of coercion.)
  2. Making a fuss over an office romance that has ended
  3. Being embarrassed or feeling the tension of sexual attraction to another person and choosing not to act on it

II. Sexual harassment can be seen as an issue of power
  A. Harassment is by definition integrated within a social context in which women as a group have a disproportionately small share of wealth and authority and social advantages compared to men as a group
  B. As power increases, the perceived ability to act on one's wishes without suffering the consequences increases
  C. Persons in hierarchical positions of authority (usually men) can use their roles to place conditions of compliance (sexual or otherwise) on their subordinates
  D. In hierarchies, where there are power differentials, top management may fail or refuse to see the destructive actions of subordinates-actions that result in high turnover rates and that fail to make use of the full competencies of 40% of the workforce
  E. Women must use energy to fend off unwanted behaviors instead of applying their capacities to performance on the job
  F. Sexual harassment may be seen as a power play, a conscious or unconscious way of expressing authority and dominance
  G. *Harvard Business Review* readers rate supervisors' behaviors as more serious and threatening than the same behaviors by peers
  H. Men conspire to keep silent about one another's conduct in this area—the power to obscure or deny reality

III. Some believe that the sexual harassment issue is a side issue
  A. Many fear that this issue might get in front of other minority rights issues.
  B. Some say that at least a few women ask for such treatment through a desire for some personal advantage such as a promotion or special favors
  C. At least one woman has been found guilty and punished for sexually harassing a man
  D. Some say this exemplifies the power of a special interest group to exaggerate the importance of a minor reality
  E. Cries of sexual harassment could be used as a defense to cover issues of incompetence and poor work performance

IV. Sexual harassment can be traced throughout the history of the human race.
  A. Contrary to anthropologists' claims, the lifestyle of the cave dwellers may not have depended on the superior strength of the male hunters so much as on the steady food gathering behaviors of the females

Figure 13.8b (Continued)

Knowledge task description

Job or Program **Sexual Harassment Policies and Responses** Page **3** of **5**

Location _____**St. Paul**_____ Effective Date _____**M/D/Y**_____

Department _____**Company-wide**_____ Cancels Page Dated _____**N/A**_____

Analyst _____**D. Gradous**_____ Approved By _____**F. Parker**_____

    B. In the middle ages, lords claimed the "right of first night" with the brides of their serfs

    C. Slave owners often shared their women slaves with male visitors

    D. Women working in cottage industries were dependent on the goodwill of middlemen who brought them supplies and picked up the finished goods—men who threatened the women with cutting their supplies or with bringing inferior materials, and so on

    E. During the Industrial Revolution, women in factories were denied privacy to go to the bathroom and then were blamed for unseemly behavior

    F. In 1915, Carrie Davis, a housemaid, shot her employer because he "ruined her character"

    C. From 1950 to 1965, women worked in the "pink ghetto" as waitresses, sales clerks, and office workers and suffered sexual harassment in silence—this after being welcomed as workers during World War II

V. The action against sexual harassment beings

    A. In 1964, the Civil Rights Act made sex discrimination illegal and sexual harassment came to be seen as a subissue of discrimination

    B. In 1976, *Redbook* magazine surveyed its readers on the subject of sexual harassment and experienced an avalanche of replies

    C. In 1978, Judge Finesilver found Johns-Manville guilty of permitting sexual harassment in the workplace

    D. In 1980, the Equal Employment Opportunity Commission issued guidelines defining and outlawing sexual harassment in the workplace

VI. Many of the legal solutions for sexual harassment are costly and relatively ineffective

    A. Under Section 703 of title VII of the Civil Rights Act of 1964, which prohibits discriminatory employment practices based on race, sex, religion, or national origin, only a handful of suits have been tried

    B. The EEOC guidelines of April 1980 define and prohibit sexual harassment for private employers of fifteen or more employees and all federal, state, and local government workers

    C. Harassed persons may file civil suits under tort law because employers are deemed responsible for the actions of their employees; however, strong prevention programs by employers may mitigate against collecting damages.

    D. In the case of rape or assault, the employer may be held responsible for failing to provide a safe place to work

    E. In Minnesota today when a woman files a civil suit and it is her word against his, she is presumed to be telling the truth of her experience of sexual harassment

    F. The law is male oriented and may perceive certain male behaviors to be socially acceptable

Figure 13.8c (Continued)

Knowledge task description

Job or Program **Sexual Harassment Policies and Responses** Page _4_ of _5_	
Location _____**St. Paul**_____ Effective Date _____**M/D/Y**_____	
Department _____**Company-wide**_____ Cancels Page Dated _____**N/A**_____	
Analyst _____**D. Gradous**_____ Approved By _____**F. Parker**_____	

VII. Collective action by women is possible
    A. In 1977, Working Women United Institute was formed as a network for referrals, legal advice, and job counseling service for victims of sexual harassment
    B. Picketing and leafleting to expose sexual harassment (public embarrassment) are somewhat effective in convincing management that this is a personnel issue
    C. Unions represent at least the potential for protection by providing sanctions through the contracting process

VIII. Action internal to an organization is possible
    A. Organizational leaders can establish policies, guidelines, and grievance processes to limit sexual harassment in the workplace
    B. Such policies must cover all types of harassment
    C. The grievance process must be simple and visible to encourage legitimate complaints
    D. To assure effectiveness, the Chief Executive Officer must endorse the policies and processes, action must be taken against the offenders, and the victim must be protected against retaliation
    E. The organization must offer support through the process so that the injured employee does not exit the organization or seek outside support before exhausting internal steps
    F. Documentation on the part of the victim is essential because it forces the organization to behave responsibly
    G. Women must begin to tell the men they work with that a remark is not funny, a touch is not welcome, and a gesture is not appropriate, but they will not do so unless organizational policies support and make clear what behaviors are not permitted

Figure 13.8d (Continued)

Knowledge task description

Job or Program **Sexual Harassment Policies and Responses**   Page **5** of **5**

Location _____ **St. Paul** _____	Effective Date _____ **M/D/Y** _____
Department ___ **Company-wide** ___	Cancels Page Dated _____ **N/A** _____
Analyst _____ **D. Gradous** _____	Approved By _____ **F. Parker** _____

Resource list

Print materials

Backhouse, C., & Cohen, L. *Sexual harassment on the job: How to avoid the working woman's nightmare.* Englewood Cliffs, NJ: Prentice Hall, 1981.

Collins, E. C., & Blodgett, T. B. "Sexual harassment ... some see it ... some won't." *Harvard Business Review*, March–April 1981, pp. 77–94.

Cunningham, M. "Corporate culture determines productivity." *Industry Week*, May 4, 1981, pp. 82–84, 86.

Driscoll, J. B., & Bova, R.A. "The sexual side of enterprise." *Management Review*, July 1980, pp. 51–54.

"Sexual harassment lands companies in court." *Business Week*, October 1, 1979, pp. 120, 122.

Renick, J. C. "Sexual harassment at work: Why it happens, what to do about it." *Personnel Journal*, August 1980, pp. 658–662.

Rowe, M. P. "Dealing with sexual harassment." *Harvard Business Review,* May–June 1981, pp. 42–44, 46.

Safran, C. "Sexual harassment: The view from the top." *Redbook*, March 1981, pp. 45–51.

Woodrum, R. L. "Sexual harassment: New concern about an old problem." *Advanced Management Journal*, winter 1981, pp. 20–26.

Zemke, R. "Sexual harassment: Is training the key?" *Training, February* 1981, pp. 22, 2728, 30–32.

Interviews

Fred Gradous, Remmele Engineering, Inc.
Larry Johnson, Dorsey, Windhorst, Hannaford, Whitney, & Halladay Dixie Lindsey, General Mills, Inc.

Figure 13.8e (Continued)

Case Example: Knowledge Task of Performing as a Shipping Team Member

We have also used examples from the job of "Shipper" in Viola Inc. in this book. By itself, Figure 13.9 illustrates an analysis for the knowledge task of "Performing as a Shipping Team Member."

Analysis plan for knowledge task
Step 1. Select job task • Achieve teamwork and greater collaboration among shippers **Step 2. Search for and analyze exports** • Interview 3 shippers and 3 managers about teamwork • Consult a teamwork expert • Questionnaire to current and former Acme team participants • Analyze the who, what, when, where, how, and why of teamwork among shippers **Step 3. Search for and analyze literature** • Review research on teamwork • Read recent teamwork literature • Call industry association for information on teamwork, if any • Write important ideas from the literature in my own words • Include prerequisites, methods, and outcomes of successful teamwork **Step 4. Create synthesis** • Select and use one or more of the methods for synthesizing information **Step 5. Prepare knowledge task description** • Write a comprehensive, detailed outline or narrative on teamwork based on the analysis and synthesis steps

Figure 13.9a –h Example of a Shipper's Knowledge Task *(Continued)*

Knowledge task description

Job or Program **Shipper**	Page **1** of **7**
Location **St. Paul, Minn.**	Effective Date **(M/D/Y)**
Department **Shipping**	Cancels Page Dated **(M/D/Y or "None")**
Analyst **R. Torraco**	Approved By **Department head**

Task #6-Perform as shipping team member

Performance standard
When confronted with difficult substitution problems, shipping process problems, or shortfalls in daily production, shippers will work in teams to remedy the problems using the Plan-Do-Check-Act Cycle

1. Definitions of *team, teamwork*, and *team building*
  A. A *team* is a group of people who have as their highest priority the accomplishment of team goals. This is contrasted with a nonteam, which tends to be a group of people with personal agendas that are more valuable to the individuals than to the group as a whole. Teams are characterized by members who support each other, collaborate freely, and communicate openly and clearly with one another
  B. Common kinds of teams:
    (1) *Committees* usually serve as investigative or advisory bodies reporting to the person or agency that has appointed or organized them
    (2) *Task forces* are temporary problem-solving groups formed to deal with issues or projects that cross functions or lines of authority. A task force may, for its life, be full time or part time
    (3) *Process improvement teams* are groups of employees and supervisors who identify and solve problems to increase the effectiveness of their work groups through improved quality and higher productivity (adapted from Quick, 1992)
  C. *Teamwork* is a method by which two or more people accomplish work. It is characterized by collaboration, shared bases of power and decision making, clear and open methods for communicating and dealing with conflict, and consensus on the goals to be achieved
  D. *Team building* is the attempt to assist the work group to become more adept at its own problems by learning, with the help he of a process consultant, to identify, diagnose, and solve its own problems (Baker, 1979)
  E. *Team building* is a set of activities whereby members of a work team:
    (1) begin to understand more thoroughly the nature of group dynamics and effective teamwork, particularly the interrelationship of process and content, and
    (2) learn to apply certain principles and skills of group process toward greater team effectiveness (Burke, 1982)

2. The benefits and importance of teamwork
  A. Teamwork results in benefits both for the members of a team and for the organization in which they work. Collaboration—people working well together and supporting one another-is a primary benefit of teamwork
  B. Improved communication is a benefit of teamwork. Team members communicate openly with information flowing freely in all directions up, down, and laterally

Figure 13.9b (Continued)

Knowledge task description

Job or Program __Shipper__	Page _2_ of _7_
Location __St. Paul, Minn.__	Effective Date ___(M/D/Y)___
Department __Shipping__	Cancels Page Dated __(M/D/Y or "None")__
Analyst ___R. Torraco___	Approved By ___Department head___

> C. Teamwork allows a more efficient application of resources and talents to identifying and solving problems. With the cooperation and pooling of resources by team members, whenever one member lacks resources or expertise, another member is there to pick up the slack. Open communication prevents duplication of effort
>
> D. Quality improvement is often the result of teamwork. Team membership instills team pride in members, and they want to make the team look as good as possible. Solving work problems using teamwork, decision making based on data, and the support of top management can result in tangible improvements in quality
>
> 3. Prerequisites for successful teamwork include the following:
>   A. Teamwork and team-building efforts must be supported by top management. The organizational culture must reflect a democratic style of leadership
>   B. Successful teams require the support and commitment of the formal team leader(s). Team leaders must have expertise in team building and in all phases of team development
>   C. Team members must want involvement in teams—that is, participation in teams must be voluntary, not through involuntary assignment.
>   D. Teams are more highly motivated if they are currently facing problems. Conversely, teams lose focus and interest in the absence of problems requiring solutions
>   E. Successful teams require adequate time for team development (approximately a year) and adequate time to accomplish their prescribed goals
>
> 4. The stages of team growth (adapted from Scholtes, 1988)
>   A. *Forming.* This initial stage is characterized by a transition from individual to team member status and by the formal and informal testing of the team leader's guidance. At team formation, there may be feelings of pride in team membership, feelings of anxiety, fear, and suspicion about what lies ahead, as well as some anticipation and optimism about the team's capabilities
>   B. *Storming.* This is likely the most difficult stage for the team. Members realize the task is different and perhaps more difficult than they expected. Not yet exhibiting true teamwork, members rely solely on individual experience rather than collaboration to address problems. Other behaviors exhibited during the storming phase include resistance, defensiveness, questioning the selection of the project and of the other members who appear on the team, disunity among members, and lack of consensus on the purpose and goals for the group

Figure 13.9c (Continued)

Knowledge task description

Job or Program **Shipper**	Page **3** of **7**
Location **St. Paul, Minn.**	Effective Date **(M/D/Y)**
Department **Shipping**	Cancels Page Dated **(M/D/Y or "None")**
Analyst **R. Torraco**	Approved By **Department head**

C. *Norming*. Initial tension and competition are replaced by acceptance of the team, acceptance of individual roles and membership on the team, and relief that everything is apparently going to work out. As members begin to confide in each other and identify common experiences, a sense of trust and team cohesion begins to develop. Team members collectively establish team ground rules and boundaries (the "norms"), and finally the group can begin to make significant progress in addressing the project

D. *Performing*. At this point, members have discovered each other's strengths and weaknesses and begin to exhibit a collaborative approach to solving problems. Change necessary for team progress is more readily identified and implemented. Since the team now has the ability to prevent or work through obstacles to performance, work is being done and group goals are beginning to be achieved. Members feel pride and satisfaction at the team's progress

5. Team-building roles (adapted from Quick, 1992)

A. *Supporting*. As the team develops, there is a realization that support and encouragement of other members results in more and better contributions from them. Mutual support among members leads to an increased sense of self-worth and enhanced team performance

B. *Confronting*. It is not uncommon for an individual's behavior to be detrimental to team progress. One member may attempt to prevent or discredit the contributions of another. Unkind comments about members or their ideas may surface. Team members can constructively confront this undesirable behavior, as long as the confrontation is confined to the *undesirable behavior* and not directed at the offender's *personality*

C. *Gatekeeping*. At times, group dynamics are such that certain members monopolize a discussion so completely that others can't enter it or are so intimidated that they remain silent. In this case, a gatekeeper may say to monopolizers, You have clearly expressed quite a number of ideas. I'd like to hear what some others have to say. For example, Carol appears to have something she wishes to say"

D. *Mediating*. Intense or prolonged disagreement can occur during interactions among team members. When disagreement between members becomes so polarized that they can't move toward each other's point of view, mediation between the members is needed. Another team member acting as the mediator intervenes to illuminate and clarify each point of view. First, the mediator asks for permission from opposing members to interpret their positions, and then does so for each side of the argument. After clarification, the mediator asks if the clarified versions reflect each disputant's argument. Each member then has an opportunity to revise or correct what was said. This often clarifies real differences or areas of disagreement that may not have been acknowledged. When team members get stuck in personal disagreements, mediation can break the impasse and move discussions forward

Figure 13.9d (Continued)

Knowledge task description

Job or Program **Shipper**	Page **4** of **7**
Location **St. Paul, Minn.**	Effective Date **(M/D/Y)**
Department **Shipping**	Cancels Page Dated **(M/D/Y or "None")**
Analyst **R. Torraco**	Approved By **Department head**

E. *Summarizing*. During group problem-solving sessions, it is not uncommon for groups to get lost in details and become confused as to the overriding issue or problem. During such confusion, a team member intervenes to sum up what has been discussed so far. This summary allows the group to reframe the real question to be answered and restores confidence in the group's purpose. Other members may add to the summary and provide additional data on which further work can be based

F. *Process observing*. The "processing" of group interaction is a review of what the group is doing effectively and what the group is doing ineffectively. The process observer is usually a facilitator who provides members with feedback, both positive and negative, about how they are functioning as a team. "Process" information highlights the team's strengths and weaknesses and allows the team to improve its effectiveness

6. Team-subverting roles (adapted from Quick, 1992)
   A. *Shutting off*. Shutting off is a way that one member can quickly silence another. Through interruption or at a pause in discussion, the speaker is ignored or contradicted by another member. The speaker often responds to shutting-off behavior with anger or withdrawal. Because of the personal animosity it engenders, this behavior has a destructive effect on teambuilding efforts
   B. *Dominating*. Domination is a common obstacle to the effective functioning of teams. The member in the role of dominator wants to take over the team discussion and may be heavyhanded in his or her efforts to do so. The major obstacle to the continued effectiveness of the team is that the dominator is more interested in pursuing personal agendas than in achieving the team's goals. If the dominator succeeds in monopolizing the team discussion, participation of other members will noticeably decline
   C. *Labeling*. Labeling is the practice of putting a label on behavior or suggesting that another member has a particular attitude or unworthy motive. Labeling is very counterproductive to team progress because it elicits defensiveness and negative feelings among team members. Labeling can sidetrack useful discussions and even cause a team discussion to be terminated
   D. *Naysaying*. Unfortunately, the power of no often has disproportionate weight in many team deliberations. The team may be considering an option or proposal that has merit but that may also be unusual or risky. In this situation, the team may be susceptible to the naysayer who, for whatever reason, is opposed to idea arid provides the team with a reason for abandoning it. Naysaying is a shortsighted and counterproductive behavior. For the moment, it allows the team to escape from meaningful decision—making

Figure 13.9e (Continued)

Knowledge task description

Job or Program **Shipper**   Page **5** of **7**

Location **St. Paul, Minn.**   Effective Date **(M/D/Y)**

Department **Shipping**   Cancels Page Dated **(M/D/Y or "None")**

Analyst **R. Torraco**   Approved By **Department head**

---

7. Elements and practices of successful teams

A. The problem-solving process can become more productive in the following ways:

   (1) Keep the group small. Full participation is more readily achieved in a small group than in a large group. Experts recommend that optimum group size is between five and nine members (Quick, 1992)

   (2) Create a plan for team action with input from members. The team's action plan sets a timetable for achieving team objectives and determines what advice, assistance, materials, training, and other resources the team will need

   (3) Announce team meetings in advance. Define the issue to be addressed at the meeting and encourage r members to come prepared with ideas the and possible solutions. Individual preparation maximizes the time and energy for group work and decision making

   (4) Groups are generally better at evaluating ideas than generating them; individuals are better at coming up with ideas. Encourage members to discuss an idea with the group, not with the originator. Other members should not put undue pressure on the originator to defend or argue for the idea

   (5) Team members should have cues or reminders about the objectives toward which the team is working. Timely agendas or key words that have meaning for the group should be referred to or made visible in the team's work area

B. Optimal group dynamics and teamwork can be developed in the following ways:

   (1) Achieve consensus on team goals. The goals of the team should be consistent with its original mission. Goals should be clarified and discussed until full consensus among members is achieved. Unacceptable or unworkable goals must be modified or eliminated from the team's agenda

   (2) Establish basic guidelines for team behaviors. Team members should agree on a few basic guidelines for how members will work together as a group. Written guidance clarifies what behaviors the group considers desirable versus those it considers unacceptable. For example, a broad range of ideas and opinions should be encouraged, while individual domination of discussion and criticism of other members should be identified as unacceptable

   (3) Define the roles of team members. Once the talents, experiences, and interests of team members are apparent, work will proceed most efficiently if team roles are clearly defined. The roles of team leader, facilitator, technical expert(s), quality advisor, and others must be formally designated

   (4) Encourage discussion and constructive criticism of ideas and proposals. If necessary, rephrase criticism in a positive way. The nature of criticism is such that it is often expressed in negative terms. Yet critical thinking is needed to reach team goals

Figure 13.9f (Continued)

Knowledge task description

Job or Program **Shipper**	Page **6** of **7**
Location **St. Paul, Minn.**	Effective Date **(M/D/Y)**
Department **Shipping**	Cancels Page Dated **(M/D/Y or "None")**
Analyst **R. Torraco**	Approved By **Department head**

(5) As an integral part of group development, all team members should achieve awareness of the group process and experience their own sense of responsibility for team progress. All team members are accountable for teamwork and for contributing to the achievement of group goals. Any member can intervene to correct a problem in how the team is functioning. The team's process and outcomes are the responsibilities of each individual member (adapted from Scholtes, 1988)

8. Evaluating and rewarding teamwork

A. The team's performance must be based on the progress of the team against agreed-on goals, not on the activity of individual members. Evaluation of performance that is activity based gives a self-defeating message: that the results of teamwork are not important Evaluation should encourage collaboration and teamwork. Team performance can be evaluated in several ways

   (1) The team as a whole should track their progress against the objectives they have established. This occurs most effectively when progress charts based on the initial objectives and timetable are regularly assessed and updated by the team

   (2) The performance of individual team members can be evaluated by peers. Peer evaluation is valuable because members are knowledgeable about the impact of the behavior of others. Peer evaluation can be both written and oral and can occur individually or through a group evaluation session. The advantage of a group setting is that all team members are present to hear feedback and are free to ask a member-evaluator why they have been given a particular assessment of performance. Of course, a disadvantage of evaluation in group settings is that a member who receives several unfavorable performance assessments may feel threatened and react negatively to an open evaluation

   (3) The most commonly used method is evaluation of the individual member by the team leader. This is based on the traditional model of performance appraisal where feedback on performance comes primarily from a single evaluator. This method carries with it the biases of evaluator perceptions (e.g., "halo effects"), low recognition of systems effects on individual performance, and other methodological problems

B. Rewarding successful team performance is a matter of the equitable distribution of rewards *to the team as a whole*. Again, the rewards and reinforcement of performance are based on team output, not individual input. There are many possible ways of rewarding a team for its efforts:

   (1) Meaningful praise and recognition of the team from top management

   (2) Monetary and salary rewards; time off from work; new and better furnishings and equipment

   (3) More responsibility and control over the scheduling and performance of work

   (4) Training and development for new or advanced work responsibilities; career opportunities for team members

   (5) Further opportunities for the team to address meaningful work problems

Figure 13.9g (Continued)

Knowledge task description

Job or Program **Shipper**	Page _7_ of _7_
Location **St. Paul, Minn.**	Effective Date **(M/D/Y)**
Department **Shipping**	Cancels Page Dated **(M/D/Y or "None")**
Analyst **R. Torraco**	Approved By **Department head**

Resource list

Print materials

Baker, H. K. (1979). The hows and whys of team building. *Personnel Journal*, 58, 367-370.

Burke, W. W. (1982). *Organization development: Principles and practices.* Boston: Little, Brown.

Dyer, W. C. (1987). *Team building: Issues and alternatives.* Reading, MA: Addison-Wesley.

Quick, T. L. (1992). *Successful team building.* New York: AMACOM.

Scholtes, P. R. (1988). *The TEAM Handbook: How to use teams to improve quality.* Madison, WI: Joiner Associates

Interviews:

Larry Blomberg, Shipper, Acme, Inc., St. Paul, MN 55101

Ken Kirschner, Shipper, Acme, Inc., St. Paul, MN 55101

Eric Lauderdale, Shipping Supervisor, Acme, Inc., St. Paul, MN 55101

Susan Mancusi, Shipper, Acme, Inc., St. Paul, MN 55101

Ronald Reed, Shipping Supervisor, Acme, Inc., St. Paul, MN 55101

Barbara Jensen, Johnson & Associates, 168 Fifth St., S.E., Minneapolis, MN 55414

Frederick Tracey, Action Consulting Group, 1211 Franklin Blvd., Chicago, IL 60609

Christopher Voeltz, Distribution Manager, ACME Seat Cover Co., St. Paul, MN 55101

Figure 13.9h (Continued)

☑ **Checkpoint**

The following exercise is included so that you can check your understanding of the procedure used in completing a knowledge task analysis. In the spaces provided, write the letter of the knowledge task analysis step (a–g) that captures the analysis activity (1–15). Compare your responses with those at the end of the list.

a Task or subject matter
b Expertise search (methods and sources)
c Expertise analysis methods
d Literature search (methods and sources)
e Literature analysis methods
f Synthesis model(s)
g Knowledge task description (format and features)

___ 1. Decided that some important features of organization could be shown by a diagram of the numbers and types of communications between departments
___ 2. Discarded two articles from among twenty on the topic of job design because they were written by authors who did no research
___ 3. Listed in a well-organized format all that is known about the potential for job redesign in this organization so that a coherent report to the vice president could be written
___ 4. Listed the sources of information so that others could verify or duplicate the same search-and-analysis steps
___ 5. Wrote a complete outline of the information gathered and organized
___ 6. Compared the results of 20 interviews
___ 7. Realized that she had defined eight factors that showed the vice president was on the right track in challenging the current organizational design and eight factors that showed he should take another look before making changes
___ 8. The company vice president reported from his performance improvement proposal that "this organization needs some organizing."
___ 9. Interviewed many people to find out where in this organization certain policies are developed
___10. Made a two-axis matrix showing the relationships among several dimensions in common among various organizational theories, and the reality of those same dimensions in this organization

___11. Found two books and five articles on organizational theory

___12. Watched an organizational development training film

___13. Examined the differences between the organizational theories of two well-known experts

___14. Sent a questionnaire to one hundred employees asking them to identify who makes certain policies in this organization

___15. Checked the results of the employee questionnaire against the results of the interviews

Answers: 1. f; 2. e; 3. g; 4. g; 5. g; 6. c; 7. f; 8. a; 9. b; 10. f; 11. d; 12. d; 13. e; 14. b; 15. c

Tips for the Analyst

We did not say that analyzing knowledge work tasks would be easy. Neither do we want to leave you with the impression that the process is too difficult. To succeed as a performance analyst, you will need perseverance and curiosity to explore many aspects of a subject and performance at work as it relates to that task; research skills for locating information in the literature and in the organization; an analytical bent for taking information apart and discovering the relationships of the pieces to one another; the courage to live with ambiguity—you must not feel the need to oversimplify or to pull the data together too soon; the capacity to tolerate disorder while finding meaning and organization in the data; the power to organize, combine, limit, and see new arrangements, frames, or ideas in the data; and the ability to synthesize.

Conclusion

Knowledge work has become the most critical work in today's economy. Knowledge work requires expertise—the capacity to do things with knowledge, not just to have information. The most important feature of the knowledge task analysis method is the connection of information to expertise and of both to performance.

Chapter 14

Multidimension and Cross-Function Tasks

Chapter Sections

- **Multidimension Tasks**
- **Cross-Function Tasks**
- **Conclusion**

The contemporary management literature describes the struggle organizations have in connecting their leadership roles and organization systems to intellectual capital and workplace expertise of individual contributors—the fuel of an organization (Locke & Pearce, 2023). The previous three chapters provide specific tools for detailing the three types of work tasks. Additional thoughts acknowledge that:

- Some work tasks are multidimensional requiring more than one task analysis tool.
- Some work tasks are cross-functional with coworkers each having discrete roles within the task.

This chapter goes beyond the established job description, task inventory, and task analysis approaches. The focus here is to highlight two variations among work tasks.

It is becoming more common in today's workplace to encounter tasks that might be part procedure, part system, and part knowledge—or any combination of the three. All work tasks do not have to fit neatly into one of the three task analysis categories. Some tasks require more than one-task analysis approach in order to achieve completeness.

It is also important to recognize individual tasks can involve more than one job holder. Some tasks reach across jobs and require collaboration across job functions to achieve the intended performance outcomes.

DOI: 10.4324/9781003518532-18

Multidimension Tasks

There are some cases in which an effort to fully document expertise can benefit from more than one type of task analysis. Task examples could include (1) making xyz computer entries and (2) facilitating strategic planning.

Making XYZ Computer Entries

This typical computer-related task will most likely require unique and important task details to be successful. The specific workplace computer hardware and software will require linear steps to complete the entry task. This aspect calls upon *procedure task analysis* for documentation. The judgment as to what data should be entered would be specified through *knowledge procedure analysis*. Together, the two analyses create complete expertise documentation.

We have all experienced instructions and manuals that run through a stream of step, step, step details without us ever knowing about data input decisions along the way.

Facilitating Strategic Planning

A worker in charge of organizational strategic planning has a complex job. The task of facilitating a strategic planning session with a team of high-level coworkers has several dimensions. First,

- Strategic planning expertise
- Group process facilitation expertise

The obvious interesting point is that there are two major realms tied into this work task. By the task title, facilitating is the task's main focal point. Another task on pure strategic planning will exist that most likely calls upon *knowledge task analysis* for strategic planning conceptual documentation and *system task analysis* for organization design documentation. In contrast, group process facilitation would likely utilize the same two task analysis tools but aimed at facilitation expertise.

It is common for people to look at work or life tasks through single lenses. The computer geek can rattle off steps and ignore the fact that she/he has a deep conceptual understanding of "the" system that allows them to put those steps into context. That person jumps right to those steps when sharing their expertise.

Cross-Function Tasks

The notion of continuously improving organization processes has become deeply ingrained in organizations (Quick, 2019). Although varying in approaches, the idea that processes should be identified, analyzed, and improved is deemed essential for improving performance. The methodologies and tools of process improvement have been proven to be quite effective (see Chapter 7).

However, one problem with process improvement strategies is that they often have weak links to specifying and developing the expertise required of multiple functions in the process. This is because they involve the expertise of more than one individual connected through a process to achieve a larger task outcome. Combining the tools presented in this book up to this point is needed to document the varying expertise required for a task that cuts across job functions. We call these cross-function tasks. A basic observation is that worker expertise should be focused on the tasks related to core organization processes—and those core process tasks often involve multiple workers.

The Health Care Insurance Sales case in Chapter 7 illustrated tasks involved multiple workers Figure 14.1. The figure illustrates how 22 flow-charted tasks were shared among six job holders.

At the point of execution, multiple workers simultaneously focus cross-function tasks. Their roles can vary. For example, one worker carries out the procedure steps and another has the responsibility of assessing/reporting success. These two elements are hard-wired to the work task with one aspect requiring procedure task analysis and the other knowledge task analysis. In another organization work requires oversight task responsibility on one worker in another, there are two. Each team member to have clarity of each other's performance expectations. Especially in the context of a technology change, with high stakes, that clarity is crucial.

Workers within Process	Phase 1: Integrated Flowchart of a Major Business Procedure As It Exists (22-process-step example)																					
	1	2	3	4	5	6	7	8	9	10	11	12	13	14	15	16	17	18	19	20	21	22
Job 1.	X		X		X		X					X					X	X				
Job 2.			X					X		X	X			X	X							
Job 3.	X	X		X				X		X			X			X	X	X	X		X	
Job 4.			X	X		X	X											X				
Job 5.	X			X	X	X		X		X						X	X	X			X	
Job 6.			X		X			X		X			X	X			X	X	X		X	X

(Process Activities over Time)   X means contributor.

Figure 14.1 Integrated Flowchart of Existing Work Process

Conclusion

How many times have you been impacted by your employer's decision to adopt a new technology? Probably more times than you wanted to, and you will certainly be impacted by this type of change again, and again. It is easy to imagine that the complexity of moving data from an old system into a new system requires a cross-functional team working together to complete this complex task. This usually involves more than one job and multiple task analyses. Technology changes are reported as having the highest impact on business performance (Schaedler, Graf-Vlachy, & König, 2022)—reportedly more than competition, politics, or economics. Conducting accurate task analyses for digital transformation projects may be one of the most valuable skills readers of this book may deliver for their companies or clients.

With the overall multidimension and cross-function tasks identified, they can be distributed into job classifications (new or existing). The tasks can also be individually analyzed in terms of what a person must know and be able to do to perform each task—whether procedure, systems, and/or knowledge in nature. Performing this kind of cross-function task analysis also forces the awareness of understanding how an individual task and individual worker fits into a larger work system. This detailed analysis requires tasks to be documented in detail using one of the three methods presented in the following three chapters, with an overall understanding of the larger multidimension and cross-functional task variations.

Part V

Managing Analysis Work to Improve Performance

Chapter 15

Organizing and Prioritizing Analysis Work for Maximum Performance Impact

Chapter Sections

- Principle 1: Engage Partners
- Principle 2: Defining the Performance Requirements Is Half the Battle
- Principle 3: Mission and System, System, System
- Principle 4: Choose the Right Tools
- Principle 5: If It's Worth Doing, Do It!
- Principle 6: Good Solutions Make Heroes (and Good Analyses Make Good Solutions)
- Principle 7: Benefits Should Exceed Costs
- Conclusion

Analysis for improving performance is a systematic process of diagnosing organization performance and for documenting workplace expertise. In terms of the analysis of organization performance, it offers a five-phase process highlighted by (1) the organization, process, team, and individual levels of performance and (2) the performance variables of mission/goal, systems design, capacity, motivation, and expertise. These variables come together in the performance diagnosis matrix, which is the goal of organization analysis. Related to the analysis of expertise, a six-component process includes the job description, task inventory, and three unique task analysis tools. The task analysis tools have the capability of analyzing the full range of contemporary workplace expertise including knowledge and systems work, not just procedural work. And further, these tools can be combined for tasks that may benefit from multiple approaches to analysis or in cases where the task stretches across jobs.

All the tools presented in this book should now be warmed up and ready to go. However, just because you have them in your toolbox does not mean you should use them for every situation. The blanket use of all these tools for every performance issue is not recommended. The critics of analysis

DOI: 10.4324/9781003518532-20

would argue that the contemporary workplace is so dynamic that investing too much in analysis is foolish. They might suggest jumping from organization diagnosis to determining performance requirements and to hiring workers who have expertise while firing those who are not able to perform at work. This is often an option. Hopefully, the preceding chapters have made the case that documenting workplace expertise is now more important than ever. Simply replacing employees as an overall workforce strategy just doesn't work.

We contend that much of the work that is labeled changing and fluid is simply the result of poorly defined work systems and less-than expert workers. As mentioned earlier, jobs and the inventory of job tasks typically get shuffled at a rate that exceeds the change in requirements within the tasks that are being reassigned. Organizations, processes, teams, and individual jobs are less stable than workplace tasks. If there is no documentation surrounding the task, and it is reassigned to another worker, that expertise is in danger of being lost to the organization. These losses are being experienced day in and day out by large and small organizations. The accumulated performance losses are enormous. The application of performance diagnosis along with work process and workplace expertise documentation should put an organization on the path to improving its situation. We have also addressed the increasingly common use of extremely vague and ill-defined job descriptions. We have described these as mainly human resource management job descriptions intended to protect the organization from various forms of litigation. Elevating these to performance improvement job descriptions is a critical step.

We also contend that changing requirements should not force an organization into hiring and firing as the only means of staying ahead of the competition. Dynamic organizations may need to create management and human resource systems analogous to flexible manufacturing systems. Referring again to the increase in vague and ill-defined job descriptions, there should be a negotiation between the potential employee and employer, ultimately arriving and clear roles and responsibilities, tasks, and performance outcomes. Flexible management and human resource systems would facilitate having the right people working on the right projects and enrolling the right people in the right development activities. Systematic analysis of workplace expertise would then be focused on the task and task modules that could quickly be configured into job assignments and training programs.

In managing the work of analysis for improving performance, like any other human activity, you should use your judgment about how to handle individual situations. The methods presented in this book have been used successfully in many organizations for diverse purposes. This chapter provides more insight into how to do this by discussing seven principles for managing the analysis:

1 Engage partners
2 Defining the performance requirements is half the battle
3 Mission and system, system, system
4 Choose the right tools
5 If it's worth doing, do it!
6 Good solutions make heroes (and good analyses make good solutions)
7 Benefits should exceed costs

These principles highlight why analysis for improving performance is important, which methods and personnel are best for specific situations, and when a rigorous analysis isn't worth the effort.

Principle 1: Engage Partners

Too many people in the consulting and performance improvement business want to hold on to their secrets of success and therefore restrict participation in their realm of activity. They often enjoy the power that comes with having and dispensing information. There is no question that some experts will protect their expertise to stay valuable and relevant.

Never conduct a performance diagnosis by yourself. The person in charge of the organization you are diagnosing should be your partner in managing the diagnosis. As much as possible, he or she should be active in accessing and interpreting analysis information. It is critical that the performance improvement proposal come from that person and you (with both names on the proposal) as it is presented to the host organization for approval. You and the person you are working for in the organization need to become a team working together for the organization.

Also, consider using unbiased third-party professionals for interviews and surveys. A local consultant or performance improvement graduate student intern could be just the right person for some of this labor-intensive work. It is conceivable that the project can speed up and the costs go down as a result.

In the best of conditions, the analysis tools in this book are used in conjunction with experts. However, organization decisions to implement new processes or work systems can often leave the analyst without a ready expert. The logic of the three task analysis methods helps substitute for the missing expert. Under these conditions, the analyst pieces together a variety of "partial experts" in the organization to capture the components of expertise. Then the analyst weaves together the components into the complete documentation of expertise required to perform the job and its tasks.

The reality is that most of the tools described in this book can be learned by average people. There have been extraordinary successes in teaching the use of these tools to workers (blue-collar and white-collar) as well as to professional analysts. In one case, a consultant was working with a top management team as partners in diagnosing the organization performance. Together they flowcharted a core process of a company and identified the 15 critical jobs within the process. Then expert job incumbents (mostly high school and technical school graduates) in each job were taught the analysis of expertise tools, and they themselves analyzed the expertise required of each of their own jobs. They didn't think they could do it. Out of fear of failure, they tried to drag the consultant into their workplace. That would have put them in a team mode, with the consultant as analyst and the workers as subject experts. Instead, after teaching them the tools, the consultant withdrew and just stayed in touch via e-mail. They transmitted their work to him; he commented on it and sent it back. It worked. All 15 of the critical jobs were documented to a high standard in record time.

In another situation, where production waste was sky-high, the substandard-performing workers themselves used the task analysis tools to document the expertise required to do their work. They were going to produce a training program based on the analysis. They did the analysis, and as they did it, they learned their jobs in the process. Their production waste went to almost zero, and they ended up not needing training for themselves. Their analysis did serve to train others. Doing the analysis produced learning analysts, an effective job aid, and documentation to produce training for others.

Many of the horror stories about choosing the wrong people revolve around the overutilization of committees and the use of "political appointees." Avoid these options.

Principle 2: Defining the Performance Requirements Is Half the Battle

For most of us, doing the kind of analysis work described in this book requires an understanding of, and commitment to, performance. If you were not engaged in analysis work, you could easily find other ways to spend your time. So, producing an analysis that will not be used is a wasteful way to spend your time.

A clearly confirmed performance requirement establishes the general need for analyzing and documenting workplace expertise. It also offers direction in choosing the appropriate task analysis tools. Finally, establishing clear performance requirements and performance standards sets you up to measure the effectiveness of your interventions. The following true incident illustrates the necessity for a clearly defined performance requirement:

The president of XYZ Corporation tells his vice president of operations that he emphatically wants to see a reduction of emails and electronic document flow in the firm. With a click of his heels, the vice president assembles a task force to reduce the flow of communication. Their tentative solutions include the following:

- A poster campaign,
- Employee newsletter articles, and
- A work-group discussion program

The president chose the poster campaign. Many four-color posters were designed, produced, and displayed around the facility. The response was nonexistent. Not once did these highly paid corporate sharpshooters ever pin down the president to find out what he meant by "excess" communication, or what types of documents/e-mails, or what level in the organization he was referring to. Whether or not there were important work behaviors that needed to be understood and improved was never resolved. Because the performance issue was never clearly defined, the activity that followed was doomed to failure.

Thus, development and delivery of interventions should be clearly linked to performance requirements. Some situations that would push you toward a clear definition of a performance requirement include these:

- Lack of clarity regarding exactly what is involved in a work performance situation.
- Nonperformance or substandard performance, causing critical difficulties in the organization or marketplace.
- New equipment, new work systems, new employees.
- The desire to bring the performance level of all workers up to that of an exemplary performer.
- A search for less costly methods of performance being forced by competition.

It is interesting to note that at some time later, using the analysis tools in this book, it was quickly discovered that the real reason for the excess communication was the fear and paranoia caused by the president himself. His judgmental management style caused everyone to want to cover their bases when it came to addressing his wrath.

Principle 3: Mission and System, System, System

The perceived performance requirement will start you thinking about what to analyze. The actual performance requirements, as defined by the careful diagnosis, will frame the plan for performance improvement and the possible need to analyze specific workplace expertise. The following items are inherent in all organizations and may yield opportunities to gain surprisingly large benefits from a competent and thorough analysis:

Corporate culture, or people's attitudes and habits at work
Equipment use, misuse, maintenance, and their effects on performance
Work system analysis and performance improvement
Personnel policies and practices and their effects on performance
New technology planning
Safety issues
Use of time at work

Quality analysis for improving performance has its results. The proof is ultimately in the new understanding of performance at work and any resulting solutions that maintain or improve that performance.

Time is the demon in the corporate picture. It seems that the only constant in industry and business is the pressure of time. "Have it done yesterday!" is the battle cry. Insufficient time is the most common objection to analysis work—the very analysis work that has the potential to define the specific requirements and work behaviors for significant gains. Thus, analysts who fail to link their analysis work to important performance requirements and performance results will never make much of a difference to their organizations.

(1) The principle "Mission and system, system, system" highlights the importance of looking at the big picture. You must come to grips with the connection of your role in the organization and (2) the connection of your tools to that role. A sound mission carried out by a fully implemented mediocre system will outstrip a brilliant system that is not honored and worked on a day-to-day basis. Better yet, buy into the best system, master it, honor it, and work it.

Principle 4: Choose the Right Tools

You have learned how to conduct analysis for diagnosing organizations and documenting workplace expertise. Hopefully, you have also learned where each tool can most usefully be applied.

Early and conscious estimates as to what analysis tools will be required will help you define and control the work. Creating a simple selection of the right tools for each performance improvement project will outline the initial planning. The specific tools come from the following dimensions:

- Diagnosing organizational performance
- Documenting and improving work process(es)
- Documenting workplace expertise

The injunction to "Choose the right tool" holds true for all forms of work. It is doubly important for the neophyte. An old craftsperson once told me that the newest and best tools are needed by beginners; only skilled old-timers can use less precise or worn tools and still produce good results. If you are new to analysis, carefully choose the best and most appropriate analysis tools.

Principle 5: If It's Worth Doing, Do It!

Wanting others to do things the right way and wanting them to get it right the first time is a perspective on work held by most work performance analysts. They should expect no less of themselves.

We are not talking about perfection—perfection is an elusive goal. But excellence is within your reach. Decide to do your best in the time allotted. The old saying "Pay now or pay later" could have been written for the analyst. It takes time to do quality analysis, and your boss may not understand why you need to do all that, but let reason prevail. You are the one who will live with the results, so pay now or pay later. We hope you are willing to pay the price for good analysis work and then reap the benefits. Do it!

We often use the taxonomy of performance (understand, operate, troubleshoot, improve, and invent) to gain personal clarity as well as to help decision-makers think about their situation. The taxonomy can be used to talk about the present state, desired state, and the appropriateness of various interventions. For example, for people who cannot but need to be able to troubleshoot the system, an intervention aimed at understanding the system will not be enough to get to the troubleshooting level.

Principle 6: Good Solutions Make Heroes (and Good Analyses Make Good Solutions)

Analysis for improving performance requires understanding and commitment. By itself, analysis is rarely rewarded. Management rewards solutions, not analysis. Management sees the costs of analysis in time and dollars and a pressing need for solutions. Unfortunately, time is the nemesis of business and industry; therefore, the time for thorough analysis must be snatched from the organization. Taking the time to analyze will ensure good solutions.

Good solutions are grounded in good analysis. More than anyone else in your organization, you understand what it takes to conduct good analyses. Others will neither know nor appreciate the demands of good analysis work. Do not expect management to support your requests for resources without a proven record of delivering on promises of performance improvement.

As a neophyte, you will need to hold your ground in the analysis phase so you can obtain hero status at the solution phase. The major strategies are to (1) focus on present performance problems, (2) have an internal partner that "owns" the performance problem in the diagnosis phase, and (3) wisely use available internal and external resources for both the performance diagnosis and the expertise documentation phases.

Principle 7: Benefits Should Exceed Costs

Cost analysis by itself is just plain useless. The name of the game in industry and business is cost–benefit analysis—getting a good return on your investment. Figure 15.1 provides an example of a cost–benefit chart. Which option would you choose when investing your own money?

Quite frankly, if we didn't have $1,000 readily available, we'd find it quickly so that we could take advantage of high-cost option D. Options A and B are bad investments. Just because an option is expensive, however, don't think that it's the best. See Figure 15.2 for a comparison.

These are real figures from the forecasted costs and benefits of a small performance improvement intervention. The shrewd performance improvement manager went with the low-cost model, not because it was inexpensive but because of the cost–benefit ratio (Swanson, 2001).

The performance analyst in industry and business is a businessperson first and should think as one. If you want to succeed in your organization, you will need to play by the rules of the organization. Knowing what the problems are, what truly constitutes good work performance, and how to link solutions to performance requirements through analysis will be of tremendous value to both you and your organization.

One more bit of advice about the reality of costs and benefits: From this book, you may get the impression that we would like you to analyze all work performance from every angle. This is not so. Excessive or inappropriate analysis can result in paralysis through analysis. Decide when or at what point analysis is not worth the effort. A decision matrix can be useful (see Figure 15.3).

Wouldn't it be great to be able to earn a high return on a low investment? Imagine a tough performance problem in a manufacturing plant, one that results in high waste of an expensive product that is almost totally linked

Option	Cost $ (Investment)	Return $ (15 days later)	Return %	Benefit $
A	1.50	1	−50	−0.50
B	10	10	0	0
C	500	600	+20	+100
D	1,000	2,000	≠100	+1,000

Figure 15.1   Financial Analysis of Investment Alternatives

Option	Cost $	Return $	Return %	Benefit $
A	60	180	300	+120
B	120	180	150	+60
C	300	180	60	−120
D	1,000	180	18	−820

Figure 15.2   Financial Comparison of Performance Improvement Options

Figure 15.3   Decision Matrix

to the lack of worker expertise. You approach the situation through a quick performance diagnosis and the careful analysis of the critical work task. This is then used to efficiently correct the problem. Hero status for you!

If you are new in the organization and must "hit the ground running," a few discrete inquiries will net many identifiable work performance problems. I recommend that you plot all of them on a two-axis, cost–benefit matrix. Wisdom dictates that you choose for your first performance improvement effort one that falls within the low-cost, high-benefit quadrant. If the problem is urgent, so much the better.

Conclusion

It is important to look before you leap into the work of analysis for improving performance. Our goal has been to provide you with all the tools you need to complete it successfully. The potential for return on your investment of time and talent is enormous. Enjoy your analysis expertise and its ability to make a difference in your organization.

Chapter 16

From Analysis to Performance Improvement

Chapter Sections

- Phases of Performance Improvement in Review
- Performance Variables in Review
- Performance Improvement in Practice
- An Important Note about Artificial Intelligence
- Bottom Line Take-Away from This Book
- Conclusion

The process of moving from analysis to improved performance can be challenging, interesting, and fun. Conducting an analysis is almost as rewarding as the final accomplishment. But not everyone feels that way, especially those without a well-equipped, up-front analysis toolbox for performance improvement.

Serious scholars in the area of problem-solving tell us that the odds of success are increased when you use powerful analysis methods for defining problems and opportunities. They also tell you that your mental health is enhanced when you are in control of the front-end definition and framing of a problem leading to a sound solution. Simply stated, good up-front analysis leads you to success and helps you feel more confident along the way.

Phases of Performance Improvement in Review

The five phases of improving performance, first presented in Chapter 2, are to (1) analyze, (2) design, (3) develop, (4) implement, and (5) evaluate. Figure 16.1 once again illustrates performance improvement as a process that parallels and enhances core organizational processes (e.g., product development, customer acquisition, production, and order fulfillment) for the purpose of improving performance.

The bookend phases of performance improvement—*analysis and evaluation*—connect to the basic organizational inputs and outputs.

DOI: 10.4324/9781003518532-21

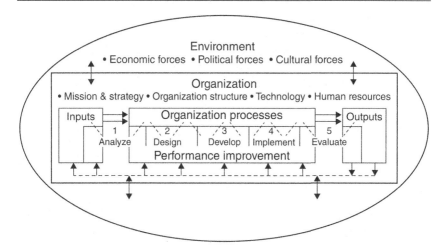

Figure 16.1 Systems Model of Performance Improvement—Interacting with Organizational Processes

Performance improvement interventions that are not accurately connected to organization goals at the analysis (input) phase have no chance of finishing the race, let alone winning the race.

Unfortunately, many organizations learn the importance of analysis after spending large amounts of time and money in the design, development, and delivery phases—only to find that their crowd-pleasing, analysis-less interventions had little or no positive impact on performance.

Interventions such as human resource development, quality improvement, reengineering, knowledge management, and performance technology that are fixated on the *design, development, and delivery phases* (pursued apart from analysis) are almost always deficient. They are generally sophisticated and costly interventions in search of an ill-defined performance opportunity or problem. Perhaps a great solution to some other organizational problem?

Audits of such development efforts invariably drive decision-makers to ask, "How did we ever get involved with this?" (Torraco & Swanson, 1997). The answer often is that there was an emotional decision, a hasty decision, a high-pressure sales pitch, or an arm twisting from the top.

Performance Variables in Review

To avoid such errors, it is important to emphasize that inside each goal and intervention are multiple performance variables at work. Thus, the performance variables of mission/goals, systems design, capacity, motivation, and expertise help guide the performance diagnosis, focus the documentation of expertise, and help ensure the inclusion of the critical dimensions required of an effective intervention. Being able to accurately respond to the questions under each variable enables the performance improvement professional to move closer to success:

Mission/Goal

- Does the organization's mission/goal fit the reality of the economic, political, and cultural forces?
- Do the process goals enable the organization to meet organization and individual mission/goals?
- Are the professional and personal mission/goals of individuals congruent with the organization?

Systems Design

- Does the organization system provide structure and policies supporting the desired performance?
- Are processes designed in such a way as to work as a system?
- Do the individuals face obstacles that impede job performance?

Capacity

- Does the organization have the leadership, capital, and infrastructure to achieve its mission/goals?
- Does the process have the capacity to perform (quantity, quality, and timeliness)?
- Do the individuals have the mental, physical, and emotional capacity to perform?

Motivation

- Do the policies, culture, and reward systems support the desired performance?
- Does the process provide the information and human factors required to maintain it?
- Do the individuals want to perform no matter what?

Expertise

- Does the organization establish and maintain selection and training policies and resources?

- Does the process of developing expertise meet the changing demands of changing processes?
- Do the individuals have the knowledge and expertise to perform?

Performance Improvement in Practice

In thinking about strategy and performance, the bad news is that the organization leaders simply flirting with improving performance end up with a poor report card. The good news is that the know-how for systematically improving performance is available and ample guidance is available for dramatically increasing success.

The arguments for a performance improvement are loud and clear. The real challenge is integrating the message of need into a personal understanding of performance that is backed up by a professional performance improvement toolbox. There are rival visions of performance improvement that run the continuum:

- Performance improvement as a major organization process—something an organization must do to succeed
- Performance improvement as a value-added activity—something that is potentially worth doing
- Performance improvement as an optional activity—something that is nice to do
- Performance improvement as a waste of organization resources—something that has costs exceeding the benefits

What follows are profiles of organization case studies that illustrate overall performance improvement journeys (not just the analysis phase) that include starting and ending points as well as key steps.

Case 1: From Evaluation to Performance Situation

A major insurance company had been spending significant resources on communication training for all sales personnel. A decision was made to evaluate the program's effectiveness. Once that decision was made, a number of important questions were asked and actions taken that resulted in improved performance.

Starting Point

Management was questioning the value of sales training. The training staff had attended a popular four-level evaluation workshop but could not get beyond the "level 1" happy sheets. They then turned to the human resource development financial assessment system (Swanson, 2001). The financial assessment system required that they specify the business outcome and think beyond training. They then conducted a performance analysis and completely revised the performance improvement intervention.

Ending Point

There was a 4:1 return on investment in less than a year. Participant knowledge and expertise exceeded the goals, as did the organizational performance. Upper management increased its investment in the program.

Key Steps along the Way

- Identifying the outcome variable of "sales"
- Facing the lack of understanding of the communication breakdown in the sales process
- Quickly studying the communication breakdown in the sales process
- Altering the communication training to match the new understanding
- Gaining management support to implement the new sales communication techniques
- Evaluating the communication expertise of participants before training, at the end, and back on the job
- Tracking actual sales attributable to the training
- Having the CFO provide the net value of each sale
- Providing a two-page executive summary evaluation report to all key personnel

Case 2: From Satisfaction to Performance Situation

This Fortune 50 corporation is seen as a leader on a number of fronts, including its enlightened view of investing in the development of its workforce. Participant satisfaction with development efforts has always been high. Even so, with large amounts of money being spent on quality improvement, organization development, and training efforts, the top managers thought they should "check up" on their investment. They commissioned an audit by a team of researchers to evaluate their investment.

Starting Point

An auditing model designed to compare existing practices and ideal or "best practices" was selected. A team of two external auditors with expertise in performance improvement and auditing conducted the on-site audit.

Ending Point

There are two major ending points. The first was the three-hour presentation of the audit results to the 12-member top management team. This was a very emotional truth-telling session, with management team defensiveness and admissions of less-than-desirable conditions. The second ending point was captured in a letter from the top manager to the lead auditor three years after the audit. The letter reported the fact that the audit report was still functioning as their benchmark and that major HRD staff development investments and major changes in the way HRD work was being done had taken place.

Key Steps along the Way

- Having an internal champion of the effort
- Having a clear and straightforward auditing method
- Having external auditors
- Having auditors with HRD expertise
- Having the company developers provide all documentation
- Having all top managers in the room for the audit report
- Having a company with a history of integrity
- Having a continuing dialogue with the auditors after the audit

Case 3: From Analysis to Performance Situation

A large sales organization had been experiencing major changes in products, information systems, customer requirements, and market competition. Clearly, the work had changed, and it seemed as though only selected "superstar" sales personnel were able to regularly succeed. A decision was made to do a comprehensive up-front performance diagnosis.

Starting Point

Things were not going well, and nobody was willing to take on the challenge. The new VP of performance consulting walked right into the middle of the situation without adequate staff competence to do a performance diagnosis of the major sales business process. The VP hired a consulting firm to work with him.

Ending Point

The core sales process was documented and improved, and it survived two leadership changes. The roles of the people working in the process were clarified, with process activities clustered into assignable and trainable tasks.

Training and certification programs directly tied to the defined and improved sales process are in place.

Key Steps along the Way

- Having an internal champion who also brings the performance partners to the table
- Underestimating the power of a "culture of relationships" relative to a "culture of analysis and improvement"
- Using the power of process documentation to reveal leadership gaps
- Using people who want to and have the capacity to be "students of the business" as part of the team
- Managing the demand for quick action (with or without results)

An Important Note about Artificial Intelligence

Artificial intelligence (AI) is the ability of a computer or computer-controlled robot to perform tasks that are commonly associated with the intellectual processes characteristic of humans, such as the ability to reason. Although there are, as yet, no AIs that match full human flexibility over wider domains or in tasks requiring much everyday knowledge, some AIs perform specific tasks as well as humans (Copeland, 2024).

At the time of this writing there are two assessments of AI worth highlighting.

1 "A.I. produces spectacular images and is fun to play with, but it's neither reliable nor safe (yet)." (Sommer, 2024, *New York Times* 3/15/2024)
2 "Artificial Intelligence (AI) could be as transformational as the printing press, steam engine, electricity, computing, and the internet." (Chloe, 2024, *Inc.* 4/9/2024)

Clearly, AI will impact organizations and the work requirements of those functioning in them. It already has, to some degree, as computer programs and robotic machines move from being precisely controlled to gathering information and learning. Exactly, how this will play out over time in impacting the analysis processes and actual performance improvement interventions is hard to predict.

AI pre-cursers have been challenging the human mind for decades (think of the "human versus computer" chess game challenges). Focused computer programs to aid in work tasks abound. Also, the incredibly large YouTube information and learning tool utilizes contributed ready-made problem solutions of varying quality (think "how to replace a sink faucet or making safe financial investments"). We are sure each of you can attest to the excellent help you have received through YouTube. On other occasions, not that good. Thus, "buyer beware" in terms of the quality of the YouTube postings and reliance on early AI programs.

One area that is seeing a boon is AI writing. Matt Ellis highlights on a *Grammarly* blog that AI can be used for 19 writing tasks (2023). Using a request with prompts—AI can produce an e-mail, birthday card, thank you note, press release, and so on with impressive results. When confronted with specific organization, work systems, and individual work details—AI writing is simply inadequate.

Bottom Line Take-Away from This Book

It is natural to think that organizational problems can be resolved easily and swiftly with authoritative decision-making. This book has made the case that to fully understand organizational problems related to human expertise requires much more. Unilateral decisions will not cut it when it comes to the expertise required for essential tasks. Further, in the age of the highest turnover of expertise we have ever seen, tools for capturing the relevant expertise are more important than ever. We have laid out several processes for capturing expertise (e.g., overall problem analysis, techniques for data gathering, work process analysis, procedural, systems, knowledge, and cross-functional task analyses), and these tools are all intended to capture critical knowledge required for any firm to remain competitive and to survive. If you take nothing else away from this book, consider the following:

1 The problem that you are experiencing is probably much deeper in the organization than you think.
2 Use the tools provided in this book to substantively understand those problems.
3 Consider which jobs and related tasks are most strategic to organization success.
4 Use the tools provided in this book to document them in detail—such detail that if your most valued employees (in terms of expertise) were to leave the organization, you would have a basis on which to start train, promote, and hiring replacements.

It is inevitable that your most expert and valued employees (whether direct reports or executives) will move on at some point. What will you do when they leave? What is your plan for trying to replace their expertise?

Analysis is the key. First, analyzing and isolating problems along with their causes through deep understanding, and second, by analyzing the expertise required of workers to excel.

Conclusion

Analysis is the "sextant" of performance improvement. The triangulation of data and observations provides the definition and direction for successful performance improvement efforts. The follow-up assessment and evaluation of results address the ultimate worth of performance improvement investments. When all is said and done, the conclusion drawn from evaluating a performance improvement intervention should be that:

- the organization performs better,
- the process performs better,
- the team performs better, and/or
- the individual performs better.

References

Academy of Human Resource Development. (1999). Academy of human resource development standards on ethics and integrity. Bowling Green, OH: Author.

Academy of Management. (2005). The academy of management code of ethical conduct. Briar Manor, NY: Author.

Argyris, C. (1993). Knowledge for action: a guide to overcome barriers to organizational change. San Francisco, CA: Jossey-Bass.

Bartlett, K. R. (2005). Survey research: Foundations and methods of inquiry. In R. A. Swanson, & E. F. Holton (Eds.), Research in organizations: Foundations and methods of inquiry (pp. 97–113). Berrett-Koehler.

Bassi, L. J., & McMurrer, D. P. (2006). Employers' perspectives on human capital development and management. Advances in developing human resources. San Francisco, CA: Berrett-Koehler.

Becker, G. S. (1993). Human capital: a theoretical and empirical analysis with special reference to education (3rd ed.). Chicago, IL: University of Chicago Press.

Bereiter, C., & Scardamalia, M. (1993). Surpassing ourselves: an inquiry into the nature and implications of expertise. Chicago, IL: Open Court.

Bertalanffy, L. V. (1968). General systems theory as integrating factor in contemporary science. Akten des XIV. Internationalen Kongresses für Philosophie, 2, 335–340.

Bjorkquist, D. C., & Murphy, B. P. (1987). Teach how to conduct a needs assessment in industry: learning by doing. Journal of Industrial Teacher Education, 24(2), 32–39.

Boulding, K. E. (1956). General systems theory: the skeleton of a science. Management Science, 2(3), 197–207.

Brache, A. P. (2002). How organizations work: taking a holistic approach to enterprise health. New York, NY and Hoboken, NJ: John Wiley & Sons.

Brannick, M. T., & Levine, E. L. (2002). Job analysis: methods, research, and applications for human resource management in the new millennium. Thousand Oaks, CA: Sage.

Brinkerhoff, R. O. (Ed.). Evaluating training programs in business and industry (pp. 71–82). New directions in program evaluation, no. 44. San Francisco, CA: Jossey-Bass.

Buckingham, M. (2022, June). Designing work that people love. Harvard Business Review. https://hbr.org/2022/05/designing-work-that-people-love

Buckley, W. (Ed.). (1968). Modern systems research for the behavioral scientist. Aldine: Chicago.

Camp, R. C. (1995). Business process benchmarking. Toronto: Irwin.

Campbell, C. P. (1989). Job analysis for industrial training. Journal of European Industrial Training, 13(2), 115–132.

Campbell, J. P., Campbell, R. J., & Associates (1988). Productivity in organizations: new perspectives from industrial and organizational psychology. San Francisco, CA: Jossey-Bass.

Center for Accelerated Learning (1992). Accelerated learning 1992. Lake Geneva, WI: Author.

Chermack, T. J. (2003). Mental models in decision making and implications for human resource development. Advances in Developing Human Resources, 5(4), 408–422.

Chermack, T. J. (2011). Scenario planning in organizations: how to create, use, and assess scenarios. San Francisco: Berrett-Koehler Publishers.

Chloe, A. (2024, April 9). Jamie Dimon predicts AI will be as transformational as electricity. https://www.inc.com/chloe-aiello/jamie-dimon-predicts-ai-will-be-as-transformational-as-electricity.html

Clarke, D., & Crossland, L. (1985). Action systems: an introduction to the analysis of complex behavior. London: Methuen.

Coleman, N. (2006, May 2). McGuire gives himself a clean bill of health. Minnesota, MN: Minneapolis Star Tribune.

Copeland, B. (2024, April 10). Artificial intelligence. Encyclopedia Britannica. https://www.britannica.com/technology/artificial-intelligence.

Crawford, M. B. (2006). Shop class as soulcraft. The New Atlantis, 13, 7–24.

Cummings, T. G., & Worley, C. G. (1993). Organizational development and change (5th ed.). Cincinnati, OH: South-Western College Publishing.

Cummings, T. G., & Worley, C. G. (2016). Organization development & change.

Davenport, T. H. (1993). Process innovation: reengineering work through information technology. Cambridge, MA: Harvard Business School Press.

Deming, W. E. (1986). Out of the crisis. Cambridge, MA: MIT Press.

Diamantidis, A. D., & Chatzoglou, P. (2018). Factors affecting employee performance: an empirical approach. International Journal of Productivity and Performance Management, 68(1), 171–193.

Dillman, D. A. (2000). Mail and internet surveys: the tailored design method (2nd ed.). New York, NY: Wiley.

Dirkx, J. (1996). Human resource development as adult education: fostering the educative workplace. In R. Rowden (Ed.), Workplace learning: debating five critical questions of theory and practice (pp. 114–137). San Francisco, CA: Jossey-Bass.

Dooley, C. R. (1945). The training within industry report, 1910–1945. Washington, DC: War Manpower Commission Bureau of Training, Training within Industry Service.

Drazin, R., Glynn, M. A., & Kazanjian, R. K. (2004). Dynamics of structural change. In M. S. Poole & A. H. Van de Ven (Eds.), Handbook of organizational change and innovation (pp. 114–137). Oxford: Oxford University Press.

Drucker, P. F. (1964). Managing for results: economic tasks and risk-taking decisions. New York, NY: Harper & Row.

Dubois, D. (1993). Competency-based performance improvement. Amherst, MA: HRD Press.

DuPont (1989). ISO 9000 is coming!!! The answers to your questions. Wilmington, DE: Quality Management and Technology Center, DuPont.

Ellis, M. (2023, July 27). 19 writing tasks you can do with AI. Grammarly. https://www.grammarly.com/blog/ai-writing-tasks/

Ericsson, K. A., & Smith, J. (1994). Toward a general theory of expertise: prospects and limits. Cambridge: Cambridge University Press.

Falayi, F. (2019, July 9). It's time we finally do away with performance improvement plans. *Forbes*. https://www.forbes.com/sites/forbescoachescouncil/2019/07/09/its-time-we-finally-do-away-with-performance-improvement-plans/?sh=573d249b50b2

Fernandez de Henestrosa, M., Sischka, P. E., & Steffgen, G. (2023). Predicting challenge and threat appraisal of job demands among nurses: the role of matching job resources. International Journal of Environmental Research and Public Health, *20*(2), 1288.

Fine, S. A., & Cronshaw, S. F. (1999). Functional job analysis: a foundation for human resources management. Mahwah, NJ: Erlbaum.

FitzGerald, J. M., & FitzGerald, A. F. (1973). Fundamentals of systems theory. New York, NY: Wiley.

Flanagan, J. C. (1954). The critical incident technique. Psychological Bulletin, 51, 327–358.

Forelle, C., & Bandler, J. (2006). The perfect payday. Wall Street Journal, A1.

Forester, J. (2006). UnitedHealth debt outlook lowered. *St. Paul Pioneer Press*, B1.

Forster, N. (1994). The analysis of company documentation. In C. Cassell & G. Symon (Eds.), Qualitative methods in organizational research (pp. 147–166). London: Sage.

Fuchsberg, G. (1993, September 10). Executive education: taking control. Wall Street Journal, R1–R4.

Gagne, R. M. (1962). Military training and principles of learning. American Psychologist, 17, 83–91.

Gallup. (2022, December 15). State of the global workplace. Retrieved December 20, 2022, from https://www.gallup.com/workplace/349484/state-of-the-global-workplace.aspx

Gilbert, T. F. (1996). Human competence: engineering worthy performance. Washington, DC: International Society for Performance.

Gilley, J., Dean, P., & Bierema, L. (2000). Philosophy and practice of organizational learning, performance, and change. Cambridge, MA: Perseus.

Gleick, J. (1987). Chaos: making a new science. New York, NY: Penguin.

Goldberg, R. M. (2022). Negotiating family resilience amidst caretaking and employment constraints: a qualitative analysis of African American employed caregivers. Community, Work & Family, 25(3), 279–301.

Gradous, D. B. (Ed.). (1989). Systems theory applied to human resource development. Alexandria, VA: American Society for Training and Development Press.

Gupta, A., & Baksi, A. K. (2022). HR metrics and quality of hire in human capital market: a case study. Specialusis Ugdymas, 2(43), 1872–1883.

Hammer, M., & Champy, J. (1993). Reengineering the corporation: a manifesto for business revolution. New York, NY: HarperCollins.

Harless, J. H. (1980). An ounce of analysis is worth a pound of objectives. Newnan, GA: Harless.

Harrington, H. J. (1992). Business process improvement: the breakthrough strategy for total quality, productivity, and competitiveness. New York, NY: McGraw-Hill.

Harvey, R. J. (1991). Job analysis. In M. D. Dunnette & L. M. Hough (Eds.), Handbook of industrial and organizational psychology (2nd ed., Vol. 2, pp. 71–163). Palo Alto, CA: Consulting Psychologists Press.

Hayes, B. E. (1992). Measuring customer satisfaction: development and use of questionnaires. Milwaukee, WI: ASQC Quality Press.

He, W., Li, S. L., Feng, J., Zhang, G., & Sturman, M. C. (2021). When does pay for performance motivate employee helping behavior? The contextual influence of performance subjectivity. Academy of Management Journal, 64(1), 293–326.

Hergenhahn, B. R., & Olson, M. H. (1993). An introduction to theories of learning (4th ed.). Englewood Cliffs: Prentice Hall.

Herling, R. E. (2000). Operational definitions of expertise and competence. In R W. Herling & J. M. Provo (Eds.), Strategic perspectives on knowledge, competence, and expertise: advances in developing human resources (pp. 8–21). San Francisco, CA: Sage.

Holton, E. F. (1996). The flawed 4-level evaluation model. Human Resource Development Quarterly, 7(1), 5–21. https://doi.org/10.1002/hrdq.3920070103

Holton, E. F. (2001). Theoretical assumptions underlying the performance paradigm of human resource development. Human Resource Development International, 5(2), 199–215.

Holton, E. F. (Eds.). (2005). Research in organizations: foundations and methods of inquiry (pp. 97–113). San Francisco, CA: Berrett-Koehler.

Holton, E. F., & Baldwin, T. L. (Eds.). (2003). Improving learning transfer in organizations. New York, NY: Wiley.

Holton, E. F., & Phillips, J. J. (Eds.). (1995). In action: conducting needs assessment. A snapshot of needs assessment (1–12). Alexandria, VA: ASTD.

Holton, G. J. (1998). The advancement of science, and its burdens: with a new introduction. Boston, MA: Harvard University Press.

Jacobs, R. L. (1989). Theory: systems theory applied to human resource development. In D. B. Gradous (Ed.), Systems theory applied to human resource development (pp. 27–60). Alexandria, VA: American Society for Training and Development Press.

Julliard, C. (2004). Human capital and international portfolio choice. Princeton, NJ: Princeton University (Unpublished manuscript).

Juran, J. M. (1992). Juran on quality by design: the new steps for planning quality into goods and services. New York, NY: Free Press.

Kaplan, S. N., Sørensen, M., & Zakolyukina, A. A. (2022). What is CEO overconfidence? Evidence from executive assessments. Journal of Financial Economics, 145(2), 409–425.

Kinkel, S., Baumgartner, M., & Cherubini, E. (2022). Prerequisites for the adoption of AI technologies in manufacturing—evidence from a worldwide sample of manufacturing companies. Technovation, 110, 102375.

Kirkpatrick, D. L. (1979). Techniques for evaluating training programs. Journal of the American Society of Training Directors, 13, 21–26.

Kirkpatrick, D., & Kirkpatrick, J. (2006). Evaluating training programs: the four levels. San Francisco, CA: Berrett-Koehler.

Korten, D. C. (1995). When corporations rule the world. San Francisco, CA: Berrett-Koehler.

Kotter, J. P. (1990). What leaders really do. Harvard Business Review. https://hbr.org/2001/12/what-leaders-really-do

Kouzes, J. M., & Posner, B. Z. (1987). The leadership challenge: how to get extraordinary things done in organizations. San Francisco, CA: Jossey-Bass.

Krueger, R. A. (1988). Focus groups: a practical guide for applied research. Newbury Park, CA: Sage.

Kusy, M. (1986). The effects of type of training evaluation and support of training among corporate managers. St. Paul, MN: Training and Development Research Center, University of Minnesota.

Lavarakas, P. J. (1987). Telephone survey methods: sampling, selection, and supervision. Newbury Park, CA: Sage.

LeCounte, J. F., Prieto, L. C., & Phipps, S. T. (2017). CEO succession planning and organizational performance: a human capital theory approach. Journal of Leadership, Accountability and Ethics, 14(1).

Lewis, T., & Bjorkquist, D. C. (1992). Needs assessment: a critical reappraisal. Performance Improvement Quarterly, 5(4), 33–54.

Locke, E. A., & Pearce, C. L. (Eds.). (2023). Handbook of principles of organizational behavior: indispensable knowledge for evidence-based management. Hoboken, NJ: John Wiley & Sons.

Lyau, N. M., & Pucel, D. J. (1995). Economic return on training investment at the organization level. Performance Improvement Quarterly, 8(3), 68–79.

Mager, R. F., & Pipe, P. (1984). Analyzing performance problems. Belmont, CA: Lake.

Marsh, S. (2021, February 5). Why remote work is here to stay. Forbes. https://www.forbes.com/sites/forbestechcouncil/2021/02/05/why-remote-work-is-here-to-stay/?sh=31d649e41ec2

Marshall, A. (1949). Principles of economics (8th ed.). New York, NY: The Online Library of Liberty.

McLean & Company. (2020, December 8). HR trends for 2022. Retrieved February 7, 2023, from https://www.prnewswire.com/news-releases/mclean--company-reveals-the-hr-trends-for-2022-301439740.html#:~:text=Top%20research%20take aways%20from%20the%202022%20HR%20Trends%20Report%3A&text=For%20 non%2Dremote%20jobs%2C%20organizations,attraction%20has%20been%20 negatively%20impacted

McLagan, P. (2003). New organizational forces affecting learning transfer. In E. F. Holton & T. L. Baldwin (Eds.), Improving learning transfer in organizations (pp. 39–56). New York, NY: Wiley.

McLagan, P. A. (1989). Systems model 2000: matching systems theory to future HRD issues. In D. B. Gradous (Ed.), Systems theory applied to human resource development: theory-to-practice monograph (pp. 61–82). Alexandria, VA: American Society for Training and Development Press.

McLean, G. N. (1988). Construction and analysis of organization climate surveys. St. Paul, MN: Training and Development Research Center, University of Minnesota.

McLean, G. N. (2005). Organization development: principles, processes, performance. San Francisco, CA: Berrett-Koehler.

Merriam-Webster's Collegiate Dictionary. (2003). Merriam-Webster's collegiate dictionary (11th ed.). Springfield, MA: Merriam-Webster.

Micklethwait, J., & Wooldridge, A. (1996). The witch doctors: making sense of management gurus. New York, NY: Times Books.

Miles, M. B., & Huberman, A. M. (1984). Qualitative data analysis: a sourcebook of new methods. Newbury Park, CA: Sage.

Miller, C. P. (2021). Performing class: domestic labor in working-class modernism (Doctoral dissertation, Brandeis University). https://doi.org/10.48617/etd.60.

Miller, D., & Xu, X. (2016). A fleeting glory: self-serving behavior among celebrated MBA CEOs. Journal of Management Inquiry, 25(3), 286–300.

Miller, D., & Xu, X. (2019). MBA CEOs, short-term management and performance. Journal of Business Ethics, 154, 285–300.

Mills, G. E., Pace, W. R., & Peterson, B. D. (1988). Analysis in human resource training and development. Reading, MA: Addison-Wesley.

Miner, J. (2002). Organizational behavior: foundations, theories, and analyses. Oxford: Oxford University Press.

Mintzberg, H. (2017, February 22). MBAs as CEOs: some troubling evidence. Henry Mintzberg. https://mintzberg.org/blog/mbas-as-ceos#:~:text="...we%20find%20that%20MBA%20CEOs,rewarded%20for%20this%20"performance

Murphy, B. P., & Swanson, R. A. (1988). Auditing training and development. Journal of European Industrial Training, 12(2), 13–16.

Nadler, D. A., Gernstein, M. S., Shaw, R. B., & Associates (1992). Organizational architecture: designs for changing organizations. San Francisco, CA: Jossey-Bass.

Nadler, L., & Nadler, Z. (Eds.). (1990). The handbook of human resource development (2nd ed.). New York, NY: Wiley.

Nehls, K., Smith, B. D., & Schneider, H. A. (2015). Video-conferencing interviews in qualitative research. In Hai-Jew, S. (Ed.), Enhancing Qualitative and Mixed Methods Research with Technology (pp. 140–157). Hershey, PA: IGI Global.

Nichols, T. (2017). the death of expertise: the campaign against established knowledge and why it matters. Oxford: Oxford University Press.

Nohria, N., & Berkley, J. (1998). What ever happened to the take-charge manager? Harvard Business Review on Leadership, 199–222.

Nutt, P. C. (2003). Why decisions fail: avoiding the blunders and traps that lead to debacles. San Francisco, CA: Berrett-Koehler.

Oxford English Dictionary. (2004). Oxford English dictionary (2nd ed.). Oxford, UK: Oxford University Press.

Parker, B. L. (1986). Evaluation in training and development. Journal of Industrial Teacher Education, 23(2), 29–55.

Passmore, D. L. (1997). Ways of seeing: disciplinary bases of research in HRD. In R. Swanson & E. Holton, Human resource development research handbook (pp. 114–137). San Francisco, CA: Berrett-Koehler.

Peters, T. J., & Waterman, R. (1982). In search of excellence: lessons from America's best run companies. New York, NY: Harper & Row.

Pfeffer, J., & Sutton, R. I. (2000). The knowing-doing gap: how smart companies turn knowledge into action. Cambridge: HBS Press.

Phillips, J. J. (1996). ROI: the search for best practices. Training & Development, 50(2), 42–48.

Phillips, J. J., & Phillips, P. P. (2016). Handbook of training evaluation and measurement methods. London: Routledge.

Phillips, P., Phillips, J. J., Stone, R., & Burkett, H. (2006). The ROI fieldbook. London: Routledge.

Porter, M. E. (1980). Competitive strategy: techniques for analyzing industries and competitors. New York, NY: Free Press.

Quick, T. (2019). Brief history of continuous improvement. The Journal for Quality and Participation, 42(1), 1–2.

Rossett, A. (1990). Training needs assessment. Englewood Cliffs, NJ: Educational Technology Publications.

Rummler, G. A., & Brache, A. P. (1995). Improving performance: how to manage the white space on the organization chart (2nd ed.). San Francisco, CA: Jossey-Bass.

Rummler, G. A., & Brache, A. P. (2012). Improving performance: how to manage the white space on the organization chart. Hoboken, NJ: John Wiley & Sons.

Ruona, W., & Swanson, R. A. (1998). Theoretical foundation of human resource development. In R. Miller (Ed.), Human resource development (pp. 114–137). Alexandria, VA: University Council for Research in Vocational Education.

Sætre, A. S., & Van de Ven, A. (2021). Generating theory by abduction. Academy of Management Review, 46(4), 684–701.

Saldis, F. P., & Kerzner, H. (2017). Project management workbook and PMP/CAPM exam study guide (12th ed.). New York, NY: Wiley.

Sanchez, J. I., & Levine, E. L. (2000). Accuracy or consequential validity: which is the better standard for job analysis data? Journal of Organizational Behavior, 21(7), 809–818.

Schaedler, L., Graf-Vlachy, L., & König, A. (2022). Strategic leadership in organizational crises: a review and research agenda. Long Range Planning, 55(2), 102156.

Schwartz, P. (1991). The art of the long view: planning for the future in an uncertain world. New York, NY: Doubleday.

Senge, P. M. (1990). The fifth discipline: the art and practice of the learning organization. New York, NY: Doubleday.

Senge, P. M. (1993). Transforming the practice of management. Human Resource Development Quarterly, 4(1), 5–32.

Sisson, G. R., & Swanson, R. A. (1990). Improving work performance. Educational Technology, 30(5), 16–20.

Sleezer, C. M. (1991). Developing and validating the performance analysis for training model. Human Resource Development Quarterly, 2(4), 355–372.

Sleezer, C. M., & Swanson, R. A. (1992). Culture surveys: a tool for improving organization performance. Management Decision, 30(2), 22–29.

Sommer, J. (2024, March 15). If Nvidia keeps rising like this, it will be bigger than the global economy. *New York Times.*

Stolovitch, H. D., & Keeps, E. J. (Eds.). (1992). Handbook of human performance technology: a comprehensive guide for analyzing and solving performance problems in organizations (pp. 602–618). San Francisco, CA: Jossey-Bass.

Stuart, M., Spencer, D. A., McLachlan, C. J., & Forde, C. (2021). COVID-19 and the uncertain future of HRM: furlough, job retention and reform. Human Resource Management Journal, 31(4), 904–917.

Sullivan, H. (2022). Expertise, agency, and collaboration. In Collaboration and public policy (pp. 129–156). Cham: Palgrave Macmillan.

Swanson, R. A. (1981). Analyzing non-observable work behavior. Journal of Industrial Teacher Education, 18(4), 11–23.

Swanson, R. A. (1982, November). High technology, training, and crystal balls (pp. 1–2). Criterion.

Swanson, R. A. (1985). A business person first. Performance and Instruction Journal, 24(7), 10–11.

Swanson, R. A. (1987). Training technology system: a method for identifying and solving training problems in industry and business. Journal of Industrial Teacher Education, 24(4), 7–17.

Swanson, R. A. (1989). Everything important in business and industry is evaluated. New Directions for Program Evaluation, 1989(44), 71–82.

Swanson, R. A. (1990a). Experience: a questionable teacher. Human Resource Development Quarterly, 1(1), 1–4.

Swanson, R. A. (1990b). HRD paranormal interventions. Human Resource Development Quarterly, 1(3), 207–208.

Swanson, R. A. (1991). Ready-aim-frame. Human Resource Development Quarterly, 2(3), 203–205.

Swanson, R. A. (1992a). Demonstrating financial benefits to clients. *Handbook of human performance technology*, 602–618.

Swanson, R. A. (1992b). Pick a system, any system. Human Resource Development Quarterly, 3(3), 213–214.

Swanson, R. A. (1993). Scientific management is a Sunday school picnic compared to reengineering. Human Resource Development Quarterly, 4(3), 219–221.

Swanson, R. A. (1995). Human resource development: performance is the key. Human Resource Development Quarterly, 6(2), 207–213.

Swanson, R. A. (1996a). Analysis for improving performance: tools for diagnosing organizations and documenting workplace expertise. San Francisco, CA: Berrett-Koehler.

Swanson, R. A. (1996b). In praise of the dependent variable. Human Resource Development Quarterly, 7(3), 203–207.

Swanson, R. A. (1997a). TADDS short (theory application deficit disorder). Human Resource Development Quarterly, 8(3), 193–195.

Swanson, R. A. (1997b). Human resource development research handbook: linking research and practice. San Francisco, CA: Berrett-Koehler Publishers.

Swanson, R. A. (1999). Foundations of performance improvement and implications for practice. In R. J. Torraco (Ed.), Performance improvement theory and practice: advances in developing human resources (pp. 1–25). Thousand Oaks, CA: Sage.

Swanson, R. A. (2001). Assessing the financial benefits of human resource development. Cambridge, MA: Perseus Publishing.

Swanson, R. A. (2022). Foundations of human resource development (3rd ed.). Oakland, CA: Berrett-Koehler.

Swanson, R. A., & Chermack, T. J. (2013). Theory building in applied disciplines. Berrett-Koehler Publishers.

Swanson, R. A., & Gradous, D. B. (1986). Performance at work: a systematic program for evaluating work behavior. New York, NY: Wiley.

Swanson, R. A., & Gradous, D. B. (Eds.). (1987). Adapting human resources to organizational change. Alexandria, VA: American Society for Training and Development Press.

Swanson, R. A., & Gradous, D. B. (1988). Forecasting financial benefits of human resource development. San Francisco, CA: Jossey-Bass.

Swanson, R. A., & Holton, E. F. (1997). Human resource development research handbook: linking research and practice. San Francisco, CA: Berrett-Koehler.

Swanson, R. A., & Holton, E. F. (1999). Results: how to assess performance, learning and perceptions in organizations. San Francisco, CA: Berrett-Koehler.

Swanson, R. A., & Holton, E. F. (2005). Research in organizations: foundations and methods of inquiry. San Francisco, CA: Berrett-Koehler.

Swanson, R. A., Holton, E. F. III, & Holton, E. (1999). Results: how to assess performance, learning, and perceptions in organizations. San Francisco, CA: Berrett-Koehler.

Swanson, R. A., Horton, G. R., & Kelly, V. (1986). Exploitation: one view of industry and business. Journal of Industrial Teacher Education, 25(1), 12–22.

Swanson, R. A., & Sleezer, C. M. (1987). Training effectiveness evaluation. Journal of European Industrial Training, 11(4), 7–16.

Swanson, R. A., & Sleezer, C. M. (1988a). Determining financial benefits of an organization development program. Performance Improvement Quarterly, 2(1), 55–65.

Swanson, R. A., & Sleezer, C. M. (1988b). Organizational development: what's it worth? Organizational Development Journal, 6(1), 37–42.

Swanson, R. A., & Sleezer, C. M. (1989). Measurement practice meets measurement science. In C. M. Sleezer (Ed.), Improving human resource development through measurement (pp. 1–4). Alexandria, VA: American Society for Training and Development Press.

Swanson, R. A., & Torraco, R. J. (1994). The history of technical training. In L. Kelly (Ed.), The ASTD technical and skills training handbook (pp. 114–137). New York, NY: McGraw-Hill.

Tenner, A. R., & DeToro, I. J. (1997). Process redesign: the implementation guide for managers. Reading, MA: Addison Wesley.

Thomas, J. C., Kellogg, W. A., & Erickson, T. (2001). The knowledge management puzzle: human and social factors in knowledge management. IBM Systems Journal, 40(4), 863–884.

Thurow, L. (1993). Head-to-head: the coming economic battle among Japan, Europe, and America. New York, NY: Warner Books.

Tichy, N. M. (1983). Managing strategic change. New York, NY: Wiley.

Tolman, E. C. (1932). Purposive behavior in animals and men. New York, NY: Naiburg.

Torraco, R. J. (1992). Accelerated training 1992: buyer beware. Human Resource Development Quarterly, 3(2), 183–186.

Torraco, R. J. (1994). The development and validation of a theory of work analysis. St. Paul: University of Minnesota Training and Development Research Center.

Torraco, R. J. (1997). Theory building research methods. In R. Swanson & E. Holton (Eds.), Human resource development research handbook (pp. 114–137). San Francisco, CA: Berrett-Koehler.

Torraco, R. J. (2005). Theory development research methods. In R. A. Swanson & E. F. Holton (Eds.), Research in organizations: foundations and methods of inquiry (pp. 114–137). San Francisco, CA: Berrett-Koehler.

Torraco, R. J., & Swanson, R. A. (1991). Auditing the strategic alignment of quality improvement, organization development, and training programs to the business. St. Paul, MN: Training and Development Research Center, University of Minnesota.

Torraco, R. J., & Swanson, R. A. (1995). The strategic roles of human resource development. Human Resource Planning, 18(4), 10–21.

Torraco, R. J., & Swanson, R. A. (1997). The strategic audit of HRD as a change intervention. In E. F. Holton (Ed.), Leading organizational change (pp. 99–121). Alexandria, VA: American Society for Training and Development Press.

Tribus, M. (1985). Becoming competitive by building the quality company. Kingsport, TN: American Quality and Productivity Institute.

Turner, J. (2022, July 6). 6 ways the workplace will change in the next 10 years. Gartner. https://www.gartner.com/smarterwithgartner/6-ways-the-workplace-will-change-in-the-next-10-years

U.S. Bureau of Labor Statistics. (2022, February 7). Employment situation summary. Retrieved February 7, 2022, from https://www.bls.gov/news.release/empsit.nr0.htm

von Bertalanffy, L. (1962). General system theory: A critical review. General Systems: Yearbook of the Society for General Systems Research, 7, 1–20.

Weick, K. (1995). Sensemaking in organizations. London: Sage.

Weisbord, M. (1987). Productive workplaces: organizing and managing for dignity, meaning, and community. San Francisco, CA: Jossey-Bass.

Wheatley, M. J. (1992). Leadership and the new science: learning about organization from an orderly universe. San Francisco, CA: Berrett-Koehler.

Wickens, C. D., Helton, W. S., Hollands, J. G., & Banbury, S. (2021). Engineering psychology and human performance. Milton Park, UK: Routledge.

Work Institute. (2022, March 15). 2022 retention report: how employers caused the great resignation. Retrieved April 15, 2023, from https://info.workinstitute. com/hubfs/2022%20Retention%20Report/2022%20Retention%20Report%20-%20 Work%20Institute.pdf

Yin, R. K. (1993). Applications of case study research. Newbury Park, CA: Sage.

Zemke, R., & Kramlinger, T. (1982). Figuring things out: a trainer's guide to needs and task analysis. Reading, MA: Addison-Wesley.

Index

Printed in the United States
by Baker & Taylor Publisher Services